St. Mark's
AND THE
Social Gospel

St. Mark's

AND THE

Social Gospel:

Methodist Women and Civil Rights
in New Orleans, 1895–1965

ELLEN BLUE

THE UNIVERSITY OF TENNESSEE PRESS / KNOXVILLE

All figures courtesy of Helen Mandlebaum except as noted.

Part of this volume was first published as "The Citizens Forum on Integration: 'Underground' Methodist Response to the *Brown* Decision," *Methodist History* 43, no. 3: 213–26. Used by permission of *Methodist History.*

Part of this volume was first published as "True Methodist Women: Reflections on the Community at St. Mark's," in *Louisiana Women: Their Lives and Times,* edited by Janet Allured and Judith F. Gentry (Athens: University of Georgia Press, 2009.) Used by permission of the University of Georgia Press.

Library of Congress Cataloging-in-Publication Data
Blue, Ellen.
St. Mark's and the social gospel: Methodist women and civil rights in New Orleans, 1895–1965 / Ellen Blue. — 1st ed.
p. cm.
Includes bibliographical references (p.) and index.
ISBN-13: 978-1-62190-107-5
1. St. Mark's United Methodist Church (New Orleans, La.)—History.
2. Women in church work—Louisiana—New Orleans—History.
3. Women in church work—Methodist Church—History.
4. St. Mark's Community Center—History.
5. Civil rights—Religious aspects—Methodist Church—History.
6. Social gospel—Louisiana—New Orleans—History.
7. New Orleans (La.)—Church history.
I. Title.
II. Title: Saint Mark's and social gospel.

BX8481.N46B68 2011
261.7088'2870976335—dc23

2011020835

CONTENTS

Part IV

Post-1965 and Conclusion

ILLUSTRATIONS

ACKNOWLEDGMENTS

No project of this magnitude is completed without assistance from many people. Thanks are due to the late Reverend Ms. Alexis Brent and to the Reverend Mr. Gregor Dike, who initially granted me access to the records at St. Mark's United Methodist Church (UMC). The oral history project that Margery Freeman, a member of the congregation, performed in 1979 was absolutely invaluable; funding by the UMC's General Commission on Archives and History (GCAH) for her project bore fruit in this study, as well.

I received funding assistance for my own work, and I am grateful for the GCAH's "Women in United Methodist History" research grant, awarded in 2003. It allowed me to spend additional time at the Brooks-Howell Home for retired deaconesses in Asheville, North Carolina, working in their archives and interviewing deaconesses.

This study began as research for my Ph.D. dissertation at Tulane University in New Orleans, where my studies were supported in part by a Dempster Fellowship awarded by the UMC's General Board of Higher Education and Ministry (GBHEM); the John M. Moore Fellowship, administered by trustees at Southern Methodist University; and a four-year fellowship at Tulane. Tulane also awarded me the Lurcy Travel Grant to present a paper at the Gulf South History and Humanities Conference in October 2000. I presented other papers based on this research at the southwest regional meeting of the American Academy of Religion (AAR) in March 2002; at the Sider Institute of Anabaptist, Pietist and Wesleyan Studies at Messiah College in Grantham, Pennsylvania, in May 2002; at the "Struggle, Faith and Vision" conference at the Scarritt-Bennett Center in Nashville in March 2007; and in many more public settings. I am grateful for comments of those who attended.

Material from chapter 5 appeared as an article entitled, "The Citizens Forum on Integration: 'Underground' Methodist Response to the *Brown* Decision," in the April 2005 issue of *Methodist History*. It was reprinted in volume C of *New Orleans and Urban Louisiana,* which is volume 14 of the Louisiana

Purchase Bicentennial Series in Louisiana History, Samuel C. Shepherd Jr., editor (Lafayette: Center for Louisiana Studies, 2005). Permission for reprinting is gratefully acknowledged.

Material based on my research for chapters 1, 2, 3, and 4 is included in an essay entitled, "True Methodist Women: Reflections on the Community at St. Mark's, 1895–1939," which appeared in a volume called *Louisiana Women: Their Lives and Times,* edited by Janet Allured and Judith F. Gentry (Athens: University of Georgia Press, 2009). Permission for reprinting this material is gratefully acknowledged.

Many individuals granted me interviews, and I am especially grateful to the late Reverend Mr. Andy Foreman for devoting two full afternoons to answering my questions and for granting me access to his extensive personal collection of records. Former community center staff members had maintained personal collections, which they shared with me. They include Laura Smith, Julia Southard Campbell, Dorothy Lundy, and Mary Frances Fairchild Tooke. Warren Calvin provided particularly vital information about the center's records. The Honorable Lindy Boggs visited with me about her relative, Mary Morrison. Leila Werlein Stone, Ann Werlein, the late Betty Werlein Carter, Lorraine Werlein Moore, and John Parham Werlein shared information about Mary Werlein and the Reverend Dr. S. H. Werlein. Parker Schneidau aided me in learning more about his grandmother, Harriet Rowland Parker, and provided a photograph for use in this volume. Isabel Gardner Larue and Beach Carré were exceptionally helpful in providing information about their ancestor, Elvira Beach Carré, and Isabel and her daughter, Susan Larue, provided photographs of Elvira.

Many archivists and librarians assisted this project. They include: Dale Patterson, Tracey Del Duca, Jocelyne Rubinetti, and most especially, Mark Shenise at the GCAH, Drew University, Madison, New Jersey; Debra McIntosh at Millsaps College, Jackson, Mississippi; Brenda Square and Mark Phillips at the Amistad Research Center, Tulane University, New Orleans; Margery Wright, Kyle Labor, and Sharon Chevalier at Magale Library, Centenary College, Shreveport, Louisiana; Pamela Arceneaux and Mary Lou Eichhorn at the Historic New Orleans Collection; Lester Sullivan at Xavier University, New Orleans; Danny Gamble at the *New Orleans Times-Picayune;* and three archivists at Emory University, including Anne Graham at the Pitts Theology Library,

Kathy Shoemaker in Special Collections at the Robert W. Woodruff Library, and Naomi Nelson in the Manuscripts, Archives and Rare Book Library. Particular thanks are due to Harry Miller at the Wisconsin Historical Society in Madison and Dr. Elaine Caldbeck at the Garrett Evangelical Theological Seminary archives in Evanston, Illinois. Sandy Shapoval and Clair Powers of the Phillips Theological Seminary library deserve special thanks for their help and their joy in providing it.

Deaconess Mary Lou Moore, former director at the Scarritt-Bennett Center's Laskey Library in Nashville, went to great lengths to facilitate my research there. Steve Gateley, director of the new research library opened in 2007, provided assistance, and I was delighted to be the first person to use the materials when it opened. Dr. Carolyn Oehler saw that the center's hospitality was provided to me while I was in Nashville for research trips. Deaconess and historian Dr. Barbara Campbell devoted time during one of her own visits to Scarritt (before her interim presidency) to introduce me to the resources there.

The former librarian at Brooks-Howell, Anne McKenzie, was extraordinarily accommodating. I also received assistance from Naomi Wray, Ann Janzen, and others at Brooks-Howell. Helen Mandlebaum requires special mention; she provided not only her own memories and memorabilia from St. Mark's, but also names and addresses of many other individuals connected with its history, and many of the photographs are from her personal collection. This project would not have happened without her. I thank all the residents and staff at Brooks-Howell for their hospitality and for the opportunity to be in a room with that many powerful women.

Volunteer historians of the United Methodist Women and its predecessor organizations in Louisiana allowed me to use their materials, especially Seola Callahan, the conference UMW historian who maintained records housed at the Louisiana Conference Center in Woodworth, and Norma Winegeart, a former conference historian who shared some of her personal memorabilia with me. The Reverend Mr. William Earl Nolan shared material from his and from his late mother, Mildred Nolan's, extensive collections of material on the history of Louisiana Methodism.

Several present and former members of the Tulane community contributed to the success of this venture, most especially my advisor, Dr. Randy Sparks;

Dr. Clarence Mohr; Dr. Nicholas Bloom; and Donna Denneen. Other scholars were generous with time and knowledge, including Dr. Catherine Wessinger of Loyola University in New Orleans, who fostered my understanding of women and religion in America and carefully read and commented on my dissertation. Others who read the dissertation and offered encouragement include Dr. Elizabeth Box Price; Graham R. D. Price; and the Reverend Dr. William W. Hutchinson, bishop of the Louisiana area of the UMC. Dr. Charles M. Wood of Southern Methodist University not only read the work, but also helped in a number of important ways during its preparation. Dr. Robin Roberts and Dr. Carolyn De Swarte Gifford read this manuscript and made extremely helpful comments.

My student research assistants at Phillips, the Reverend Dr. Delana Taylor McNac and Tiffany Kirkland, spent many hours checking the accuracy of the references, and their successor, Barbara Schwartz, also assisted in research for this project, including initial construction of the index. Kristi Susanna Simpson assisted greatly in the final preparation of the manuscript. I very much appreciate their work and their attention to detail.

The early research phase could not have been completed without the cooperation of the Reverend Ms. Carole Cotton-Winn and the Reverend Mr. Freddie Henderson, past superintendents of the New Orleans District of the UMC, and the people of St. Paul's UMC in Harahan and of Metairie UMC. My husband, the Reverend Mr. Jim Wilson, attended to many of my pastoral responsibilities in the early years of this work so that I could pursue my research and writing, accompanied me on countless research trips and, not least, fought with microfilm copiers in several states on my behalf.

This book is dedicated to the Methodist women who built and staffed St. Mark's and who labored to make us see that the Kingdom *is* at hand—and especially among them, Alexis Brent.

ABBREVIATIONS

CFI	Citizens Forum on Integration
GBGM	General Board of Global Ministries of the United Methodist Church
GCAH	General Commission on Archives and History of the United Methodist Church
IWO	Independent Women's Organization
MEC	Methodist Episcopal Church
MECS	Methodist Episcopal Church, South
MFSA	Methodist Federation for Social Action
MFSS	Methodist Federation for Social Service
NAACP	National Association for the Advancement of Colored People
NOCA	*New Orleans Christian Advocate*
SCEF	Southern Conference Educational Fund
SCHW	Southern Conference on Human Welfare
SOS	Save Our Schools, Inc.
UMC	United Methodist Church
UMW	United Methodist Women
WCTU	Woman's Christian Temperance Union
WP&HMS	Woman's Parsonage and Home Mission Society
WSCS	Woman's Society of Christian Service
YWCA	Young Women's Christian Association

INTRODUCTION

The story of St. Mark's Community Center and the St. Mark's congregation is a story about women. It is a story about white, southern women, about Methodist women, women who were products of their own time and place but who also challenged the prevailing culture in both subtle and dramatic ways, and who brought about substantial change in New Orleans.

St. Mark's and the Social Gospel is not a traditional biography, because not one of these women—not those who worked in 1895 nor those who worked in 1965, nor any of their sisters in between—was regarded as biography material. No one collected their papers and archived them. By the turn of the twenty-first century, finding enough information about any one of them to fill a book proved impossible. Yet that circumstance is precisely the story of women's most powerful work, work that is performed collaboratively, using the hours and talents and nickels and dimes of many women joined together.

The white southern Methodist women in this study established and ran a settlement house. Settlement houses were not, as the name might imply, focused on providing housing for the needy. Rather, they were facilities that allowed well-educated women to live in low-income neighborhoods, learning from their neighbors as they got to know them about what their true needs were. Settlements were designed on the one hand to provide an oasis of calm and beauty for people whose daily lives in dirty factories and crowded tenements tended toward chaos, but they were also designed to give the settlement workers a deep, experiential understanding of how they could best help the neighborhood. Hull House, established in Chicago by Nobel Peace Prize recipient Jane Addams, is the best known of all settlement houses in this country, but other nonsectarian settlements came to be identified with famous workers like Lillian Wald and Florence Kelley, and even Eleanor McMain, who ran Kingsley House, the nonsectarian settlement in New Orleans.

Traditional history has neglected the women who are the focus of *St. Mark's and the Social Gospel,* for several reasons. Those reasons include the dismissal

of religious settlements by social historians and nonsectarian settlement workers of the time (for being too religious) and by the church at large (for not being
religious enough); the fact that Methodist deaconesses, like Methodist preachers, were moved around from location to location by the larger church, which
prevented any one woman's story from becoming indistinguishable from that
of St. Mark's (and vice-versa); and the fact that the laywomen of Methodism did
their work collaboratively, as an organization, an approach that is only beginning to garner some of the historical attention it deserves. Furthermore, as discussed in the following pages, the history of the deaconess movement within
Methodism overall has received very little consideration by historians, and despite the importance of their ministries in southern cities, even less research
has been done on Methodist deaconesses in the South. The fascinating history
of their groundbreaking work has been lost, along with the names of the individual women who accomplished it.

Since the second wave of feminism began, many have debated the topic of
what feminist leadership styles should look like. Early in this movement, many
women in the workforce absorbed the message that to achieve success in what
was "still a man's world," they should make themselves appear, in work style

Fig. 1. A postcard of St. Mark's produced by C. B. Mason sometime
between 1923 and 1926.

if not in dress, as much like men as possible. Feminist theology, on the other hand, began to question relatively early whether men's experience and perspective is indeed "the human situation" for women.[1] Over time, the concept of "woman-church" emerged, with reflection on what a nonhierarchical church might look like. Today, feminist theologians tend to focus on the interconnectedness of lives and souls. They tend to value community over individuality, *not* as a way of demeaning a woman's self, but as a way of acknowledging that hierarchical structures have not been good for the church, and most especially for women or any other marginalized group.

In part from necessity and in part from theological conviction, the Methodist women of New Orleans from 1895 onward worked as collaborators to achieve dramatic results in their city. This book focuses in part on women whose careers as professional church workers brought them to the city for a time, and in part on laywomen who lived in New Orleans all their lives. Like fabric that needs strength in both warp and woof, Methodist women's endeavors required, for success, both trained professionals, who could devote full time and considerable expertise to the work, and highly dedicated laywomen, who could raise funds and build lasting local networks. The professionals included Methodist deaconesses like Mary Lou Barnwell, Nettie Stroup, Margaret Ragland, and all the others whose names appear in these pages. New Orleanians whose work undergirded St. Mark's included Mary Werlein, Elvira Beach Carré, and Hattie Parker, strong women who were motivated by religious devotion and a "call" to the Social Gospel. Profound questions about what the mission of the church should and should not be have been reflected in the relationships between St. Mark's and the larger Methodist community and even, at times, between St. Mark's and the entire city. The laywomen supported the deaconesses, and not just financially; they backed radical activities verbally and in other substantive ways. The professional deaconesses and the laywomen forged not only working alliances that enabled them to ease the harsh living conditions of immigrants and laborers, but also deep and lasting friendships. These relationships created a community of women who understood and appreciated each other's abilities, desires, and commitments to social change.

As its subtitle indicates, this book follows St. Mark's from its inception during the Social Gospel era—a time at the turn of the twentieth century when the

Fig. 2. The center's staff gathered on Easter 1930
included Lillian Addison, Wortley Moorman, Nettie
Stroup, Margaret Marshall, and Bess Sargent.

church reached out to address unprecedented social problems in cities as a
result of industrialization, urbanization, and immigration—to its extremely
controversial activities during the civil rights era. It also documents the decades in between. Because St. Mark's began as a classic product of the Social
Gospel and was also deeply involved in the school desegregation crisis in New
Orleans in 1960, *St. Mark's and the Social Gospel* provides an unusual and valuable lens for viewing the relationship between the two movements and demon-

strates positive links between them, as the women of St. Mark's dared to break the race barrier that the American South deemed sacrosanct.

Overall, scholars and society at large have seriously undervalued women's work at Methodist settlement houses. The stories of the women who for decades mellowed the wood of the stair railings with their hands, and who dreamed on the third-floor sleeping porch with the sounds of the French Quarter surrounding them, are worth hearing not just for their own value, and not just for their power to inspire the listener, but also because they offer significant correctives to previous understandings of important historical eras in the history of the United States and in the history of the church. Histories of the Social Gospel movement tend to focus on male theologians, primarily from the northeastern United States.[2] When the Methodist Episcopal Church, South (MECS) women of New Orleans who lived out its mandates are considered among the movement's central practitioners, as they most definitely were, and the movement is observed through their history, a much fuller view of the Social Gospel emerges. I argue that examining the work of southern Methodist women calls for a serious reshaping of how the Social Gospel has been understood. Viewing the movement through the lives of women who embodied it clarifies several things, especially the dating of its "demise." This study of St. Mark's shows that the work of the Social Gospel remained in full swing in the 1920s, and that it was not until the New Deal in the 1930s, when government took over some of the work previously done in the private sector by volunteers, that the Social Gospel began a significant decline. Because of these white women's surprising stances on race relations in the first half of the twentieth century, the history of St. Mark's also contributes significantly to the ongoing discussion about whether the Social Gospel was intrinsically racist.

Their training in the Social Gospel made the women of St. Mark's far more radical than other Louisiana women. The story of these "True Methodist Women" shows how powerful an agent for transformation religious motivation can be, for their devotion is what allowed them to push for real social change even when that put them in conflict with the values of their segregated and sexist society.[3] It is precisely that religious motivation that separated them from the upper-class women whose lives have recently been studied by other historians. Though John Patrick McDowell astutely noted three decades ago that the MECS women were driven both by theology and by culture, the actual relationship between the two factors and the ability of theology to trump even cultural expectations has not previously been carefully examined. Even at the turn of the twenty-first century, it is difficult for churchwomen to act outside cultural norms, and the task was infinitely harder for women who "stept out of their place" at the turn of the twentieth.[4] Understanding their motives and experiences deserves far more attention than has previously been applied.

SPANNING THE CENTURY

The building that St. Mark's Community Center and St. Mark's United Methodist Church shared on North Rampart Street is sacred space. It is holy not because it is isolated from the rest of the famous French Quarter of New Orleans, but because it has been so deeply embedded within it. Despite sharing that structure where North Rampart meets Governor Nicholls Street, the community center and the church were separate entities; nevertheless, they were so interrelated, at least throughout most of their histories, that it was usually only by means of context that a New Orleanian could decide which entity a speaker who simply said "St. Mark's" actually meant.

St. Mark's UMC is a worshipping congregation that remains affiliated with the Louisiana Annual Conference. Deaconesses who worked at St. Mark's Community Center played key roles in the congregation's lay leadership until the mid-1960s, but throughout most of the twentieth century, its pastors were male. In the twenty-first century, after Hurricane Katrina, the community center reorganized as the North Rampart Community Center, and the new board governs its activities; the Women's Division of the church's General Board of Global Ministries (GBGM) still owns it.[5] Methodist women have been responsible for its ministries since 1895, when the local women's societies assumed control of an already extant but failing mission on Tchoupitoulas Street, where city missionary Lillie Meekins served the poorest residents of the city's Irish Channel section.[6]

Over the next two-and-a-half decades, Methodist women nurtured that struggling outpost into a thriving ministry. It was in 1909 that the women first expanded their work to the French Quarter, establishing a settlement house that served Italians and white immigrants from twenty-four other nations. Additional expansions, changes of name, and changes of location occurred before 1923, when the women opened the facility at 1130 North Rampart that was widely considered the finest settlement house in the South, and where both black and white New Orleanians were openly served in its health clinic. Margaret Ragland, the first Methodist deaconess to serve St. Mark's, was assigned in 1909, and deaconesses continued to run the facility until Fae Daves retired in the mid-1960s.[7]

When Katrina made landfall in August 2005, St. Mark's still occupied that same building and still provided some of the same types of services to disadvantaged residents of New Orleans. It was no longer a true settlement house, but it still provided vital services for its neighbors.

The Role of the Methodist Deaconess

Lucy Rider Meyer established the first training school for Methodist deaconesses in Chicago in 1885, operating almost totally on faith that God would provide for their needs. She was also trusting that the church would eventually recognize the contribution that trained women could make to its ministries. The Methodist Episcopal Church created the office of deaconess in 1888, and it consecrated its first deaconesses that year. Their initial mandate was "to minister to the poor, visit the sick, pray with the dying, care for the orphan, seek the wandering, comfort the sorrowing, and save the sinning."[8]

Although the Civil War had been over for two decades when Meyer opened her school, Methodism had not yet healed the prewar split of 1844, when the Methodist Episcopal Church, South (MECS) broke off from the Methodist Episcopal Church (MEC), primarily over the issue of slavery. The southern women were close behind their northern sisters in establishing a school to train women as Christian workers. As soon as she visited Meyer's new school in Chicago, the MECS women's leader, Belle Bennett, began to raise funds for the Scarritt Bible and Training School, which would educate the majority of the deaconesses who served St. Mark's. The MECS created the office of deaconess in 1902 and consecrated its first deaconesses in April 1903. Although the MEC had congregations in New Orleans and even conducted work among the Italian community similar to (and predating) the work of St. Mark's, St. Mark's was entirely a mission of MECS women. Because of their leadership on issues surrounding race and ethnicity, it is important to remember that all the women who served St. Mark's prior to the denominations' reunification in 1939 were members of the southern church.[9]

The office of deaconess still exists today in the United Methodist Church (UMC). Women are consecrated as deaconesses each year, and their number is slowly climbing after a sharp decline in the decades after Methodist women won the right to be ordained. In 2007, there were 138 United Methodist deaconesses in service. In 2010, 152 women were active deaconesses, and 109 were retired.[10]

Considering its impact on church and society, the history of the deaconess movement within Methodism has been the subject of very little research, and most of that has focused on northern women and their training schools. Appendix A discusses the scholars who completed this work. One of these, Sarah Kreutziger, demonstrated that the work of Methodist deaconesses helped lead to professionalization of the field of social work, but there is less agreement on whether the creation of deaconess orders helped or hindered the professionalization of women's work within the church itself.[11] Some feminists think that the deaconess office represented a sop to keep women from agitating too strongly for positions that offered real power. The MEC created it during the same decade when requests from Anna Howard Shaw and Anna Oliver for full ordination resulted not only in denial of their request, but also in the rescinding of all "exhorter's licenses" that had previously been issued to women. It was created at the same General Conference (1888) where the first five women elected as delegates were not seated because the all-male body decided that "laymen" referred only to men.[12] Others, however, believe that the creation of a class of professional, albeit not ordained, women in the church was an important step toward professionalization of women's efforts and eventual ordination. A case can be made to support either belief. There were men who believed at the time that the office of deaconess would occupy women's attention and divert them from seeking ordination, while other men feared that creating the office would eventually lead to the presence of women bishops within the Methodist episcopacy. (More than a half century later, developments proved the second group correct.)

Without doubt, the way that Lucy Rider Meyer organized the deaconess program opened it to criticism by later feminists. She insisted the women

Fig. 3. Berta Ellison (left) and Margaret Young wearing
deaconess attire. The man standing between them in
front of St. Mark's is unidentified.

should not be paid for their work, so no one could say they performed it for
monetary gain. Early MEC deaconesses received their room and board and
an allowance of eight dollars per month to cover all their other needs, including the habit-like uniforms they were required to wear up until about 1925.[13]
(Southern women earned a slightly higher stipend.) In early twentieth-century
New Orleans, as in other locales, the deaconesses were easy to spot as they
made home visits in impoverished neighborhoods, wearing their characteristic black dresses and bonnets, with a white bow underneath their chins. One
writer observed, "Any discussion of deaconesses sooner or later turns to a
discussion of the 'garb' and its advantages and disadvantages." Meyer initially

required the uniform as a "distinctive sign; giving its wearers the protection which is so well known to be extended to the Romish Sisters of Charity." She thought there was no other mode of dress that would be "so economical; both as to money, and that which is worth more than money, time and thought. It would also promote sisterly equality among the workers.... Last of all it would be a badge of sisterly union." Methodist deaconesses wore no jewelry, she said, because it would present too great a temptation in the poverty-stricken areas where women served.[14]

THE WOMEN'S SPHERE

When Meyer alluded to the "protection" that their dress extended to Roman Catholic nuns, she may have seen it as a deterrent not only against being accosted on city streets, but also against being accused of having stepped outside the proper "women's sphere" of the late 1800s. Charisma "is typically the first means by which women gain authoritative positions" in religious organizations.[15] I suggest that the dark, drab uniforms may have been intended—or at least have served—as a nonverbal sign that deaconesses did not aspire to be powerful individuals who sought control in church matters; the garb may thus have allowed them to appear as somewhat less threatening to male authority (though this would not be enough to save St. Mark's head resident Margaret Ragland's job in 1911–12).

Barbara Welter's research for her classic article on the "Cult of True Womanhood" helps explain many of the cultural barriers that deaconesses faced as they attempted to carve out a niche for themselves in a mainstream southern denomination. In a dramatic overturning of traditional Christian teaching that from the second century had held that women were more sinful than men, the women of the nineteenth-century United States came to be regarded as more deeply spiritual and religious than men, and thus to serve as the "keepers" of their families' souls. However, this new standard still prohibited their religious leadership, because that would take them out of the proper "women's sphere" and violate the expectation that women should demonstrate not only piety, but also the characteristics of domesticity and submissiveness. Discussing the ideal of the "True Methodist Woman," Jean Miller Schmidt suggested that individual Methodist women responded to such expectations in one of three ways: 1) by attempting to meet the ideal as it was presented to them; 2) by protesting against the whole notion of separate spheres for men and women; or 3) by working within the women's sphere but "testing the elasticity of its boundaries." Using Susan Hill Lindley's terminology of "soft feminism" among female religious leaders, Schmidt argued that the office of deaconess, "while offering a public ministry to women, was . . . an interesting combination of traditional and modern images of Christian womanhood." Schmidt sees deaconesses as enlarging the influence of women in the Methodist tradition. This history of St. Mark's clearly shows that while the women who worked there acted directly on many issues of concern to them, they often used less-direct influence to subvert the existing order of society.[16]

Toward Reworking Parameters for the Social Gospel

Readers who want more context for the discussion of women's roles in that fascinating time in U.S. and church history when the Social Gospel was in flower may want not only to read this section, but also to turn to Wendy J. Deichmann Edwards's and Carolyn De Swarte Gifford's *Gender and the Social Gospel*. That volume contains a good literature review on the topic.[17]

One contribution of this study is its thorough contradiction of some earlier church historians' assertions that there was no manifestation of the Social Gospel in the South. The Methodist laywomen who funded St. Mark's Community Center studied substantive Social Gospel texts in their societies, and the deaconesses who ran it were thoroughly trained in Social Gospel theology, including that of Walter Rauschenbusch, widely regarded as the movement's premier theologian. In her insightful 2001 essay, "Deciding Who Counts," Susan Hill Lindley considered the standard definition for the Social Gospel movement: the application "of the teaching of Jesus and the total message of Christian salvation" not just to individuals, but also "to society, the economic life, and social institutions." Lindley pointed out the need to "unpack" that definition in light of recent reconsideration of "who counts" as a Social Gospel practitioner. She concluded that "Social Gospel" might remain a "multileveled term" whose usage in American religious history would have to be "clarified in particular contexts."[18]

Yet despite the changes that may appropriately occur in our understanding of the movement as it is viewed in different contexts—moving, for instance, from the world of northern male academics and theologians normally viewed as its primary actors, to the world of southern churchwomen who actually took the concepts to the streets of the Irish Channel and the French Quarter—it is still possible to describe the Social Gospel in basic ways. The movement is usually seen as a response to the increasing industrialization and urbanization in the United States in the nineteenth century, and to the social problems and pressures that accompanied them. References to "economic life" and "social institutions" point to arenas where Christians endeavored to make human society more nearly resemble what they believed the coming Kingdom of God would be like. Social Gospelers believed they were supposed to help institute such a Kingdom on Earth, and practically speaking, the Social Gospel's primary transformation of Protestant Christianity lay in the area of how, and indeed whether, the church should meet "material" needs of people who are poor, along with needs more readily categorized as "spiritual." Typical ministries included food and clothing banks, health clinics, English lessons, vocational education and job placement for adults and youths, and kindergarten. The greatest doctrinal change the Social Gospel fostered was to swing emphasis away from personal salvation in the hereafter toward the salvation of society as a whole in the here and now.

It was once commonly accepted that the Social Gospel movement ended at the time of World War I (1914–18), because the futility of that conflict led to worldwide disillusionment. However, I believe this closing date was assigned in large part because several of the most prominent male thinkers and writers died at around that time and, naturally enough, stopped publishing. The failure of historians to distinguish between practitioners of the Social Gospel and other Progressive reformers has also contributed to the problem. Examination of the work at St. Mark's shows that after surviving a serious challenge in 1911–12 from men concerned both about widening female influence and the overall aims of the Social Gospel, the movement's duration in New Orleans extended well past World War I—indeed, Methodist women were on the upswing of their Social Gospel work in 1923, when they opened their new facility on North Rampart Street.

The 1920s were a time of prosperity for much of the nation, but immigrants continued to pour into the country and the majority of them struggled with economic deprivation. They faced greater and better-organized opposition in that decade, because of the resurgence of the Ku Klux Klan and anti-immigrant political organizations, and because of a growing acceptance of the idea that the immigrant was a "problem," an opinion reflected even in the speech of bishops and other church leaders. Inspired by human needs and by their own theological convictions, the women continued their Social Gospel activities and service directed toward immigrants throughout the 1920s. It was only the onset of the New Deal in the 1930s that convinced a number of them that they could more efficiently serve the needy by working through government agencies than by continuing to pour their efforts into the programs of the church. The "Americanization" work performed during this era has undergone much scrutiny and justifiable criticism in recent decades, but the goals and attitudes of the deaconesses at St. Mark's were very different from those of many who were intent on Americanizing immigrants.

In 2003's *Gender and the Social Gospel,* Edwards and Gifford pointed out that the scholarly studies of the Social Gospel movement that have not considered the work of women are inadequate. They insist that the task of retelling the movement's history "with a full cast of players and complete slate of issues" has only just begun. Studying the Social Gospel only through "theological treatises, sermons, and philosophical monologues" led to a truncated understanding of the entire movement. They call for investigation of the movement by means of primary research, using minutes of women's meetings; the publications produced by women's home missionary, temperance, and other organizations; women's periodicals; and journals, novels, poetry, and letters.[19] This study of St. Mark's does exactly that.

St. Mark's, built during the Progressive Era and still in operation when Katrina made landfall, offers a unique lens onto the Social Gospel's legacy. Although stereotypical female reformers of the Progressive Era were present among the women who supported St. Mark's, this study reveals that many of the deaconesses and other leaders among the Methodist laywomen of New

Orleans held beliefs that cast serious doubt on previous suppositions about the conservative political, theological, and ideological tendencies of Social Gospel reformers. Further, examining the deaconesses' work casts light on how their Social Gospel origins shaped the St. Mark's congregation's reactions to events in the civil rights era.

EXPLANATION OF METHODIST TERMINOLOGY AS USED IN THIS STUDY

Despite the fact that when women took charge of the work on Tchoupitoulas Street in 1895, three decades had elapsed since the end of the Civil War, the Methodist church had not yet reunited from its prewar split. As noted earlier, the Methodist Episcopal Church, South (MECS) broke off from the Methodist Episcopal Church (MEC) in 1844, primarily over the issue of slavery. Methodism's founder, John Wesley, had adamantly opposed slavery and the slave trade in England, and the MEC forbade (at least in principle, though unfortunately not always in practice) owning, buying, or selling slaves. The two branches did not reunite until 1939, when they and the Methodist Protestant offshoot came together to form The Methodist Church (table 1).

The MECS is often rightfully referred to as "the southern church," but the MEC is often erroneously referred to as "the northern church." The MEC was simply the main body of Methodism founded in 1784, and after the Civil War, numerous MEC congregations existed in many southern cities, including New Orleans. Though it is technically inaccurate, "the northern church" is in some instances the clearest way of designating the MEC, especially in oral communication, so Methodists often hear that term.

Splits and mergers among the United Methodist Church's predecessor denominations inevitably resulted in name changes for Methodist organizations and publications, including those related to women's groups. To complicate matters further, there were occasional non-merger-related name changes, as well. This can make Methodist nomenclature virtually incomprehensible to non-Methodist historians and confusing even to those steeped in Methodist history. This study, therefore, uses terms chosen to help the reader understand what group or publication is being mentioned, even though this is sometimes

---

TABLE 1

Relevant Splits and Mergers in Methodism	
1784	Methodist Episcopal Church (MEC) established in Baltimore, Maryland
1844	Methodist Episcopal Church, South (MECS) breaks off over slavery
1939	MEC, MECS (and Methodist Protestants) reunite, form The Methodist Church
	Race-based Central Jurisdiction is created
	Louisiana Annual Conference A, white membership churches, assigned to South Central Jurisdiction
	Louisiana Annual Conference B, black membership churches, assigned to Central Jurisdiction
	Women's Society becomes Woman's Society of Christian Service (WSCS)
1968	The Methodist Church unites with Evangelical United Brethren (EUB), forming the United Methodist Church (UMC)
	Women's Society becomes United Methodist Women (UMW)
1970	Louisiana Annual Conference A and Louisiana Annual Conference B merge, forming the Louisiana Annual Conference

accomplished at the expense of accuracy regarding the exact name that may have been in use during a given period. As one example, rather than referring to the women's home mission society as the Woman's Parsonage and Home Mission Society in one place and the Woman's Home Mission Society, the Woman's Society of Christian Service, the Wesleyan Service Guild, or the United Methodist Women in others, the terms "woman's society" and "women's society" are usually used to refer to the Methodist women's mission organization. It is crucial to remember that the term "woman's society" when used in this book with reference to events during the existence of the MECS (1845–1939) always refers to the women of the southern church unless otherwise specified. Further, it always refers to white women's societies; changes in the racial makeup of the societies that accompanied mergers are discussed later.

TABLE 2

Name Changes and Other Important Dates in the St. Mark's Story	
1886	Women's society formed in the Methodist Episcopal Church, South (MECS)
1890	Name changes to Woman's Parsonage & Home Mission Society (WP&HMS), portfolio expanded
1891	WP&HMS chartered in Louisiana
1895	Women adopt the struggling "Tchoupitoulas Mission" in the Irish Channel
1902	MECS creates office of deaconess
1906–7	Women rename ministry on Tchoupitoulas Street the Mary Werlein Mission
1909	Women open settlement house, St. Mark's Hall, on Esplanade Avenue First deaconess is assigned
1918	Laity (voting) rights for women approved in MECS
1923–25	St. Mark's moves to new structure at 1130 North Rampart Street. Building is formally dedicated Community Chest (later United Way) is established in New Orleans St. Mark's Community Center officially separated from the congregation, St. Mark's Methodist Episcopal Church, South in order to receive Community Chest funds
ca. 1926	Mary Werlein Mission fades from existence
1956	Ordination for women approved in The Methodist Church
1960	Pastor at St. Mark's Methodist Church breaks the white boycott at William Frantz Elementary during the school desegregation crisis
1966	Last deaconess (until after Hurricane Katrina), Fae Daves, leaves community center
2005	Katrina makes landfall on August 29, and levees subsequently break
2007	Community Center reorganized as North Rampart Community Center

The Mary Werlein Mission was known as the "Tchoupitoulas Mission" when Methodist women assumed responsibility for it in 1895. In publications, it is referred to as the "Tchoupitoulas Mission," the "Tchoupitoulas Street Mission," and the "Tchoupitoulas Street Church." Sometime in 1906 or 1907, the women officially changed its name to the "Mary Werlein Mission," but it was occasionally called that even earlier. In this book, except where the name is part of a quotation, the pre-1906 facility is always referred to as the "Tchoupitoulas Mission" and post-1906 as the "Mary Werlein Mission" (table 2).

When it was located on Esplanade Avenue, the St. Mark's settlement house was known as "St. Mark's Hall," and when it moved to North Rampart Street, it became known as "St. Mark's Community Center." Because records are so scanty, it is not clear exactly when the "Church of All Nations" congregation attached to St. Mark's Hall officially became known as the St. Mark's congregation, but at the time this occurred, it was St. Mark's Methodist Episcopal Church, South (MECS). After the 1939 reunification, it became St. Mark's Methodist Church. In 1968, The Methodist Church merged with the Evangelical United Brethren and the congregation received its current designation, St. Mark's United Methodist Church. The name of the Community Center was not affected by any of these mergers.

In the lived experience of most United Methodists, the most significant organizational unit of the Methodist church is the Annual Conference, a yearly gathering of clergy and lay members in a particular geographical region. Although all Methodist clergy and laity are bound by the provisions of the *Book of Discipline,* which is amended and approved by the General Conference (a worldwide gathering of representatives from each Annual Conference that meets every four years), the Annual Conference makes meaningful decisions about rules and practices within its own boundaries. The boundaries of the Louisiana Annual Conference happen to be the same as the boundaries of the political entity, the state of Louisiana. At the time the *New Orleans Christian Advocate (NOCA),* a source frequently cited in this study, was being published, there were two Annual Conferences in the state of Mississippi, and both were cosponsors of *NOCA,* along with the Louisiana Annual Conference.

In the United Methodist Church, bishops are assigned to "areas" rather than to Annual Conferences, and some areas contain more than one Annual

Conference. For a time, Louisiana was included with Arkansas in such an area. The inclusion and later exclusion of Arkansas in the Louisiana bishop's area had no effect on this project.

Jurisdictions, composed of several Annual Conferences, are the next largest entity in the UMC. The conferences are grouped together based on geography. However, between 1939 and 1968, a jurisdiction existed that was based solely on the race of its members. At the time of the 1939 MEC-MECS merger, the church made a tragic concession to racism. To ensure that no white pastor would have to serve under a black bishop or district superintendent, all black-membership churches in the United States were assigned to the racially defined Central Jurisdiction, no matter into what geographic jurisdiction they would otherwise have been assigned. Thus, in Louisiana, the white-membership churches belonged to the Annual Conference (Louisiana A) that was affiliated with its geographically determined jurisdiction, while Louisiana Conference B, made up of only black-membership churches, was affiliated with the Central Jurisdiction.

In 1968, terms of the merger of The Methodist Church with the Evangelical United Brethren necessitated the abolishment of the Central Jurisdiction, and its congregations were assimilated into the geographically based Annual Conferences and jurisdictions to which they would otherwise have belonged. The primary effect on this study was the subsequent merger—and the prior separation—of the women's societies of the two racially divided Annual Conferences in Louisiana. Because St. Mark's began as a white-membership congregation and served primarily white clientele in its social service activities at that time, its woman's society was all white throughout the first half of the twentieth century and beyond, and it was part of the conference-wide and denomination-wide, all-white woman's society structures. Thus, when the term "woman's society" is used in this book in reference to events prior to 1970, it is referring *only* to the white women's organization in the New Orleans District and/or Louisiana Annual Conference A. After 1968, the black and white membership groups became one, and post-1968 references to the "woman's society" refer to the integrated group.

ARRANGEMENT OF THE TEXT

Some topics explored in this study lent themselves to closer scrutiny in one time period than in others. As a result, I have used a combination of chronological and topical approaches, and this requires both some backtracking and some foreshadowing of later events in several chapters, rather than rigidly chronological narratives.

Part I covers the period between 1895 and World War I. In it, chapter 1 focuses on the Mary Werlein Mission on Tchoupitoulas Street, adopted by the woman's society in 1895, where city missionary Lillie Meekins served residents of the Irish Channel. It documents early Social Gospel activities among Methodist women in New Orleans. Chapter 2 recounts the opening of St. Mark's Hall on Esplanade Avenue in 1909. Established primarily for work with Italians, the hall served immigrants from twenty-five nations. The narrative addresses a crisis in 1911–12 when St. Mark's was almost forced to close because of objections from male church leaders about the "secular" Social Gospel and the presence of strong female leadership at the settlement. Chapter 3 covers events between the end of World War I and the mid-1920s, as the mission evolved into a major settlement house. The new building on North Rampart Street was completed, and these Social Gospel practitioners made strong forward progress long after the end of World War I, when the movement is often said to have died. This chapter addresses the formal separation of congregation and community center in 1925.

Part II explores the work for gender and racial equality between the 1920s and 1960. In chapter 4, an examination of the deaconesses' training in socialist economic theory demonstrates that the Methodist women of the Social Gospel movement were more radical and egalitarian than most elite, female Progressive reformers. Gender issues are emphasized, in part because the question of the closing date for the Social Gospel movement depends on whether the movement is considered from the standpoint of northern male writers or from that of the southern females who were its hands-on practitioners. Work toward gender equality, including ordination of women, affected St. Mark's and the larger deaconess movement.

Chapter 5 is set in the 1950s and ends with the onset of the school desegregation crisis in New Orleans in 1960. With major emphasis on the issue of race relations, it discusses the Citizens Forum on Integration (CFI), an ecumenical group formed in New Orleans in response to the 1954 Supreme Court decision in *Brown v. Board of Education of Topeka* that mandated integration of public schools. The CFI was founded by a former Methodist clergyman who was profoundly committed to the Social Gospel and Christian socialism, and it was chaired successively by Methodist clergymen who were deeply influenced by deaconesses, including one who was a deaconess's son and another who would later become chair of the board of directors at St. Mark's Community Center. This chapter connects the work of white deaconesses who joined the National Association for the Advancement of Colored People (NAACP) in the 1930s during their studies at Scarritt College; the surprising work of white women's societies in the Methodist Episcopal Church, South toward improving race relations; the work of the CFI; and the basis for the relative tolerance of the St. Mark's congregation to the decision of their white pastor to leave his daughter in a newly integrated public school.

Part III tells the story of that pastor's action and the center's direct involvement in the civil rights struggle. Chapter 6 focuses on the congregation during the school desegregation crisis of 1960. Its minister, Andy Foreman, broke the white boycott of William Frantz Elementary School when a black child, Ruby Bridges, was admitted, and Foreman's daughter, Pamela, continued to attend classes there. The national media covered Foreman's actions, and the St. Mark's congregation experienced severe internal conflict as it struggled to face with integrity the ethical and legal necessity of integration. The center's own struggle in that arena is discussed in chapter 7. The history of St. Mark's illuminates connections between the Social Gospel movement and the civil rights movement. This chapter explores the links between the deaconesses who received theological training at Scarritt and Foreman, whose decision stemmed in part from Foreman's association with his own academic advisor at another Methodist school.

Part IV comprises two chapters. Chapter 8 consists of a brief look at the history of St. Mark's Community Center and the St. Mark's congregation since 1965. Chapter 9 presents the conclusions drawn from this study.

Writers of women's history often encounter insurmountable problems in their search for needed documents, owing to a long-standing and widespread devaluing of women's work and activities. Those who research the history of female leaders within the organized church tend to find the documentation even scarcer, because the church has often led, not followed, and caused, not merely participated in, the disrespect of female leaders. As is probably the case for many religious settlement houses, historical records are extremely sparse at St. Mark's Community Center, and I had to pursue many strategies to compile the data necessary for this study. Appendix A is a discussion of the sources that allowed completion of my own research despite the lack of local records, and I provide it as an aid to other researchers of churchwomen's history. Appendix B contains the Charter for Racial Justice approved by the Woman's Society of Christian Service (WSCS) in 1962.

Seeking the Kingdom of God in the City

The impact of St. Mark's on the city of New Orleans was immense. Its stories are dramatic reflections of its times, but they are not only reflections, for it was often St. Mark's that changed the picture, leading the way into different understandings of what urban diversity could and should mean.

Since 1895, the women whose dreams have shaped the reality of St. Mark's have dared to believe that despite the flawed nature of the city they loved and the church they served and humanity in general and even themselves, their lives lived together could produce a glimpse of what the reign of God might look like. In 2010, the congregation that worshipped at 1130 North Rampart Street remained a model of what a church that cares about justice might look like on Sunday morning; the changed lives of the center's youth and children still proved that the grace once called upon by women now long dead had indeed proved sufficient for the day. If the prayer "Thy kingdom come" has ever been or ever will be answered, surely evidence of that response will appear in New Orleans, where generations of "True Methodist Women" have been tending God's people at St. Mark's. The story of their labor begins here.

PART I

Methodist Women Doing
Settlement Work:
1895–World War I

1

THE MARY WERLEIN MISSION, 1895–1908

In May 1940, daily newspapers in New Orleans chronicled the death of Mary Werlein. The *States* called her "one of the most devoted charity workers this city has ever known." It began its coverage with a phrase that sounded fitting for a sermon: "Miss Mary Werlein's body turns to dust in Metairie cemetery, but her soul lives. . . ." It went on to praise her in extravagant terms: "Her religious devotion was an inspiration. Her entire life was a denial of self and a devotion to others. In her burned the zeal of the Christian Martyrs, the courage of the Crusaders. She was a flame on the altar of brotherhood. Her light still burns—in the spirit of the living."[1] Because this language might seem a bit overblown but not completely unexpected in an obituary, it is important to emphasize that this came from the publication's news coverage, not from its obituary section. Her status as a Methodist laywoman, rather than a member of a religious order, needs emphasis, as well. She was in her forties when the story this book recounts began. The groundbreaking Social Gospel ministries that she and other Methodist women created and nurtured would transform the lives of many thousands of New Orleanians and shape the city itself in important ways.

METHODIST WOMEN ADOPT A STRUGGLING MISSION IN 1895

Before my research on St. Mark's began, only a very small amount of material about its history had found its way into print. Many of those documents described St. Mark's as an outgrowth of an establishment on Tchoupitoulas Street named the Mary Werlein Mission. The founding of the mission was placed in

1907 or 1908, said to be the same year that a deaconess, Lillie Meekins, arrived as a missionary in New Orleans from the Woman's Parsonage and Home Mission Society (WP&HMS).[2] Parts of this historical self-understanding of St. Mark's, especially the dates, proved incorrect.

Linking the founding of St. Mark's with the founding of the Mary Werlein Mission is accurate, because the mission is indeed where the women learned to enact their Social Gospel theology, and the move to the French Quarter and the establishment of St. Mark's Hall can, without distortion, be seen as an expansion of the work they were undertaking at the mission. However, by 1907, the mission had been operating on Tchoupitoulas Street for at least a decade under the women's administration. Although the facility's exact origins remain unclear, it is certain that Methodist women took over administration of the Tchoupitoulas Mission in February 1895 and that it had been operating for at least a few years by that time. Mary Werlein was involved in the acquisition of a building for it in 1895. Further, by 1907, Lillie Meekins (who was never a deaconess) had been at work as a city missionary in New Orleans for more than a decade; she was serving there at least as early as 1896. Other female city missionaries were employed even earlier.

All these women were part of an emerging but already strong movement within Methodism. Formal organization for women's work was approved in the Methodist Episcopal Church, South (MECS) by the General Conference of 1886, which authorized a "Woman's Department of Church Extension" to help fund construction of parsonages. In 1890, the General Conference bestowed "the more definite title of 'Woman's Parsonage and Home Mission Society.'" With the name change came an expansion of their portfolio to encompass "any work coming under the head of missions."

Ellen Burruss Parker, who was married to Bishop Linus Parker, was appointed to establish women's work in the Louisiana Conference, and after more than a year of organizational work, the statewide society was officially established on December 3, 1891. Even before 1891, societies at several individual congregations in New Orleans had already been engaged in "some excellent work" that included the employment of female city missionaries.[3] The newly chartered organization elected officers, including Mrs. F. A. Lyons, president; Mrs. C. W. Carter, recording secretary; Miss Mary Werlein, corresponding secretary, and Mrs. L. K. Widney, treasurer.[4]

Soon afterward, the group established an industrial school run by "our City Missionary, Miss Susie Burbank, an earnest, zealous, Christian woman." The *New Orleans Christian Advocate* called Susie Burbank "a consecrated young lady" whose salary was funded by donations from the various women's society groups in the city, and the article observed, "Her usefulness can not be overestimated. No one doubts her fitness or call to the work."[5] Burbank and a number of volunteers kept the school open even in the hot summer months, helping children acquire abilities that could move them from a status as unskilled laborers to skilled artisans.[6] MECS women were also involved in the larger issue of child labor legislation. For instance, in 1900, noted settlement worker Florence Kelley spoke on "The Factory Problem" and led a discussion about child labor at the annual meeting of the Woman's Board of Home Missions held in New Orleans.[7]

In 1894, Mary Werlein, a thirty-nine- or forty-year-old, single laywoman who resided at her family's home at the corner of Nashville and St. Charles avenues and who was the solicitor for subscriptions to the churchwomen's magazine, *Our Homes,* also held the office of state organizer for the WP&HMS. The women thought that designating a state organizer was "the best way to build up the work; because nothing but active, personal effort will multiply our societies, and develop that strength which we need." Early that year, the state president and Werlein made a trip around Louisiana to form additional local units of the society. They acknowledged that part of their success would depend on the assistance of pastors "in presenting the work favorably, to the women of their charges."[8]

In February 1895, the *New Orleans Christian Advocate* (hereafter referred to as *NOCA*) published an account of how the barely three-year-old women's organization came to oversee the mission that would later bear Werlein's name and from which St. Mark's would be spawned.[9] At a "very important" meeting of the New Orleans District WP&HMS, at which every society in the district was represented, the women heard a letter from the treasurer of the Tchoupitoulas Mission. He wrote that the board that had elected him had ceased to exist, and that his responsibility would end when the current lease on the building expired at the middle of that month. He recommended that the woman's society assume responsibility for the mission, which would cost them about $300 a year. The presiding elder of the New Orleans District (who would today be called the district superintendent) was on hand, and he urged the women to take charge of the facility. They also heard an appeal from Hadley Harrison, the mission's superintendent, who had been "actively connected" with the ministry there for three years. Harrison explained that four evening services were held at the location each week. He claimed that "Sinners have been converted" and joined local churches, and that an average of ninety children were attending Sunday school there. He attributed much of the success to "the faithful work of Miss Burbank, who has labored in the neighborhood of this mission for eight months."[10] Indeed, Burbank's work in providing educational opportunities through the industrial school was no doubt a key part of the mission's attractiveness to young people and their families.

Harrison urged the women not to abandon the work, and they voted unanimously to adopt the mission. Three women, Miss Mary Werlein, Miss Lizzie Watson, and Mrs. S. A. Montgomery, formed a committee "to secure a building and make all necessary arrangements for the ensuing year." They designated Hadley Harrison to continue as superintendent at the mission and elected Mary Werlein as their district treasurer.[11]

THE WOMAN'S SOCIETY GAINS STRENGTH

The fact that the men of the church hierarchy believed the women could rescue the mission speaks to the powerful nature of the women's group then in place in New Orleans. Their unanimous adoption of the project demonstrates a high level of self-confidence in their ability to accomplish the tasks involved, including the fund-raising. Sure enough, within two months, *NOCA* was editorializing that under the women's leadership, the mission was doing "a noble work." Revival services held during the previous two weeks had resulted "in many conversions." The "powers that be" had decided to charter an MECS congregation housed at the mission, and people were already applying for membership. "Our sisters of the Woman's Parsonage and Home Mission Society have cause to rejoice as they behold the fruits of their labors," the writer concluded. "The work of the Lord has prospered in their hands."[12]

Further evidencing the group's strength, in the fall of that year, the *New Orleans Christian Advocate* published a special double issue called the "Woman's

Edition" that paid tribute to the society on the cover. The editorial material mentioned the extra weight of the issue and the extra work involved in getting it out, and reported that so many businesses had desired to advertise in it that even with a double issue, some of them still could not be accommodated.[13]

One of the WP&HMS members, Mrs. H. A. Kennedy, wrote a history of the organization for this edition. She said that the newly organized church at the mission, eight months into the women's administration, now had a pastor, the Reverend J. M. Henry, and that three evening services were held each week. "The proceeds of this Woman's Edition of the New Orleans Advocate will be used as a building fund for a permanent house of worship in that neighborhood," she explained.[14]

MARY WERLEIN AS SOCIAL GOSPEL ACTIVIST

Kennedy said the society had organized a "training school for Christian workers" that the members attended. Local pastors and physicians lectured for a half hour each week, for a total of five months, and "[m]uch valuable instruction was obtained and put into practical use." She also discussed the reading list adopted by the group and admonished, "We must equip ourselves for service if we would be efficient workers in God's vineyard." The list comprised three books: *Our Country: Its Possible Future and Its Present Crisis* by Josiah Strong; *Prisoners of Poverty: Women Wage-Workers, Their Trades and Their Lives* by Helen Campbell; and *Applied Christianity: Moral Aspects of Social Questions* by Washington Gladden.[15]

The presence of works by Strong and Gladden, two of the better known Social Gospel thinkers, demonstrates that New Orleans Methodist women, even laywomen like Werlein who were not employed for pay in mission work at any level, were being grounded in Social Gospel theory. This helps to refute the former conventional wisdom that there was no manifestation of the Social Gospel in the South.

The frequent mentions and tributes paid to her in the pages of the *New Orleans Christian Advocate* and the society's decision to name the mission after her while she was still alive are indicative of the prominent role Werlein played in the women's organization, and particularly in the mission endeavor on Tchoupitoulas. An 1897 *NOCA* report said that she was "by individual efforts" raising about $25 per month to pay the rent and gas bills, and speculated that the mission might be able to leave its rented facility and move into "a home of its own" during the year. It implied that Werlein would hold primary responsibility for the acquisition of a new building and noted, "Miss Werlein, whose life, talents, and money are consecrated to the service of her Master, has contributed $1,000 to a loan fund in memory of her sainted parents."[16]

Exhibiting many of the classic, if not stereotypical, characteristics of female Progressive reformers, Werlein, who was born in 1853, never married and spent her time engaged in good works. Her great-nieces, Lorraine Moore and the late Betty Werlein Carter, recalled that Mary visited regularly in the parish prison and held religious services there. She was also a benefactor of St. Anna's Asylum, a residence for the elderly located at the corner of Prytania and St. Mary streets, where she gave many hours of volunteer service.[17]

Leila Werlein Stone of Vicksburg, Mississippi, another great-niece of Mary Werlein, remembers her great-aunt as "one of those women who got better looking as she got older. She was a tiny woman, with blue, piercing eyes and gorgeous, snow-white hair which she kept immaculately groomed." On occasion, Stone would accompany her aunt to St. Anna's, where, she recalled, "the old ladies just adored her. She would go down there and play the piano for them. She loved to play 'O Happy Day.'"

Despite the fondness residents of St. Anna's felt for Mary Werlein, she was not universally regarded as the soul of kindness. As Stone said, "The book of Jude begins with a prayer that the saints might be preserved. I heard a pastor read that once and say that some of the saints were preserved in sugar and others were preserved in vinegar. Aunt Mary was a vinegar saint."[18]

Werlein was known for walking to St. Anna's and to other destinations, even when they were some distance away, so that she could save the carfare and donate it to missions. Stone concurred: "She was very frugal, very frugal. She would spend each summer with my grandfather and grandmother at their summer home in Biloxi, and when she was in New Orleans living with Ethel May, she was very constrained, but in Biloxi—my grandmother was a very kind and loving person, and Aunt Mary just ruled the roost. If I'd reach for the butter at the table, down would come her bony little arm on mine, and 'I'll help you, Leila, Jr.' she would say. She'd give me one little pat of butter that never quite covered my piece of bread."[19]

Other than letters published in *NOCA,* none of Werlein's papers appear to have survived. Her family has no written records about her, and most relatives have few memories of her. The extant letters, then, are a particularly important window into the thinking of a lay Social Gospel practitioner, and large portions are reproduced here. The letter written by Werlein and published in the May 1895 *New Orleans Christian Advocate* demonstrates how seriously she took her work as mission treasurer (and perhaps also a bit of the "vinegar" in her own personality):

> To the friends of the Woman's Parsonage and Home Mission Societies and of the Tchoupitoulas Mission, I would say a word. To you who had subscribed to this mission are these lines especially addressed. Friends, please do not fail to hand in your amount. Because it may be but little, do not believe it does not matter whether you are prompt or not. Remember there is *"multum in parvo."* ...
> ... The rent notes and gas bills come whether there is anything in the treasury or not, and they can not be met unless you meet them. . . . Many persons say they do not believe in foreign missions. This, then, is their opportunity. Cast in your mite monthly, and go to the mission and see with your own eyes and hear with your own ears what is being done. If you will not grasp this opportunity for home mission work, then know the truth that your words are spurious and forever after hold your peace about the foreign work, for we know too well that often this is only a quietus upon the conscience.[20]

Providing detailed information on several methods by which subscribers could deliver their payments to her (and these included dropping them off at the family's music store on Canal Street), Werlein suggested that because "[t]he best of people are sometimes forgetful," subscribers should "cut this out and place it upon your looking-glass, and I will guarantee your district treasurer will not have to make a call upon you again." She signed her letter, "Yours in the work, Mary Werlein."[21]

Another letter she wrote, which appeared in the July 11, 1895, issue, offers additional insight into her life and work as a reformer. The *NOCA* editor asked Werlein to write an account of the Baton Rouge District women's conference held in Ponchatoula, Louisiana, that she had attended. She furnished him a copy of the letter she had sent to Lucinda B. Helm, editor of the churchwomen's periodical, *Our Homes,* about the event: "It was a most delightful occasion, the spiritual feature being quite marked—in fact, it was equal to a camp meeting all the way through, and we bless God for the privilege of being there. Of course, we went to represent the work of the Woman's Parsonage and Home Mission Society. Never did anything lay nearer our heart than this cause, and we feel we shall never be quite satisfied until the whole of the state of Louisiana, at least, shall be canvassed, and an auxiliary planted in every church where it is at all practicable."[22]

The original charge of the society at the time of its creation had been to help build parsonages, and Werlein continued to take that portion of the group's task to heart: "Oh, how we do long that every charge should have its own parsonage, and our brethren made somewhat comfortable! They have a hard enough time at best, and it is just as little as the women of our beloved church can do to be determined that, by the help of God, it should be done."[23] Werlein's interest in the clergy's welfare was in part personal. Though she had several close relatives who were Episcopalian clergy, her closest brother, Shepard Halsey Werlein, born two years before her, was a prominent Methodist clergyman. This is the Reverend Dr. S. H. Werlein who was Leila Werlein Stone's grandfather, and with whose family Mary Werlein spent each summer in Biloxi, Mississippi. A noted reformer, he served several of the largest southern pulpits during his career, and used his prominence to advocate publicly for laity rights for women, temperance, and other reform causes of the era. It seems likely that Werlein had him in mind as she continued her letter to Helm: "If we are too strong in our praises of our beloved ministers, pardon it, for we have always had a weak spot, and a very big one at that, in our heart for the Methodist ministers; and if there are any flaws in the characters of any of them, the outside world shall never have the knowledge of such imperfections if it waits for us to give the information."[24]

The women's five-day trip to Ponchatoula resulted in the organization of one youth and four adult societies. Werlein was convinced that "There is not much that woman cannot accomplish when she goes at it with a heart full of love and energy, baptized by the Holy Ghost." This letter is signed, "Yours for Christ, Mary Werlein."[25]

If this letter were the only evidence, one might conclude that it was the building of parsonages that interested Werlein most among the WP&HMS activities, and there is no reason to believe that her concern for this issue was not genuine, especially because several of her relatives were clergymen. However, the women knew that in order to establish a women's organization in a congregation, they needed the pastor's cooperation. Werlein's letter praised a pastor who had assisted the women on their organizing trip, stating, "it is due to his hearty cooperation that we had such fine success."[26]

She may have believed it was the women's efforts to build parsonages that would be most positively received by most male clergy, both because they might see positive benefits for themselves or their male colleagues and because it fit more neatly into the so-called "woman's sphere." The provision of parsonages—that is, homes—for clergy families was presumed to be a natural concern for women. Werlein's letter regarding donations for the Tchoupitoulas Mission, written only a few months earlier, clearly demonstrates her deep commitment to its programs for assisting the poor and her support for the broader field of home mission endeavor.

Though not a lot of Werlein's writing survived, the material that exists contains a number of very telling phrases, such as "baptized by the Holy Ghost" and "equal to a camp meeting." They indicate that she may have chosen Methodism rather than the Episcopal Church for her own religious expression because of a preference for more "enthusiastic" worship. Though this could be used to comment on her leanings in a particular divergence of opinion within Methodism about liturgy, that discussion is beyond the scope of this project. A more useful revelation for the purposes of this study is what it can contribute to a later discussion of whether Methodist woman's society members were motivated by a desire to replicate their social class. Werlein's rhetoric indicates that she was motivated by a desire to evangelize (that is, to bring outsiders in) rather than by a desire to make her society an exclusive organization peopled only with upper-class women.

SOCIAL GOSPEL POLICIES DEFENDED

Almost exactly one year after the meeting where Werlein and the other members of the women's organization assumed responsibility for the mission, *NOCA* printed two stories about the progress they had achieved. One included a reprint of an article from a major New Orleans newspaper, the *New Orleans Daily Picayune,* that announced the establishment of a free employment bureau. Persons who needed jobs were urged to come by the mission at 1014 Tchoupitoulas Street any day between two and four o'clock in the afternoon. Employers who needed workers were encouraged to contact the pastor. Following the reprinted story, *NOCA* provided its own content that not only praised this endeavor, but also signaled approval of other kinds of Social Gospel ministries, along with their theoretical and theological underpinnings.

"There are thousands of people in this city who are in the most abject poverty," the *NOCA* author wrote. "Some preliminary work needs to be done before these people can be brought under the influence of the gospel. They will not attend church until they have food to eat and clothes to wear." The writer went on to defend Social Gospel tactics by refuting the prevailing belief that the poor lacked resources because of a character flaw that made them "paupers by choice," and by pointing to the success of the methodology of linking social empowerment with evangelization in other places: "The success of the Salvation Army in the large cities of Great Britain is to a large extent due to the fact that while it preaches the gospel, it also, like our blessed Lord, ministers to the physical necessities of men."[27]

A separate story printed in the same issue informed readers that the Sunday school at the mission was growing not only in numbers, but also in "spirituality." It noted that large prayer and class meetings were "doing great good in developing the spiritual life of the infant church. The Sabbath services are well attended, and many, on profession of faith and by certificate, are joining the church."[28] Because the editor defended Social Gospel strategies on numerous occasions, it is reasonable to assume that his emphasis on spiritual growth at the mission may have been part of an effort to deflect criticism about secularization.

WIDENING THE WOMEN'S SPHERE

It is noteworthy that, in the course of this commentary, *NOCA* relegated the female city missionary to the role of "helper," stating that the pastor "finds an efficient helper in Mrs. Lillie Meekins, one of his members, who is also the missionary of the Woman's Parsonage and Home Mission Society."[29] A column written two months later by a woman depicted Meekins herself in a leading role; the WP&HMS annual report composed by Florence Russ noted the dangerous aspects of Lillie Meekins's service, stating, "Mrs. Meekins, the city missionary, residing in the mission, which is in one of the most depraved portions of our city, is one filled with the Holy Spirit, and works faithfully to 'seek and save that which is lost.'"[30]

The "depraved" section of the city to which Russ referred was known as the Irish Channel, and it was reputed to have a high degree of lawlessness. Mills and small factories operated amid the homes of their laborers. Because Tchoupitoulas Street runs alongside the Mississippi River, sailors and others who worked on the docks and wharves frequented the area. The Irish Channel offered a classic example of turn-of-the-century problems associated with industrialization and urbanization, the same problems to which the Social Gospel is usually deemed a response.

It is fortunate that Meekins's own description of her work on Tchoupitoulas Street, written sometime between 1893 and 1898, was preserved verbatim in a 1936 publication:

All of the families in the field are of the poorest . . . those employed barely earning sufficient to supply the necessities, none of the comforts of life. The homes consist of one room. So many are unemployed; and where these have found Christ they need constant help to sustain their faith through the many discouragements along this line and to help them to trust their heavenly Father for their daily needs. This blessed and most compensating work means to go here and there—anywhere He may lead. It means a sympathetic, cheering word to one; loving counsel to an erring one; the binding together of a broken link in a home; a prayer with a straying one; a patient listening to the daily sorrows; a story of misery, of poverty; trying to get employment for another; procuring doctor and medicine for a sick one. It means the cup of cool water; the cool cloth placed on a fevered brow; to bathe the feet, to ease pain; a cup of tea to another; perhaps to spend the night with a sick one—to indeed be made all things to these people that we might thereby lead some to salvation.[31]

The Irish Channel was also the setting for the Boarding Home for Working Women established under the auspices of the WP&HMS in early 1897. As stated earlier, the New Orleans laywomen read *Prisoners of Poverty: Women Wage-Workers, Their Trades and Their Lives* by Helen Campbell, and this examination of the plight of women employed at low wages is likely to have fueled enthusiasm for the project.

A twelve-room building was secured "to provide a comfortable and suitable home for young girls coming to this city in search of employment, to surround them with refining influences, and to help them to spend their hours of recreation in a manner both pleasant and beneficial to themselves." The home was supervised by a Mrs. Stafford, "a courteous Christian lady." Writing for *NOCA*, the WP&HMS secretary called the group's accomplishments at the facility "a grand work" and insisted that it was "especially woman's work, because it is her province to smooth by her gentle ministry the rough places of life. . . . It is her promise to keep the home-life sweet and pure by her love and prayers and to seek out those deprived of its blessed influence and surround them, as far as possible, with its protecting care."[32]

It is most interesting to see the New Orleans laywomen using the emphasis on "home," which national reformers and suffragists like Frances Willard frequently relied upon to temper resistance to otherwise "unsuitable" activities for women. Rosemary Skinner Keller noted that using language about "home protection" and making "the world more home-like" with regard to issues like suffrage "effectively released thousands of women in their callings from God." Willard herself once wrote, "Under the mold of conservative action, I have been most radical in thought." Historian Sara Joyce Myers has explored how Belle Bennett and several other women leaders in the MECS operated within the norms of female behavior, because they found their efforts more effective that way. Scholarship regarding members of nonreligious women's clubs and organizations has also identified a type of "domestic feminism," in which women enlarged their spheres of influence through couching their activities as natural extensions of their home-oriented activities. Still, the flaunting of domesticity is ironic in regard to an establishment specifically for women who would be working outside the home, and it demonstrates that the Methodist women of New Orleans took a backseat to no one in their subtle subversion of patriarchal restrictions.[33]

In 1901, the worshipping congregation at Tchoupitoulas Street, where Meekins remained employed as city missionary, consisted of 129 members; seven individuals had joined the previous year by making professions of faith, and four had transferred from other congregations. In 1903, the city mission board reported that twelve teachers were employed at the industrial school, which 255 children had attended the previous year. The number of congregational women's societies represented on the board had increased, from eight to eleven, and the amount expended for the salary of the city missionary was $200.85. They worked with a total budget of $2,278.79. By 1906, the women's society was "contemplating undertaking a much broader work at the mission. They are seeking to secure subscriptions which will total $100.00 a month, so that they may secure the services of a trained worker, and inaugurate several departments of settlement work."[34] The mention of a "trained worker" points to the women's increasing recognition of the need for professionalization of women's positions within the church.[35]

Sometime between the publications of the 1906 and 1907 *Journals,* the mission's name, which had varied among the Tchoupitoulas Street Church, the Tchoupitoulas Mission, and the New Orleans Mission, was officially changed to the Mary Werlein Mission (which it had also occasionally been called in earlier reports). The conference board of missions budgeted $300 for its operation the next year.[36] Meekins wrote: "There is ever much to be done, and ever will be, as long as this factory territory exists, with the crowded tenement conditions which ever follow such boundary. Poor wages ever require a claim on us for temporal help, and the daily discouragements which often come to these people in the monotonous drudgery of their lives require our constant strengthening spiritually; but we are leading them slowly to Christ through this mission."[37] Her critique of social conditions, low wages, and the monotony of factory jobs demonstrates that the women were thinking substantively about underlying economic structures that the Industrial Revolution had created.

THE DEATH OF MARY WERLEIN

Mary Werlein served on the board of stewards of the mission congregation until it was subsumed into the St. Mark's congregation. After the mission closed, Werlein worshipped with the Parker Memorial congregation on Nashville

Avenue, near her home, until she died of pancreatic cancer in 1940, at the age of eighty-six. Interestingly, the weekly Methodist publication, the *New Orleans Christian Advocate,* devoted far less space to her death than the city's daily newspapers. *NOCA* printed only four sentences, including: "She had lived a long, long while, and was truly one of the elect women of New Orleans Methodism."[38]

In contrast, the *Times-Picayune* and the *States* provided significant coverage of her death in their regular news sections, in addition to the expected entry among the obituaries. The *States* actually ran two longer stories on May 4, duplicating some of the copy between them. On page three, they ran a six-inch story headed, "Devout Church Worker Expires," that provided details about the funeral arrangements and noted that "one of her last requests" was for friends to send money to one of her favorite charities instead of flowers. On page four, amid a somewhat less formal look at doings around the state and nation, a shorter, more vivid story was headed simply, "Mary Werlein." It began with the observation that "Miss Mary Werlein's body turns to dust in Metairie cemetery, but her soul lives." Along with St. Mark's and St. Anna's, it included the Woman's Christian Temperance Union (WCTU) and the Travelers' Aid Society among her favored organizations. Praising her as "one of the most devoted charity workers this city has ever known," the writer said she had developed her interest in "charity work" early in life through "her membership in organizations connected with the Parker Memorial Methodist Church," an obvious reference to the women's society. As noted in this chapter's introduction, the story said "the zeal of the Christian Martyrs" and the "courage of the Crusaders" burned within her. (Today, a comparison with Crusaders would be read more negatively than positively, but clearly the *States* considered it a compliment.)[39] Under the headline, "Charity Worker of New Orleans Dies at Age of 86," the *Times-Picayune* provided five and one-half inches of more formal coverage.

Although both of the major secular newspapers used the nomenclature "charity worker" for Werlein, the *States,* with its rhetoric about "zeal of Christian martyrs" and "courage of Crusaders," may actually have come closer to an accurate depiction of how Werlein's Social Gospel–inspired activities were viewed at the turn of the twentieth century. It is possible that the author remembered some of the conflicts Werlein and the other WP&HMS women had with the Methodist establishment or with other segments of society who opposed their assistance to immigrants or their work in support of racial toler-ance or women's suffrage. "Charity worker" is inoffensive language, but the far more loaded labels "reformer," "activist," and "practitioner of the Social Gospel" could equally well have been applied to her.

In the era when Werlein and her friends were establishing settlement work in New Orleans, the ideas of the public and even of the church at large about activities like those of the WP&HMS were shaped by extremely popular So-cial Gospel novels. Unquestionably, the best known is Charles Sheldon's *In His Steps*. Published in 1897, it has influenced countless Christians. Sales estimates range up to twenty million, and in the mid-twentieth century, it appeared on one historian's list of thirteen "books that have changed America."[40] The charac-ters are prominent church members who covenant to ask, "What Would Jesus Do?" before making any decision. Their transformed lives impact an entire city.

The Tchoupitoulas Mission was very similar to the mission the novel's characters decided to support with their money, talents, and presence. Further, there are readily apparent similarities between one character, a single woman who had to decide how to use inherited money, and Mary Werlein. It would be easy to believe that Werlein and the other New Orleans women were pursu-ing their ministries because they were inspired by the writer. Therefore, it is crucial to recall that Werlein and her WP&HMS companions had already been engaged in their work for several years before the book appeared. It was art imi-tating life, rather than the other way around, and I make this point because so much evaluation of the Social Gospel movement has been based on the prem-ise that the men who wrote about it were the movement's primary actors.

ADDRESSING THE "MENACE" OF IMMIGRATION

Shortly after the turn of the century, the MECS General Missionary Confer-ence was held in New Orleans. One of the featured speakers was Belle Bennett, the Kentucky laywoman whom John Patrick McDowell has called "the domi-nant figure during the first two decades of the twentieth century" in MECS home mission efforts.[41] Delivering an address on the Woman's Home Mission Society, she laid out the organization's accomplishments of the past fifteen years. Though it was established only to build parsonages, as the means for sharing information expanded and women learned more about urban conditions, "the demand for other and purely missionary work became imperative." While they had aided in the construction of 1,147 parsonages, donating more than $107,000 and lending more than $31,000 toward that work, their 24,712 members had raised and spent more than three times as much on other projects. For example, in 1901, society members were supporting eight schools and employing thirty-two teachers, who had taught one thousand students over the years.[42]

Bennett explained the women's strategy for urban ministry, which was to organize a city mission board in every city that had two or more women's groups. Three women from each group would form the board, with the pastors and the presiding elder as advisory members. "The plan has grown in favor, and eleven cities have carried on successful missions," she said. (One of those cities was New Orleans, under the leadership of Elvira Carré, whose work is discussed later in this chapter.) The eleven city mission boards employed fourteen trained city missionaries, who visited from house to house, "getting into the home life and close to the hearts of the people." They gave Bible readings, held cottage prayer meetings, brought the needs of the sick and destitute to the notice of church members, and urged "on parents and children the importance of attending the services of the Church and the Sunday school."[43] Then she proceeded to advance a rationale for the continued existence of the women's mission board (evidence of her prescience, because it was subsumed by the men's mission board in 1910 without the women's approval, a turn of events discussed in many sources).[44]

Bennett voiced the opinion that the women's efforts had been motivated by problems that she, and many southern Methodists, saw as byproducts of a large number of "irreligious" foreign-born immigrants. She said that Chinese and Japanese immigrants to the West had come from "an idol-worshipping people" with "degrading vices." She spoke of population shifts from rural areas to southern cities with "rapidly changing industrial conditions," which also affected the racial mix. "The factory population, with its difficult problems, was enormously on the increase; and the mining camps, with their mixed and migratory multitudes of every nationality and no religion, were a growing evil. The churchgoing classes were undoubtedly growing stronger and perhaps more aggressive, but the non-churchgoing classes were certainly growing larger and more discontented."[45] Readers who are familiar with the rhetoric about immigration in the early twentieth century will recognize this as comparatively mild language. She may have included the material to help convince the men in the audience that an "all hands on deck" policy, with "all hands" including the women's mission board, would prove wise.

The women of New Orleans were already planning to expand their work at the mission by opening a second location selected to reach Italian immigrants. Bennett's omission of Roman Catholics from her list of "problem" immigrants is interesting, especially when her rhetoric is compared with that of Harry W. Rickey, the male secretary of the Louisiana Conference's Board of Missions, who provided an example of language more typical of that period. At the 1903 conference gathering, he reported:

> In Louisiana the Providence of God has wiped out the distinctions between the home and foreign missionary fields. If we will not send our money to foreign fields, God has sent the heathen to our shores. The Dago, the Chinaman, the Turk, the Indian, the Negro, the untutored European, are already here. If we are to preserve the Anglo-Saxon supremacy, we must Christianize them, or they will heathenize us. It is no longer a question of geography or of parallels of latitude and longitude, but of self-preservation, progress, retention of our rights and privileges as citizens of America and servants of God.
>
> All the problems of the foreign fields are unloaded upon us, and solve them we must, or they will dissolve us who are in Louisiana. ... We must become missionaries, or we will become, eventually, dromedaries of the Dago, the Turk, the Jew, or the German and their commercial genius.[46]

With Rickey's call to Louisiana Methodists as "citizens of America and servants of God," he demonstrates the conflating of Protestantism and nationalism so prevalent in the early decades of the twentieth century. The prejudice against Italian Roman Catholics, which allowed him to consider them "heathens" in exactly the same way he considered non-Christians as "heathens," is addressed in a later chapter, and was not usually shared by MECS deaconesses.

His proposed solution is both racist and ironic—along with more money and a wider distribution of Christian literature, he calls for "more prayer, larger inspiration, wise planning, and conscience-stirring teaching."[47]

Even the highest leadership of the MECS was not above fear-mongering about immigration. The Episcopal Address to the General Conference in 1906 called the increased numbers of immigrants flooding to New Orleans and Galveston "a perilous menace" that might reduce America to paganism unless the immigrants were Americanized first.[48]

It is significant that male church leaders who wished to call attention to the "immigrant problem" did so in terms that continued to draw division between groups. The "us-them" mentality is evident in these statements that use terms like "self-preservation" as a rationale for mission funding. In general, they appear to lack the sympathy for the immigrants as individuals, which the MECS women seem to have felt. When only utterances, writings, and actions of men are considered to comprise the Social Gospel (as has usually been the case), it is easier to support assertions that the movement was intrinsically racist. A very different picture results when we move the women who were living out the Social Gospel in the South into the center of the picture.

RACIAL AND ETHNIC TENSIONS INCREASE

New Orleans had a large number of black citizens, including some who had been slaves or descended from slaves, and some who had descended from the city's unusually large population of free people of color. In 1900, racial tensions came to a head when a disturbance occurred within a mile and a quarter of the mission. Robert Charles, a black man who was a supporter of the International Migration Society, a back-to-Africa movement, shot and killed a police officer in late July. Events escalated over the next several days to a full-scale riot with plentiful gunfire that resulted in dozens of casualties.[49] Whites were outraged, and the editor/publisher of the afternoon paper, the *New Orleans States,* called for a "FINAL SOLUTION" to "the negro problem." (This was more restrained language than he sometimes used—William Ivy Hair found he had once used the word "nigger" twenty-eight times in one editorial.) The publisher's threat meant that if blacks did not stifle their dissatisfaction, it would lead to race war, which

would in turn lead to "extermination" of the black race. Enough shared his opinion to keep the *States* the most powerful afternoon paper in Louisiana, and he
was later eulogized by his friend and supporter, the Reverend Mr. B. M. Palmer
of the First Presbyterian Church, whose own less-than-tolerant views on race
relations have been explored by other writers.[50]

Larger questions about the complicated racial structure of New Orleans
and the city's immigration history have also been addressed by various scholars. They have acknowledged that the animosity whites felt toward blacks in
that era advantaged other ethnic groups, who might otherwise have been even
more discriminated against than they were. Nevertheless, there was much in-
tolerance toward Italians.[51] Among other tensions, there was lingering distrust
over an incident in 1879. Police chief David Hennessy was assassinated and
reportedly told a fellow officer with his last words that "Dagos" did it. Large
numbers of Italians were arrested on little or no evidence, and eleven Sicilians
were eventually taken from the parish prison and lynched by a mob. Historian
Louise Reynes Edwards-Simpson implied that the persons responsible, at least
for instigating the lynching, if not for committing the deed itself, were sixty-one
members of the Pickwick Club and the Krewe of Comus, two of the most powerful private social organizations in the city.[52] Regardless of whether she is correct, the fact that this could even be seriously suggested reflects the extreme
level of tension around the issue of immigration, which affected almost every
aspect of life in New Orleans at the turn of the twentieth century.

A classic study of the Old Regulars (or Choctaws), an organization that exercised political control in New Orleans for decades, makes the point that there
were large numbers of Italians who needed services from government and who
thus became a political force in the city around the turn of the century. In 1890
there were 7,767 foreign-born Italians in New Orleans, who were "[f]or the
most part . . . of the lower classes, poor and illiterate." The author puts the Italian population at 16,500 in 1900 and 21,818 in 1920. In 1930, Italians made up
5.2 percent of the population.[53]

The majority of ethnic Italians were indeed poor, having been driven from
their homeland by economic conditions so grim that some 7 percent of Sicily's
population emigrated between 1899 and 1910. Southern Italians made up 20
percent of the 8.4 million immigrants to the United States that decade.[54] Many

had been recruited by the state-sponsored Louisiana Agriculture and Immigration Association, which distributed pamphlets like "An Invitation to Louisiana for Italian Tenant Farmers and Agriculturists" throughout southern Italy. Louisiana was among the most active and successful southern states in recruiting Sicilians as an inexpensive source of labor.[55]

One historian suggested southern Methodists, "like other southerners," were troubled by the thought of black labor being "displaced by the Italian immigrant. Although the Negroes were considered inefficient, unreliable, and unwilling to serve, southerners considered them the lesser of two evils when compared with the Roman Catholic Italians who were accused of disregarding the Sabbath, of bringing in criminal attitudes and the Mafia, and of being willing to strike."[56] However, subsequent history shows Italians eventually gained "white" status, while blacks remained segregated for decades to come. In fact, Edwards-Simpson maintains that the solidification of Jim Crow led directly to increased acceptance of Italians. "Whereas New Orleans had long perpetuated a more fluid racial caste system turn-of-the-century de jure segregation precluded subtle distinctions between Black and white categories." In 1898, the state legislature, "after much debate," exempted Italians from Jim Crow segregation. "By 1905, Sicilians began to be viewed more as backward and tradition-bound than as racially inferior. The new designation was not a major improvement in any immediate way and it was sufficiently condescending to justify the continued exploitation and ill-treatment of Sicilian immigrants." Still, the move "carried with it the possibility for the immigrants to rehabilitate themselves by internalizing modern perspectives whereas the earlier racial classification castigated Sicilians in biological terms with no avenue for uplift."[57]

METHODIST WOMEN ADDRESS THE NEEDS OF IMMIGRANTS

The MECS women of New Orleans worked hard to address the perceived problems of the diverse urban community. Progressives and reformers of the Social Gospel era have received criticism for using a "band-aid" approach to address the symptoms, rather than underlying causes, of social ills. However, to the exact extent that the women (like society in general) saw the underlying problem as the very existence of the "Other" in their midst, their failure to address the problem at the root—by exterminating minority groups, as the *New Orleans States* editor proposed, or by urging the closing of our borders—might appear a genuinely progressive, if not Christian, response. Often portrayed as conservatives for trying to "Americanize" immigrants (which they did), the southern Methodist women also tried to adapt the church to the presence of the immigrants; further, attempting to meet what they saw as the immigrants' greatest need (to adapt to America) is a moderate response, especially compared with the Ku Klux Klan and various other violent anti-immigrant groups that arose over the next few decades.

It concerned the MECS women that their work in the Irish Channel was reaching few of the Italians who were moving into the city, many of whom lived in the French Quarter. Around 1900, the part of the Quarter bounded by Esplanade, North Rampart, St. Peter, and the river (roughly the section downriver from the St. Louis Cathedral) was often called "Little Palermo," after the town in western Sicily.[58] Both the former St. Mark's buildings on Esplanade Avenue and the current facility at the corner of North Rampart and Gov. Nicholls streets are located within this section.

The year 1908 found Belle Bennett back in Louisiana, this time to address the Annual Conference gathering about home missions, where she "displayed a wonderful knowledge of the real conditions in New Orleans" and helped secure passage of a resolution submitted by the conference secretary for home missions. The resolution referred to the "evangelization" of New Orleans and especially its immigrants as "great and perplexing problems." Referring to an agreement among the Women's Home Mission Society and the General Boards of Missions and Church Extension to provide "substantial aid" for the work, she called upon the Annual Conference to cooperate with a joint commission appointed to frame policy for mission work on the Gulf Coast. That commission intended to establish "a great mission below Canal Street." The resolution was adopted, along with others that addressed financing the new enterprise.[59]

Belle Bennett, Lillie Meekins, "local philanthropists," and officials of the home mission board had evaluated the success of the Mary Werlein Mission and determined that the city needed an additional location to meet the influx of immigrants expected to occur when the Panama Canal opened. The women sought a site near the waterfront but on the other (downriver) side of Canal Street.[60] (In New Orleans parlance, this would be in the European, rather than the American, section of the city.) They selected a location at 619–21 Esplanade Avenue.[61] Though Methodist settlements for white clientele in other cities were called "Wesley House," Bennett herself named the Esplanade settlement St. Mark's Hall. Considering that St. Mark is the patron saint of Venice, where a cathedral and beautiful square honor him, it seems clear that the facility was intended to be especially hospitable to Italian immigrants, including Roman Catholics.

One historian has suggested that much of the local mission activity on the part of MECS churchwomen—work she terms "practical religion"—began in response to missionary work that MEC women initiated in the south after the Civil War and in response to a perceived need by the southerners to compete with it. Despite the extent of the urban problems the southern church faced, the southerners were not enthusiastic about the northern church's efforts to address them, and some considered the MEC's postwar missionaries to New Orleans "invaders."[62] It was probably no coincidence that MEC women had already been working with Italian immigrants for more than a dozen years in the very same block of Esplanade.

Nevertheless, there is a significant difference in the chosen vocabulary about Italian immigrants from the MECS women and the women's society of the MEC, and perhaps counter-intuitively, it is the northern women whose rhetoric is vitriolic. Using derogatory language that would have been hurtful to anyone of Italian origin was a part of the northern women's tactics for gaining support for the New Orleans ministry. In 1896–97, the MEC women's organization issued calls for additional missionaries from the northern church to reach the "densely ignorant" Italians of New Orleans, who were "dirty beyond belief" and "not so easily controlled as the Negroes." They sponsored a sewing school and a Sunday school and many of the same activities that St. Mark's would initiate nearby.[63]

MECS women did not use such language about the Italians whom they would serve, and as evidence in later chapters will show, they did not see black citizens, much less Italians, as a group that needed to be "controlled." The "social control" language that has been so troubling to some scholars was not part of the MECS women's discourse.[64] On the contrary, material written by the first superintendent of St. Mark's, Nicolas Joyner, admitted that "we, as a people, are woefully ignorant of the language, manners, and customs of other folks, and we absolutely ignore every view-point but the Anglo-Saxon." Published in the MECS publication, *The Missionary Voice*, the article decries judging all Italians by the behavior of a small criminal element and insists that most Italians are "an economical and industrious people" who are "apt to learn." The "Book Shelf" section of the same issue talks about a guide for Italian immigrants distributed at St. Mark's that "contains the simplest . . . information which we ourselves absorb unconsciously as we grow up, but for lack of which an alien may suffer or be defrauded or punished."[65]

ELVIRA BEACH CARRÉ SHAPES MECS WOMEN'S WORK

The relative tolerance, open-mindedness, and lack of class consciousness displayed by Joyner and by the other MECS women reflected the attitudes of Elvira Beach Carré, who was both Joyner's personal mentor and a woman who held an extraordinarily powerful leadership role in the New Orleans women's work. Regarded as "a tower of strength to Methodism in Louisiana" who was "universally esteemed and honored,"[66] she was chosen by the WP&HMS members across New Orleans to lead their city mission board as president for an astonishing nineteen years. Elected to the position in 1892, when the group first organized, Elvira Beach Carré shaped the Social Gospel ministries in New Orleans during three of the movement's most vital decades.

Born in Ohio in 1842, she moved to New Orleans with her family when she was four years old, attended public schools, and graduated from a "female seminary" run by a Madame Bigot. Her father, E. D. Beach, was "one of the most prominent physicians" in New Orleans. His first name, Erasmus, and middle name, Darwin, speak of well-educated parents of his own. Dr. Beach "took the highest interest in civic matters" and served as a member of the school board. He was twice elected coroner, and investigations into causes of death spurred him to work successfully for regulation of steamboat boiler construction and railroad crossings. After retirement, he continued to serve the poor.[67] He was an active Methodist layman throughout his life. A fellow congregant recalled that "[h]e was a man of strong personality" with "definite convictions and . . .

the power of independent action," and that he had done "a vast amount of good among many people of all classes and creeds."[68]

Dr. Beach's commitment to working with the poor and his concern for those "of all classes and creeds" were traits that he passed along to his daughter, Elvira, who at age twenty married a lumber mill owner about thirteen years older than she. Her husband died some fifteen years later, in 1877. In 1891, a local publication, *Louisiana Review*, profiled Carré in a section called, "What Women Are Doing—Gifted Louisiana Women" and noted that she had successfully managed the lumber mill after her husband's death. Observing that she was a slender brunette of medium height, with "large dark eyes . . . full of intelligence and kindliness," the author seemed surprised to find that she was "essentially feminine in appearance and manner and one would never imagine that beneath that gentle face and quiet manner was the strength of will and intellect of a man."[69]

As discussed in the introduction, women of the late 1800s and early 1900s were expected to confine themselves to the so-called "women's sphere," and the "Cult of True Womanhood" was deeply rooted in religious authority. The necessary qualities for "True Womanhood" were piety, domesticity, and submissiveness, and it is an interesting exercise to analyze the article about Carré in light of this description and the "True Methodist Womanhood" that Jean Miller Schmidt devised from it.[70]

Designation as a "devoted member" of her church and an "active worker" on the board of the Christian Woman's Exchange testified to Carré's piety.[71] Speaking of her life before her husband's death, the *Louisiana Review* informed readers that it "had been a quiet and secluded one up to that time, devoted to domestic duties and social pleasures." This definitely speaks of the dutiful wife who does not step out of her place.

She was the mother of seven children, including a son who died just before he turned two, and daughters who died at the ages of eight and ten. The four remaining children were sons, and it was for them that she rescued the lumber mill when it nearly failed because of poor management after her husband's death.[72] First, she hired an accountant to teach her to keep books, and then took over the running of the business herself. Nevertheless, readers were reassured that Carré was "always devoted to her home life" and that she had "never, in her busiest years, relinquished the management of her domestic affairs." Thus, she properly displayed domesticity.

Fig. 4. Elvira Beach Carré, president of the
City Mission Board for nineteen years and one
of the driving forces behind the establishment of
St. Mark's. Photo courtesy of Isabel Gardner
Larue and Susan Larue.

Gender roles put powerful limitations on the lives of southern women during Carré's lifetime. Among the options Schmidt lists for women whose lives were constrained by the expectations for the "True Methodist Woman" is one of enlarging their accepted "sphere" of activities while continuing to emphasize their devotion to traditional duties and roles. This depiction of Carré by the *Louisiana Review* reveals that she offers an excellent example of women who chose this route for shaping their identities as churchwomen.

The "busiest years" that the author referred to were busy indeed, for Carré worked at the office from ten o'clock in the morning to 4 o'clock in the afternoon "each day for four years," and later completed the same office tasks working from home.[73] Even after her sons reached the age where they could handle the business, she remained extremely active in the life of the church and community. She once served as president of six organizations at the same time and was eventually made the "Honorary Life President" of five.

The deaths of three children would not have been so unexpected in that time as it would be today, but they would remain no less devastating to a mother. Though Carré did retreat for some time to the family's vacation home at a Methodist campground in Tennessee after at least one of her daughter's deaths, she always returned to pick up her responsibilities. In fact, her activity could possibly have been a part of her strategy for coping with these losses and the loss of her husband when she had not reached age forty. However, she would have had countless choices for channeling her energies, and the selections she made among organizations other than the WP&HMS reveal much about her philosophical and theological bent. Significantly, when the Young Women's Christian Association (YWCA) first came to New Orleans, she was "a leading spirit" in organizing the local unit and served as president during its first two years; this affiliation with a group dedicated to better racial understanding signals as well as anything her commitment to the improvement of race relations. Carré died in 1924 at the age of eighty-two, having lived long enough to see St. Mark's move into its wonderful new structure on North Rampart Street and expand its services into a ministry that would serve the city for a century to come.[74] She and the other laywomen who piloted the MECS societies through conflicts and challenges both to their work and to their existence as powerful female leaders made possible the cutting-edge work toward racial progress that the deaconesses at St. Mark's accomplished, which is described in the coming chapters.

WERE FEMALE SOCIAL GOSPEL PRACTITIONERS "CONSERVATIVE"?

When the New Orleans Council of Social Agencies organized in the early 1920s, it assigned both St. Mark's Hall and Kingsley House to the committee for institutions whose primary task was "Character Building."[75] Later, the newly organized Community Chest classified them both as "Recreation and Character Building Agencies," along with the YWCA and YMCA, the Girl Scouts and Boy Scouts, the Young Men's and Young Women's Hebrew Associations, the Salvation Army, and other similar groups.[76]

Some analysts regard the function "character building" as evidence of a conservative agenda; they think it indicates a belief that poverty was the result of poor people's character flaws. On the contrary, the MECS women were convinced that poverty was *not* the result of a character flaw. Lillie Meekins attributed the poverty of her neighbors at the mission on Tchoupitoulas to the failure of factory owners in the Irish Channel to pay a living wage. The majority of the more thoroughly educated deaconesses went further, ascribing poverty's roots to an unethical economic system, namely, unchecked capitalism.

Some of those who charge that Progressive Era reformers were disguising a conservative agenda under the banner of reform use the argument that underlies a late-twentieth-century revision of the New Deal not as the socialist or quasi-socialist phenomenon that many contemporaries considered it, but rather as a cleverly conceived and played rightist strategy to shore up capitalism; New Dealers, according to this view, addressed economic problems just enough to prevent a real revolution. Similarly, elite women reformers have been depicted as beneficiaries of their fathers' or husbands' capitalist endeavors, which depended upon the maintenance of the economic and political status quo. Indeed, several scholars of women's history have linked the reform impulse to social class. For instance, a monograph on religious women and reform in another southern coastal city suggests it was membership in society's elite, as over against religious conviction, that correlated best with many kinds of reform activity.[77]

Diana Kendall's wonderfully illuminating 2002 study, *The Power of Good Deeds: Privileged Women and the Social Reproduction of the Upper Class,* considers the philanthropic work of elite women in southeast Texas. Kendall used interviews and her own participant observation in various social/philanthropic organizations. Her conclusions provide a most helpful clue toward understanding the differences between the elite women she describes and the individuals who were the mainstays of the MECS women's groups.[78]

The philanthropic work Kendall's organizations engage in do not emphasize personal contact with those in need; instead, they specialize in fund-raising. A large annual event for the membership involves the "coming out" of young women whose mothers have devoted sufficient time and energy to the group. Participation as a debutante or her escort is understood to pave the way for suitable marriages and thus the preservation of the elite class of a city. The key to this class reproduction is the limited entry into the organizations she describes.

Without dispute, New Orleans has such organizations. The elitist Carnival krewes spring to mind for anyone familiar with the city's Mardi Gras traditions. Some individual MECS women were by virtue of wealth and family lineage among the social elite of New Orleans, and thus there was some duplication of "Methodist women" with "society figures" over the past century. However, these elite women poured the vast majority of their incalculable volunteer hours and enormous energy into the WP&HMS, a group that was *not* self-limiting and that deliberately brought them into direct contact with, rather than isolated them from, persons of different backgrounds and social classes.

It is true that people tend to attend church near their homes, and so it might be argued that there is some protection against "intrusion" of women from different backgrounds, because one's choice of residence is usually determined in part by one's income. However, the sites of the Rayne, Carondelet, and Parker churches (the church homes of Hattie Parker, Elvira Carré, and Mary Werlein, respectively) were at locations where income levels varied significantly within a few blocks and where Methodists at many levels of affluence would have found them the most convenient and logical places for worship. Further, Rayne Memorial is on the St. Charles Avenue streetcar line, and Carondelet relocated to St. Charles in the very early twentieth century, making both of these churches especially accessible for those who used public transportation.

The woman's society at the Rayne Memorial congregation would have claimed well-to-do women among its membership. Yet in 1908, the Rayne women's yearbook emphasized that the members were by no means hands-off philanthropists; rather, they were expected to have actual contact with "the destitute." The group's monetary contribution supported the work of a city missionary and a deaconess "who devote their entire time to relieving conditions caused by poverty, sin and suffering." But, the writer added, "our members come in close, personal touch with the needy members of the congregations, and when necessity arises they nurse the sick, comfort the sorrowing, provide funerals for the dead, clothes and food for the living." They also hand-delivered Bibles and magazines to jails and visited the female prisoners.[79]

The organizations Kendall described require invitations and sponsorships, and to maintain exclusivity, they make sure that some women who apply are *not* chosen to join the groups. In contrast, the Rayne yearbook contained this text regarding the woman's society: "The number of women actively engaged in this department of Church work is only 65 while there are probably 200 women whose names are on the Church register. Why have you not enrolled yourself as a member of the Home Mission Society? Is it because you are not interested in those who are hungry, and cold, and sick?"[80] This constitutes more than a simple invitation; it seems an active attempt to shame any woman who has not been part of the group into joining. Blanket verbal invitations during worship and printed invitations in newsletters or bulletins would also have been issued several times a year. In short, any assertion that the MECS women's society practiced anything akin to the organizations that Kendall studied with regard to intentional "gatekeeping" would prove a grievous error.

Carondelet Street (later First Methodist) member Elvira Beach Carré's wealth is evident in her ability to provide extensive higher education not just for her own sons, but for Nicolas Joyner, as well. Though much of the family's financial success came from her own daily work in the business while she was a widowed mother raising her own four surviving children and the three children of a sister who died, it is irrefutable that she was born into privilege and re-mained in a position of wealth. The Werleins were also an affluent family. Mary's father was a pioneer in the publishing of sheet music in the United States, and generations of New Orleanians acquired their first band instruments at one of the Werlein Music stores.

Both of these women chose the Methodist church over the Episcopal de-nomination, despite the fact that some of the Werlein men of Mary's generation became Episcopal clergy, and Elvira Carré's family also included individuals ordained as Episcopal priests. Both families had men ordained as Methodists as well, including Mary's brother, Shepard Halsey Werlein. It is impossible to determine with any accuracy the motives of particular members of these fami-lies who chose to affiliate with one or the other tradition, but it is possible to comment on some important differences in how the two groups are perceived. Sociologists of religion observe that choice of denomination tends to be re-lated to socioeconomic standing. Methodism was then, and still is, usually as-sociated with a somewhat lower standing than the Episcopalian church. These differences are consistent with their roots in England, where those who at-tended services at the Church of England were usually of higher social standing than the "chapel" Methodists.

This discussion began with an assertion that Methodist women did not reflect the belief of certain elite reformers that poverty resulted from flaws in character. Linking "poverty" with "low character" is not an authentically

Wesleyan position. Many of the early Methodists were very poor. In fact, Methodism's founder, John Wesley (1703–91) was the son of a Church of England cleric who was sent to debtors' prison. John never forgot this aspect of his upbringing and the pain and difficulty it caused his mother, Susanna. All his life, John Wesley was known for reaching out to those in need. His outdoor preaching brought proclamation to miners and other laborers who were unlikely to appear at the Church of England on Sunday morning. His many projects designed to help people in need included the establishment of free health clinics and a school for poor children, precisely those the WP&HMS women would pursue in New Orleans.

The ability to cross class and other social lines is considered to have been a major benefit for early Christians and one of the factors, along with care for the poor and hungry, that helped account for the success of the Jesus movement. Some of the same claims can be made regarding the early days of the fast-growing Methodist movement. John Wesley had actually hoped the members of what he termed a "select society" of Methodists, those who were especially dedicated to spiritual pursuits, would in time choose to hold all their possessions in common the way the New Testament in "Acts of the Apostles" indicates the early church members did.[81] During his lifetime, he was disturbed to watch the discipline he promoted resulting in a rise in the socioeconomic status of many of his followers.

Wesley maintained a correspondence with an English woman, Miss March, who was resisting his attempts to persuade her to visit in the homes of poor people. She offered up a series of reasons why she could not engage in such visiting, including the notion that she should spend her time in "uplifting" company and that proximity to the poor would lower, not raise, her level of spirituality. She "eventually admitted that she struggled with the fact that affiliating with the Methodists put her in connection with so many who were of 'lower character' or unrefined." Wesley was unsympathetic and directly challenged her assumption that the rich were people of better character.

He also maintained that "[a]uthentic compassion can only take form through sincere encounters with those in need. This is why Wesley emphasized the need to *visit* the poor and sick even more than he did the need to offer them aid. He recognized that failure to visit was the major contributing cause of the lack of compassion that lay behind withholding aid." [82] Likewise, the deaconess movement focused on "friendly visiting" as a major part of the work and specifically trained women for the task. The desire to learn from the residents of the neighborhoods where they lived, and to let those residents play a key role in shaping the workers' agendas, is one of the major characteristics that set all settlement women apart from other kinds of reformers. Methodist women had a deep Wesleyan tradition on which they could also draw to prevent their expenditure of resources on isolating members of their social class.

The image of the Parker congregation's Mary Werlein regularly leading religious services for women imprisoned in the jails of New Orleans is enough to dispel ideas that she may have been primarily interested in social class maintenance. In fact, for Werlein, the way the denomination expressed itself in worship may also have been a key factor in her choice of Methodism. Even in more affluent Methodist congregations, neither special liturgical celebrations nor regular worship services were observed with as "high" or formal a liturgy as was common in Episcopalian churches. Recall that Werlein described the women's meeting she attended in Ponchatoula as having been so good that it was "equal to a camp meeting." Camp meetings had been the primary expression of Methodism on the frontier and were often characterized by emotional outpourings and ardent encounters with the Holy Spirit that left the worshippers physically spent. Werlein's language reveals her leanings in the widespread controversy over how "enthusiastic" Methodist religious expression should be; she talked about women who were "baptized by the Holy Ghost" and made use of terms that a reader might deem "code words," such as "energy" and "enthusiastic," as she wrote.

Overall, it is clear that the religious motivations that underlay the New Orleans women's work were what set them apart from other elite reformers of the Progressive Era. They did not perceive themselves to be on a quest through which humanity would achieve improvement and possibly perfection; rather, they saw themselves as instruments striving toward the achievement of the Kingdom of God.

2

St. Mark's Hall,

1909–1917

Although Lillie Meekins and other city missionaries had lived in the neighborhood, if not the very building, where they served, the women of the MECS moved into an ambitious new phase of settlement work in New Orleans with the establishment of St. Mark's Hall at 619–21 Esplanade Avenue and the assignment of deaconess Margaret Ragland as head resident.

The women employed the Reverend Mr. Nicolas E. Joyner as superintendent. *NOCA* reported that Joyner had visited a district meeting of the Home Mission Society two years previously and impressed the women as an "enthusiastic missionary worker."[1] It did not report that Joyner had been a childhood friend of Elvira Carré's son, Henry Beach Carré.

Joyner's father was disabled in an accident and unable to work for many years, so Joyner worked throughout his teen years to help support his family. He was licensed to preach at the Carondelet MECS (Elvira's church) at the age of eighteen. Noting his great potential for ministry, "the Carré family" helped him attend Centenary with their son. Joyner graduated with highest honors. The young men attended seminary at Vanderbilt, where they were roommates until they graduated in 1896. Then, "the two devoted friends Carré and Joyner, like David and Jonathan had to separate. Carré was going to Europe for further graduate study. Again the faithful Carré family offered to finance Joyner's going on to Europe with their son." In fact, Elvira had been widowed since 1877, so "their" son is misleading language; it would have been Elvira who made the offer.[2]

However, Joyner went instead to serve as a missionary in Monterrey, Mexico. It was this experience that impressed the women of the WP&HMS when he spoke to their group, but no doubt the high regard the president of the city mission board, Elvira Carré, had for him also played a large role in the decision to hire him at St. Mark's Hall. Once his employment was set, "local benefactors" and various church boards cooperated to send him to London so that he could study the work of Toynbee Hall, considered among the first, most successful, and most famous of all settlement houses.[3] In February 1909, the *New Orleans Christian Advocate (NOCA)* pictured Joyner on its cover, and the accompanying text described him as the "Louisiana Conference Missionary Secretary and Superintendent of St. Mark's Hall." It also noted that he had just returned from a trip to study the work of institutional churches and city missions in the urban centers of the northern United States.[4] This strategy of visiting and studying projects that were clearly manifestations of the Social Gospel provides evidence, should any more be needed, that the work of the MECS women was definitely Social Gospel–related.

An article that Joyner prepared for the November issue of the MECS Board of Missions publication, *Go Forward,* is the best extant source of information about the earliest work at St. Mark's. He wrote that 1909 had witnessed the beginning of "a new and a significant work" in the city. "It is new in that it introduces institutional and settlement methods, and significant because it indicates the turning of the attention of the entire Church to the magnificent field found in the metropolis of the South." It was his opinion that New Orleans offered "the best specimen of the 'city problem'" available to southern Methodism.[5]

Joyner explained that the location for St. Mark's Hall had been chosen to put it "in direct touch with the Italian colony and the large French element of the city's population." Describing the structure which housed it as "an old-style, three-story double dwelling, with twenty-two rooms and an inclosed [*sic*] yard some thirty feet wide and fifty feet long," he noted that it was so dilapidated that it took from January, when their lease began, until March for them to get it ready for occupancy.[6]

An MECS deaconess, Margaret Ragland, was named as the first head resident of the St. Mark's settlement house. A second deaconess was also assigned, and the two deaconesses, along with a house mother and her assistant, moved in on the first day of March in 1909. However, they had to delay their planned work so that shower baths, items to be used in a health clinic, and playground equipment for the courtyard could be installed. In the meantime, the deaconesses occupied themselves by going door to door in the neighborhood, distributing "[n]eatly printed cards, announcing the different features of the work we proposed to do."

By November, the staff had put a variety of programs into place. Seventy-two persons were enrolled in the night school, where instruction focused on English language classes. Two of the men were bartenders when they began their studies, but Joyner was pleased to report that one of them had "left the bar for another job, and is an enthusiastic member of our Sunday evening choir." The sewing school had ninety-six students who had spent the summer making dolls and other items for orphans, and a cooking school was almost ready to open. The men's club engaged in helping others through relief work. Just a month previously, St. Mark's had opened "a free clinic for women and children, a capable lady physician giving an hour three times a week to the work."

On Sunday evenings, there were worship services in the courtyard, with forty-five to fifty individuals in attendance. Joyner reported that along with singing, scripture lessons, prayers, and "short talks in English or Italian," the services also included a presentation with a stereopticon so that the congregation could "study the great paintings that illustrate the life of the Master." In summary, he said: "The first six months at St. Mark's Hall have been full of encouragement. We have . . . come into personal touch with more than three hundred men, women, and children, and over eight thousand visits have been made to the hall. As rapidly as possible the work will be extended to meet the many needs of the field we occupy. . . . *We are trying to preach the gospel by both word and deed, believing that the latter is as effective as the former.*"[7]

Although the settlement's location had been chosen to reach Italians, the worshipping congregation that met there included people from twenty-five different countries and called itself the "Church of All Nations." While later chapters address issues of race at some length, it should be mentioned here that the ethnic makeup of the congregation reflected the ethnic makeup of the French Quarter and nearby neighborhoods, and its "All Nations" label belied the absence of persons of African descent. Further, the "Italian Department" continued to pay special attention to persons from that country, and the first membership roster at the new church reflects the preponderance of Italian surnames among the congregation. There were services in Italian along with services in English, and workers distributed Bibles and tracts in Italian.[8] As part of its outreach, St. Mark's also operated an "Italian Mission" at 539 St. Ann

Street, located on Jackson Square in the heart of the French Quarter and within sight of the Roman Catholic Church's imposing structure, the St. Louis Cathedral. An Italian speaker, Rev. Zito, ministered there.[9]

Society Faces Challenges from Social Gospel Opponents

When the city mission board met in 1910, the officers from the prior year were reelected, and the *New Orleans Christian Advocate* interpreted this as approval of what the administration had been doing. In fact, the writer noted, Elvira Beach Carré (called "Mrs. W. W. Carré") was elected for her nineteenth year as president of the group, despite asking to be relieved from the "onerous duties" of the position she had already been "faithfully and efficiently" filling for eighteen years. *NOCA* observed, "We venture to say that there is not another Woman's City Mission Board in all our church that has done more, and is doing more for the salvation of the lost than this board is doing."[10]

Carré was working at that time for establishment of equal laity rights for women. The board voted unanimously to endorse a resolution from women in Savannah that would petition the next General Conference for those rights. Carré announced that one delegate from the Louisiana Conference had already agreed to vote in support of it.[11]

In 1910, work at St. Mark's Hall was progressing well. "Much relief work" was going on, and clinic work was growing "under the direction of a local physician, Dr. Ada Kiblinger, who volunteered her time." *NOCA* commented: "It affords us special pleasure to announce that the Woman's Home Mission Board did not remove any of our deaconesses from our city at its recent meeting held in Nashville. Miss Margaret Ragland is still head-resident deaconess, and Miss Daisy Duncan, trained-nurse deaconess at St. Mark's Hall." An additional woman would be joining the staff: "Miss Roberta Baker will have charge of the department of domestic science. She has taught in this department in the Wesley House at Louisville for the past three years."[12]

Robert A. Woods and Albert J. Kennedy included St. Mark's in their handbook of settlements published in 1911. They informed readers that the aim of St. Mark's was to perform "Christian social settlement work, looking to the development of a great institutional mission center similar to those maintained by the Wesleyan Church in London and other English cities." Woods and Kennedy wrote that St. Mark's Hall "Endeavors to aid in the adjustment of the foreigner to American conditions; to secure adequate enforcement of the law regulating the sale of liquor; better housing and sanitary conditions; more adequate compulsory education provision; and opportunities for wholesome play and recreation."[13]

In 1912, despite a flood that disrupted the work of the women's missionary societies around the state and delayed their meetings, the work in New Orleans seemed to be prospering. The number of local societies who were part of the city mission board had increased to ten. Margaret Ragland reported that St. Mark's Hall was operating five industrial schools, which had a total of 229 persons enrolled, and a night school that had 67 pupils, along with "two boys' clubs, two girls' clubs, one for men, and a mothers' club." She also reported "348 visits made and 281 received, 57 persons helped, [and] 63 portions of the New Testament given." At the Mary Werlein Mission on Tchoupitoulas Street, Lillie Meekins's activities were similar to those of the previous year. The recording secretary of the city mission board concluded her report by noting that while the figures showed "in part the record of the year's work," they could not "estimate the touch of personal sympathy and the mighty influence of holy living."[14]

However, in the minutes of the 1913 meeting of the state women's organization, the relatively comprehensive report that was usually published about St. Mark's Hall was simply missing. Sandwiched among comments on other ministries are a mere three sentences: "For lack of funds we came near losing our work at St. Mark's Hall in New Orleans. It was through the efforts of our Presiding Elder, James Henry, Rev. W. E. Thomas and Mrs. S. A. Montgomery that the work was kept intact. Rev. W. E. Thomas, Miss Martha Dupree, Deaconess and Miss Laura Padgett, nurse, are in charge of this splendid work among the Italians."[15]

At some point during this period, N. E. Joyner was reassigned. Presumably at the same time, the settlement house was put under the auspices of the First Methodist Episcopal Church, South and under its pastor's control. Although this pastor, J. W. Moore, received praise in the women's minutes for 1912, which included mention that he preached at their annual meeting and talked "inspiringly" about his work at the Mary Werlein Mission,[16] a letter Moore wrote to Bishop Warren Candler, who was to preside over the next Annual Conference in Louisiana, may reveal the true source of some of the problems St. Mark's Hall faced.

Moore's letterhead reveals a great deal about the new administrative structure. The main heading is for the First Methodist Episcopal Church, South at 1108 St. Charles Avenue, and it lists the staff, including a head deaconess, Miss Jennie Ducker. There is a smaller subheading to the left for St. Mark's Hall, with its address, 619 Esplanade Avenue, and the names of two staff members, Miss Margaret Ragland, head deaconess, and Dr. E. L. King, physician in charge. There is also a subheading on the right for the Mary Werlein Mission, with the address of 1026 Tchoupitoulas Street and the name of one staff member, Miss [*sic*] Lillie Meekins, head deaconess.[17]

If the letterhead can be read as an organizational chart, it would mean that Ragland and Meekins reported to Moore. This echoes the *NOCA* writer's designation of Meekins as the "efficient helper" of Brother Lallance at the mission a decade previously. In fact, although my extensive reading of minutes and reports from the MECS women's societies shows that their leaders at the local, conference, and denominational levels were always circumspect and chose their phraseology, at least for public records, to avoid any direct challenge to male and/or pastoral authority, it seems unlikely that the head residents of settlements really saw themselves as "pastor's helpers." Their positions were comparable to those of today's CEOs of busy, multitasked, nonprofit organizations. Ragland in particular was so well known and so highly regarded among churchwomen for her work with the Italian community at St. Mark's Hall that historian Mabel Howell, writing a decade and a half later, listed Ragland among a dozen individuals from across the United States whose names would "always be associated with the work carried on in these foreign communities."[18]

The new pastor-in-charge was not able to fit into the existing structure of powerful female leaders, as his letter to Candler reveals. Dated July 9, 1912, it reads:

My Dear Bishop Candler,

I am in trouble. I am in trouble with the women folks. Knowing your large influence in that quarter I want to engage your help.

St. Mark's Hall has been run largely as a Hull House and the Head Resident does not want the church introduced into her institution. I told her last week that I expected to start a Sabbath School. She said that she would resign and that she did not want any church in St. Mark's Hall. She takes the position that the church is a decadent institution and that these Settlements are to take the place of the church. I wanted a Sabbath-school and prayer-meeting. She writex [*sic*] to the women and they have called the Executive Committee together to decide the momentous question as to whether in a Mission of the M.E.C.S. a Sunday-school and a prayer-meeting are to be allowed. They tried to pull off a Boxing Contest, alias, a prize fight and had extensively advertised it when I stepped in and knocked it out the first sound [*sic*]. The Head Resident will not shake my hand but gives every evidence of a desire to shake me.

What kind of trouble do I want to get you into? You once asked me to write and I wrote. I want an article from your pen on the place of Social and Settlement work in the life of the church. I believe that with your pen you could puncture some of these silly pretensions and whilst I do not believe that you can work miracles, still some of these women might be won to sanity.

Bishop Mouzen [*sic*] promised me that I was to have no trouble with the women. Man proposes but women dispose. I think that one year is all that any man can safely endure under the dominion of those the ungallant John Knox called "The Monstrous Breed." If you have any churches needing a preacher I dare-say, that by December I shall be a statesman out of a job.

The shirt of Nessus was a loose-fitting Kimona [*sic*] compared to this hydra-headed arrangement. Nothing but a mixed metaphor could fit the case. You can show the thing up to the church and correct this secularizing evil.

With love and best wishes,
Your hen-pecked brother,
J. W. Moore[19]

For the reader familiar with the common dismissal of religious settlements by mid- to late-twentieth-century social historians because the settlements were too religious and too mission-oriented, the irony is profound. Further, because a consideration of how religious settlements have been treated by historians is a part of this study, it is important to note that one of the few historians who has mentioned the St. Mark's settlement of this era was a man who completed a 1969 dissertation on the social history of southern Methodism during the Progressive Era. He quoted from Moore's letter, which is housed among Bishop Candler's papers at Emory University, and accepted its assertions uncritically, without checking any sources that contained information provided by the women involved. The conclusion he therefore drew about the situation at St. Mark's was that "the degree of influence of the church in the settlement was slight." He attributed a probable motive to Ragland—"The head resident probably viewed the establishment of a Sunday School at the settlement as an exertion of traditionalism that would strangle the program of the mission"— that exhibits both a complete lack of data about the religious programming that was in fact carried on at St. Mark's and an equal lack of understanding of the deaconesses' mission as Christian workers.[20]

Despite Moore's claims that Ragland resisted Christianity and promoted secularization, her report to the Woman's Missionary Council for 1910 celebrated that "out of the night school has developed an Italian Bible class with a membership of twenty." Her 1911–12 report emphasized the spiritual aspects of the work at St. Mark's Hall, with information about the Sunday evening worship service with its prayer and singing, and a reference to the indwelling Spirit and the presence of the "Friend of friends" who enabled their work. Further, one of the first persons who had been converted at the hall, Mr. Lui Pagani, worked as a volunteer minister who was "at the hall on all occasions," and he and the Reverend Mr. W. E. Thomas, then pastor of Second MECS in New Orleans (and the eventual successor to Moore at St. Mark's Hall and the Mary Werlein Mission) often led religious services, conducted Bible studies and readings, and in general saw to the spiritual needs of the people. To say that Margaret Ragland forbade church functions is to contradict clear evidence presented in the contemporary women's reports in local, state-, and denomination-wide media.[21]

Ragland's conflict with Moore and this historian's later interpretation of it offer insight into larger divisions between Social Gospel proponents and traditionalists who believed that the church should have no role in social services. This 1969 dissertation on "the social history of southern Methodism" that perpetuates the idea that the women who worked at the denomination's religious settlements were unspiritual and antichurch is just one example of how the misrepresentation of women's work has been compounded over the decades.

Taken in a more complete context, Moore's words lead not to the conclusion that Ragland was irreligious, but rather to the unavoidable discovery that Moore was uncomfortable about a person of the "wrong" sex having a leadership role, especially one that some might perceive threatened his authority. It is possible that Moore could have been so convinced that social service was not appropriate Christian service that he was unable to see the evidence of the deaconesses' Christian spirituality even when it lay before him. The alternative and more likely explanation that he was so dead set against settlement work, or professional women's work, or both, that he deliberately falsified information about Ragland and the ministry at St. Mark's Hall, is even less flattering.

It is probably not coincidental that 1912 was the year when the short-lived "Men and Religion Forward Movement" was in flower in the United States. This was an attempt to recruit more men into churches and to counteract the perceived "overfeminization" of Protestantism. A number of notable figures from the Social Gospel movement, including Walter Rauschenbusch and Washington Gladden, made positive comments about the endeavor.[22]

Within the MECS, the "opening guns" of the movement to achieve laity (voting) rights for women within the church "were fired by the highly-esteemed Miss Belle Bennett in 1909. . . . As the most prominent woman in southern Methodism, Miss Bennett led the Woman's Board of Home Missions to petition the 1910 General Conference for full laity rights for women. The bishops denounced this in the Episcopal Address and the General Conference rejected the request."[23] It is easy to see the timing of the "Men and Religion Forward Movement" as related to backlash against the suffrage movement's encroachment into Protestant structures. It is unclear whether Moore was formally a part of the movement; his connection with the Louisiana Annual Conference apparently terminated in 1912, because he is not included among the list of clergy in conference journals in the years thereafter. (It is crucial that he not be confused with John M. Moore, a prominent Methodist leader who was later elected bishop; in fact, the author of the dissertation in question apparently did so, because he cites the actual John M. Moore frequently in his dissertation, but also erroneously uses "John M. Moore," rather than "John W. Moore," to refer to the author of this letter, both in the dissertation's text and in his footnotes.) Although John W. Moore's connection with the "Men and Religion Forward" movement remains unproved, it is certain that the women were facing more than just his personal negativity toward female leadership in 1911–12.

SECTARIAN SETTLEMENT WORK IS UNDERVALUED

Overtly religious settlements like St. Mark's were caught in ideological limbo in several different ways. Christians whose dualistic views of appropriately "sacred" activities posed them over against any supposedly purely "secular" concerns about meeting material needs were convinced that the women's work was not really religious work and that the church should not engage in it at any level. Thus, Moore and other pastors and laypeople who shared his ideology believed that religious settlements were not really religious. At the same time, workers at nonsectarian agencies often believed that religious settlements were not really settlements.

Many agencies, including the other New Orleans settlement, Kingsley House, were unable to cope with the tension and abandoned their religious affiliation to find acceptance in the settlement world. Now located at 1600 Constance Street, Kingsley House was founded in 1899 when five young women settled on Annunciation Street. It was also located for a time at 928 Tchoupitoulas Street, near the site of the Mary Werlein Mission. The Reverend Mr. Beverley Warner was deeply involved in establishing Kingsley House. Warner, an Episcopal rector, was "a disciple of Charles Kingsley," the English clergyman who promoted Christian socialism. The biographer of Eleanor McMain, the New Orleans educator who was its head resident, characterized the early Kingsley House as primarily the work of the clergy and members of Trinity Episcopal Church. In 1902, the facility officially became a nonsectarian settlement, and persons from several Christian denominations and a Jewish rabbi were recruited to serve on its board.[24]

Because of its nonsectarian status, Kingsley House was more widely accepted as a true settlement and had closer ties to Hull House in Chicago and the

National Federation of Settlements, which St. Mark's was not eligible to join. Indeed, Allen F. Davis wrote in *Spearheads for Reform* that McMain "divorced her settlement from its Episcopal connections" for the same reason Robert Woods changed the name of Andover House: "in order to release the settlement from certain restraints which the old name placed upon its natural progress." Davis undoubtedly agreed with McMain's decision, because he wrote: "The great majority of the social settlements in America during the progressive era were located in the large cities of the Northeast and Midwest. The South had few, and except for Eleanor McMain's Kingsley House in New Orleans, and Frances Ingram's Neighborhood House in Louisville, they were of very little importance. In addition, most of them were modified missions; religious settlements (mostly Methodist) comprised nearly 70 per cent of the total."[25]

It is ironic that Davis characterizes Kingsley House as one of two "important" southern settlements and lumps all others, including St. Mark's and other Methodist settlements, into the category "of very little importance," because the social services programming at St. Mark's and Kingsley House were almost identical. The National Federation of Settlements excluded religious settlements almost as a matter of course, with the question of how much proselytizing went on as a criterion for judging whether a religious settlement should be allowed to join. St. Mark's never joined and apparently never attempted to do so, which is not surprising, because the deaconesses unquestionably saw their work as Christian ministry.

Interestingly, there is another difference that is never mentioned in discussions of which settlements "counted"—the Kingsley House board of directors was entirely male, while the St. Mark's board was composed entirely of women. Representatives from each of the local women's society chapters made up the decision-making body at St. Mark's. Though there seems to be no admission of it in print, it seems likely that a stereotypical view of "church ladies" and their activities contributed to Davis's and other scholars' having taken Kingsley House seriously as a settlement, while not taking St. Mark's seriously at all.

I am convinced that Davis's characterization of Kingsley House as "Eleanor McMain's" and his identification of the Neighborhood House in Louisville as "Frances Ingram's" point to another factor in the disparity of historical treatments. Just as Jane Addams provided the public face of Hull House even at times when Ellen Gates Starr and others were just as deeply involved in the running of the facility, the other well-known settlements also tended to have one individual whose identity was almost synonymous with the facility's work.

An excellent example comes from a 1938 novel for young people written by Helen Dore Boylston. Part of a series of novels about a young nurse, *Sue Barton, Visiting Nurse* focuses on a year Sue spends working at the Henry Street Settlement in New York. A chapter entitled "A Minute and a Half" describes a chance encounter between Sue and Lillian Wald, the settlement's founder, at a time when Wald was no longer on the premises on a regular basis.

"Close behind [Sue] stood a woman of middle height, with graying hair and a strong, rugged face—the kindest face that Sue had ever seen, but yet a face of power and determination. The room was electric with her presence," Boylston wrote. Once Sue discovers the woman is Wald, the young nurse is in awe, finding it hard to speak, and feeling, as she must introduce herself, that her own name has paled into insignificance. When Wald smiles at one point in the brief conversation, "it was as if sunlight had fallen suddenly upon her face."

When Sue later recounts the event to her friend Kit in glowing terms, Kit asks whether, if Sue had not known Wald's identify, she would have found anything different about her. Sue insists that she felt Wald's extraordinary presence when she entered the room because Wald had "a kind of power," and she asserts, "[Wald is] the first person I ever met in my life that I *know* couldn't do a mean thing!" Kit expresses surprise that Sue has "collected" so much information about Wald in such a brief encounter. Sue explains that this is not information that is "collected" in Wald's presence; rather, she says, "It hits you like a ton of brick."[26]

There is no question that the Henry Street settlement profited from Wald's personal reputation, just as Hull House did from the international respect for Addams, winner of the Nobel Peace Prize in 1931. As over against the practice at secular settlements that became identified over the years with a powerful individual, the itinerancy system that Methodism employed from the earliest days of John Wesley and Francis Asbury, and still requires from its clergy, was also a policy of the deaconess movement. In other words, Methodist deaconesses agreed to go wherever the larger church decided they were most needed. Thus, during a period when Eleanor McMain's work at Kingsley House was acquiring the reputation that led to her listing as a "settlement leader" in *Notable*

American Women, the head residents of St. Mark's moved around from location to location, only very rarely acquiring a personal identification with any one settlement house.[27] The best-known of all the women to have served at St. Mark's, Mary Lou Barnwell, achieved prominence not for her service as head resident there, but for her subsequent service as head of the deaconess program for the whole church. There are pluses and minuses to the itinerancy system, as noted by various writers exploring the issue with regard to clergy, but with regard to the deaconesses at St. Mark's, one minus was that the settlement did not reap the benefit of having its own reputation enhanced by long-term affiliation with one powerful professional woman.

For these and other reasons, a profound divergence emerged between the historical treatment of religious settlements and that of nonsectarian ones. There has been an almost complete neglect of religious settlements in southern social history. Further, there has been a significant undervaluing of the contributions of Social Gospel settlement workers in the history of the southern church. Thus, both southern social history and southern religious history have neglected the MECS women. The yearly reports from the women at St. Mark's, taken cumulatively, reveal their own understanding that their work is both true settlement work *and* evangelistic Christian mission.

THE WOMEN RESCUE THEIR WORK

Whatever J. W. Moore's underlying understandings and motives might have been, his predictions about his short-lived tenure at First Church proved accurate. At the very next Annual Conference gathering, a new pastor was appointed to the city's premier Methodist pulpit—the Reverend Dr. Shepard Halsey Werlein, Mary's brother. S. H. Werlein had most recently been serving a large church in St. Louis, Missouri, but returned to New Orleans for the appointment that so deeply affected the survival of St. Mark's Hall. We are left to speculate about how this personnel change came to pass, but it seems highly unlikely that Mary Werlein was a disinterested party. Because the presiding elders were deeply involved in the process of appointing pastors to various charges, and because the women's brief report for 1913 gave credit to the presiding elder for helping to keep the work at St. Mark's intact, it seems likely that

Mary Werlein and other female leaders like Elvira Carré were sufficiently politically astute to recruit the person holding this position within the Methodist hierarchy to their cause.[28]

Unfortunately, Margaret Ragland also seems to have lost her appointment during the struggle. On September 1, 1912, Ragland was appointed to First MECS in Birmingham, Alabama, and deaconess Martha Nutt was named head resident at St. Mark's. Lillie Meekins remained in place at the Mary Werlein Mission, and the pastor appointed to the mission that year, the Reverend Mr. H. W. Jamieson, also served as an associate at the congregation where S. H. Werlein was senior pastor.[29]

The first annual report of the Woman's Missionary Council after Moore's departure noted that St. Mark's Hall had moved a few blocks down the street into a larger house (at 908 Esplanade), but the workforce had been reduced to only two persons. Despite adversities, the writer summarized, "we believe that the work in New Orleans is better intrenched than it ever has been in the past." The likeliest reason for their optimism is the benevolent oversight of S. H. Werlein, whose opinions about women in leadership were diametrically opposed to Moore's; for instance, the *Journal of the Louisiana Annual Conference,* 1913 contains a resolution asking for approval of full laity rights for women, and the first signature on it is S. H. Werlein's.[30]

A year later, the deaconesses celebrated that St. Mark's had "scored perhaps its most successful year" and, among other statistics, noted that 2,533 patients were treated at its clinic. The Mary Werlein Mission was profiting from some additional space, and this was the year that agitation for more space for St. Mark's began. The state women's society called on the Woman's Missionary Council of the MECS to "provide for the purchase of permanent and adequate accommodations for this work."[31]

For the 1915–16 church year, the St. Mark's staff reported that the growth of the Italian church housed in their building had been "gratifying." They included material ostensibly to clarify for the council, but no doubt really directed more toward informing non–WP&HMS readers about the relationship between the settlement house and the worshipping congregation whose activities it housed. They explained that while the council was not responsible for the workings of the congregation (which also meant that the deaconesses, by extension, were not responsible, either), the Woman's Missionary Council did allow the congregation to use space within its facility. "[E]very missionary and deaconess connected with the institution is an agent for the Church," the report added. "In other words, the activities of St. Mark's Hall result in its evangelistic enlargement and usefulness."[32] This statement may also have served to defend the women against any continuing charges of excessive secularization. (The organic connection forged by the lives of the deaconesses who worked in the settlement and who also volunteered great amounts of time and effort to the congregation is explored more deeply in chapter 8.)

The "Angel of Tchoupitoulas" Is Killed

Another setback to the women's work occurred on the day after New Year's Day, 1916, when tragedy struck the Mary Werlein Mission. It was a Sunday afternoon, and Lillie Meekins was on her way to visit her friend, Florence Russ, a leader of the missionary society. Meekins took the streetcar and got off at the corner of Camp and Foucher streets, within sight of Russ's home. Russ was standing outside, waiting for her. In an unsigned article entitled, "Mrs. Lily [*sic*] Meekins, Charity Worker, Dragged by Car: 'The Angel of Tchoupitoulas Street' Is Victim of Peculiar Accident," the *New Orleans Times-Picayune* explained: "She was in the act of stepping to the ground when the car suddenly moved, catching her skirt on the platform. She raced beside the car, screaming to the motorman to stop. Her cries were heard a block away, but the car continued on its way. After running several feet the car outdistanced her, her skirt was torn loose, and she was thrown violently to the ground."[33]

She was carrying two gifts, which she intended to deliver to children at the Seventh Street Orphanage after the visit, one for a baby who was blind. The story about the accident and a longer story printed a week later after Meekins died from her injuries made much of the fact that during her few conscious moments in the hours after the accident, she repeated, "O, my poor, blind baby, my poor, blind baby." Someone found the gifts lying on the ground and placed them at Russ's gate, where she discovered them upon returning home. Russ planned to deliver them to the orphanage, to ease Meekins's distress about her failure to complete her errand.

The *Times-Picayune* observed:

About the mission, which she has made her home during many years of devoted and unselfish labor in relieving the distressed, were gathered Sunday night many of her friends, a number of whom she had assisted when the wolf or death's angel had gone knocking at their doors. They were sorrowing and their one question was: "What can we do for her?" In that neighborhood, where distress reigns often, she has been known as the one ray of sunshine that crept down between the walls of brick lining each side of the street. To New Orleans at large she long ago become [*sic*] known as "The angel of Tchoupitoulas street."

An intense love for Mrs. Meekins was developed by every person with whom she came in contact. Along the river front and the neighborhood of the mission she was looked upon as a guardian angel. And while placing her upon this pedestal each man of the district also made himself her protector, and to even the tough character, sodden with drink, she was as one sacred. It is doubtful if a person could have spoken anything but respectfully to or of her along the river front and escaped with his life.[34]

In its front-page article about her death a week later, the *Times-Picayune* stated that the entire district had been "in gloom" all week because of her injury and impending death. It also spoke of her belief in cleanliness as a means toward "reforming men" and her constant collecting of clean used clothing, especially underwear and shirts. "If the persons seeking charity from her were not clean, she immediately provided them bath and clean clothing. In many instances it had almost magical results." The reporter provided an example: "One man who recently was discharged from jail, after serving a term in a penitentiary for safe-blowing, arrived in New Orleans with hate in his heart at the treatment he was receiving through being a former convict. He had found it impossible to obtain or hold a job on account of his record. He reached New Orleans covered with dirt from stolen rides on freight trains. He suffered the temptation to follow the criminal path again, but was saved by being brought in touch with Mrs.

Meekins. After a bath and wearing clean clothes he revived hope, and through the continuance of Mrs. Meekins' efforts obtained employment."[35]

Meekins, who was sixty-two years old when she died, had buried her only child, Nellie Meekins, "also a noted charity worker," just six weeks before the accident. Lillie, the widow of John Meekins, was born in Covington, Louisiana, as Lillie Colton and had lived in New Orleans for forty years.[36]

The stories printed at the time of her accident and death occupied far more space than the *Times-Picayune* then devoted to most other obituaries. Her death was one of the few local stories that made the front page that week, and it ran almost the entire length of the broadsheet. With the first story, the day after the accident, the newspaper carried a photograph of her. It depicts a slender woman with deep-set eyes, graying hair pulled back from her face, and a solemn, if not sad, expression. She is wearing a black blouse or dress with a white collar, which could possibly be a deaconess uniform sans the bonnet. Meekins, a widow, and a city missionary rather than a deaconess, would not have been eligible for that part of the deaconess garb.[37]

The designation by the *Times-Picayune* of Meekins as a "charity worker" is in keeping with its depiction of her activities. Her death is an interesting marker in that evolution of Methodist women's work that we might today term the movement from "mercy ministries" into "justice ministries." There were comments among churchwomen's writings from this decade about the need for "trained workers," by which they meant not women like Meekins with lived experience among the poor, but rather women who also had academic training in recognizing and combating the root causes of social problems. Such training was being developed by MECS women when Meekins died, and the post–World War I era would see an increasing number of women who sought it.

Hattie Parker Leads the City Mission Board

In April 1917, just days after the United States entered World War I, the MECS Woman's Missionary Council met in New Orleans. As far as the women were concerned, nothing but expansion of their work lay ahead. By this time, Harriet

Rowland Parker had replaced Elvira Beach Carré as president of the women's city mission board in New Orleans. The daily publication of the conference, *The Council Daily,* said Parker was "well known as a forceful thinker and speaker along the lines of social betterment."[38] It is interesting to see the adjective "forceful" used in a positive way in a church publication to describe a female in 1917.

It is a marked contrast to her description in the society pages that covered her wedding to John Burruss Parker in 1891, where she was called "a blonde of fragile type." The society reporter informed readers that both families were "amongst the most prominent in the city," explaining, "The bride's father is well known in cotton circles, and the groom is the son of the late Bishop L. Parker, a name that is a shining light in the history of Methodism." Crowding into the church for the event was "a congregation that represented the highest ecclesiastical, medical, legal and social circles of New Orleans."[39]

Parker preferred "Hattie" to "Harriet," and she is listed as Hattie Rowland Parker in a 1914 publication that called itself the first of its kind, the *Woman's Who's Who in America.* The compilers obtained their information by having the subjects themselves complete a questionnaire, which included a question about whether they supported women's suffrage. The resultant entry for Parker included a notation that she favored "woman suffrage" and said that she was "especially interested in social service, particularly in all that relates to the better protection of women and children." She was president of the Era Club and associate editor of the "New Citizen," the "official organ of the Era Club (published monthly)" and had "done magazine and newspaper work in the interest of club and missionary work."[40]

The Era group, which met in Gibson Hall at Tulane University on the second and fourth Saturdays of each month, was "devoted to the extension of suffrage among women."[41] Parker was also an officer of the Southern States Woman Suffrage Conference (SSWSC) at its 1913 inception. She is named in a study on southern suffragists as the group's corresponding secretary at the time of organization; however, she is misidentified in a footnote as the wife of the future governor of Louisiana. The man who became governor was actually John M. Parker, not John B. Parker, her husband. The SSWSC, led by Kate Gordon, is now suspect because it is associated with a ploy to have white women and not black women receive the right to vote. Gordon hoped that this strategy would win votes from white Louisiana legislators, who would see giving the

Fig. 5. Hattie Rowland Parker.
Photo courtesy of Parker Schneidau.

vote to white women as a way of maintaining a larger white majority among voters. The New Orleans suffrage groups splintered, as national groups did. In New Orleans, the conflict centered around whether amendments to state constitutions or an amendment to the national constitution was the better strategy, and Gordon's own racism was part, though not all, of the equation.[42]

It is unclear, and far beyond the scope of this study to research, how Parker's affiliations may have changed as the organization altered. However, because Parker's self-supplied information in the 1914 compilation notes her involvement with the YWCA, a group that openly declared better race relations as an important part of its portfolio, and because the MECS women's groups were far more racially progressive than the Deep South's population at large, it is important to acknowledge that her affiliation with the SSWSC is not synonymous with agreement with all of Gordon's ideologies.

Hattie's grandson, Parker Schneidau, recalled her deep involvement with the Era Club, which, as he noted, stood for "Equal Rights for All." However, Schneidau's memory is that his grandmother viewed the Era Club as primarily about child labor.[43] This may be because he went to live with Hattie after his mother died in 1925, and the Nineteenth Amendment granting women the right to vote had been in place since 1920. However, the 1917 Women's Missionary Council publication pointed to Hattie's "prominent part" in efforts to establish a separate court for juvenile offenders and in advocacy for legislation abolishing child labor. She was also known for efforts to "reduce infant mortality" and for "all that pertains to the moral and social betterment of the community."[44] In fact, Era's portfolio included a whole host of social issues. A 1940 M.S.W. thesis at Tulane listed the group's "early achievements" as "the obtaining of adequate sewerage, drainage, and pure drinking water; establishment of the Juvenile Court, and admittance of women students to Tulane University."[45]

The Era Club eventually fed into the League of Women Voters organization, but the original New Orleans chapter was not willing to follow the national rules of nonpartisan behavior. The history of these organizations has been addressed in monographs by Elna Green and Pamela Tyler, and readers who wish to have more information on women's political activities in New Orleans will find these volumes of interest.[46] For the purposes of this study, it is sufficient to note that the election of a reformer and unabashed activist such as Parker to replace Elvira Carré at the head of the city mission board confirms the approval of the New Orleans woman's society members of causes and policy that are characteristic not just of the Social Gospel, but also of the larger Progressive agenda.

AFTER STORYVILLE

Even as Europe became more deeply embroiled in World War I and the eventual involvement of the United States began to seem more likely, various types of Progressive reforms supported by New Orleans Methodists were showing signs of success. In the months immediately before the United States' entry into the war, Mary Werlein's brother, S. H., was in the forefront of a major push to rid the city of vice. A *NOCA* editorial commended those behind a movement "to create better moral conditions in New Orleans." It celebrated a citizens' meeting, the second of its kind, held at the Hippodrome on January 23, "with 1200 or 1500 persons present." S. H. Werlein presided over the event, which featured "a number of earnest speeches." Speakers claimed that cabarets and "several scores of disorderly houses" had been closed, and that saloons had kept "more nearly within the limits of the law last Sunday than perhaps they have done for years. The sentiment for reform appears to be growing—even the city dailies admit this. Let the good work go on!"[47]

These reform efforts appear to have been part of a push that came from several different quarters, some with an ugly motive lacking in the MECS women's work. One leading advocate for the closing of Storyville, the district where prostitution was sanctioned, was Philip Werlein. He was a relative and probably the brother of Mary and S. H. Werlein; several generations of Werlein fathers and sons bore the name "Philip." One was associated with the now-infamous White League, and he was almost certainly the same Philip Werlein who used a desire for white supremacy as part of his rationale for why the Storyville district, where mixed-race prostitutes were employed, should be closed.[48] Because Mary's relatives had few significant memories of her, not knowing, for instance, where or in what decade she died, it is most unlikely that differences between her and other family members could be sorted out in any helpful way, and it would contribute little to this study, at any rate.

Several of the MECS women, including Mary Werlein, were also part of organizations such as Traveler's Aid, which was formed in 1908 as an offshoot of the Era Club, "with the specific purpose of providing protection to women and girls from the white slave traffic."[49] The terminology about stopping "white slavery" may sound both overly dramatic and totally dated. This assessment is less defensible in light of the fact that sex trafficking remains a problem, even in the United States, where young immigrants from many nations are at risk. A 2008 *New York Times* opinion piece by Pulitzer Prize–winning columnist Nicholas Kristof maintains that sex trafficking "exists in all countries" and notes that it is "widely acknowledged to be the 21st century version of slavery."[50] The reality that some critics of Storyville were primarily offended by the race mixing that occurred there in no way lessens the genuine desire to protect women and children that motivated other reformers.

In the end, local advocates and opponents of closing Storyville found the matter settled at a higher level. The trump card turned out to be in the hands of the United States military. New Orleans successfully recruited a naval training station and a quartermaster depot during World War I, which benefited the city economically. However, there was serious concern about the presence of a district for licensed sex workers in a city where soldiers and sailors departed for the front lines, not least because those who contracted venereal diseases were deemed not fit to fight once they reached Europe and had to be sent back home. Mayor Martin Behrmann resisted the closure of Storyville on the grounds the military men were less likely to become diseased in a regulated district than elsewhere. However, the secretary of the navy, Josephus Daniels, sent "direct orders to close the district." Behrmann introduced the necessary ordinance to the city council, and "Storyville was officially closed on November 12, 1917."[51]

The closure of Storyville failed to transform New Orleans into a puritanical community, and it actually brought a new set of problems to the fore. The response of MECS women like Susan Elizabeth Murph Snelling to that situation is recounted in chapter 5, which discusses her influence on her grandson.

ST. MARK'S AT THE TIME OF WORLD WAR I

As war approached, the Methodist churchwomen of New Orleans still grieved the loss of Lillie Meekins but pushed steadily forward in their work. This included continued advocacy for laity (voting) rights for women, which was finally approved at the 1918 MECS General Conference.

At the local level, in March 1917, *NOCA* continued the call for a larger facility for the work of St. Mark's Hall, by now located at 908 Esplanade, explaining that the deaconesses had to use a given room for an office in the morning, as a meeting place for the clinic in the afternoon, and as a boys' playroom at night. Part of the hall's space was devoted to the activities of the worshipping congregation. A writer maintained, "They need a separate church building so that the first floor of the present building could be opened to the public for parlors and social rooms."[52]

The staff at St. Mark's Hall had been built back up since the crisis in 1912. Workers included the head resident; a second deaconess, who served as club worker and visitor; a kindergarten teacher; and a nurse. Deaconess Helen Gibson, the recently assigned head resident, reported a well-organized clinic, a sewing school, a mother's club, an "excellent" Boy Scout troop, and a Camp Fire group. Further, she said, "The social life of the community has not been neglected. On one or more occasions there have been three hundred persons at our neighborhood gathering." Gibson noted that twenty-one children had been recruited for Sunday school because of their attendance at the St. Mark's kindergarten. "The source of greatest encouragement is the fact that recruits are coming into the Church from all departments."[53]

W. E. Thomas, who was serving as pastor at both St. Mark's Hall and the Mary Werlein Mission, showed none of the objections to social service activities that J. W. Moore had evidenced; his theological stance was more in keeping with that of the first pastor assigned to St. Mark's Hall, N. E. Joyner, who asserted in 1909 his belief that preaching the gospel by means of deeds was as effective as preaching it "by word."[54] Thomas was pleased to note that the clinic had been "the greatest feeder to the Church" of all the settlement's activities. He found this to be a natural result, "since as people's physical needs are relieved it offers an opportunity for the Gospel's seed."[55]

Toward the end of the year, *NOCA* reported the presence of a new trained nurse at St. Mark's Hall and predicted that the work would yield "some very definite results" in the coming year. A new laboratory had been equipped, and an additional doctor had been recruited for general clinic work because "attendance at the dispensary has been phenomenally large." There were enough patients to keep three physicians occupied. More than one hundred children had been vaccinated, and when the hall's kindergarten opened on September 12, "the former little friends came trooping back."[56]

Inevitably, however, the United States' declaration of war began to impact life in New Orleans, and within six months, it was affecting everyday work at St. Mark's. The young people engaged in patriotic activities to show support for the war effort. The head resident reported that the girls were "enthusiastic about 'doing their bit.'" They had made three hundred visits in a canvass for a women's registration day and were given lessons in war cooking by representatives from the Government Food Preparedness Commission. The boys distributed literature and assisted in the sale of Liberty Bonds.[57]

Even dedicated Christian workers were caught up in the fervor for war. Hattie Parker, the president of the city mission board, did clerical work for the military "to free up a man to go to France and fight." When the Woman's Missionary Council of the southern church met in New Orleans in April 1917, twenty-six deaconesses and city missionaries offered a resolution that would permit them to answer the government's call "for mobilization of women for service in the struggle for world democracy." It made the women's appointments subject to change should they be accepted and assigned to active duty "along the channels of mercy and Christian social service." Signers included Helen Gibson, then head resident at St. Mark's, and Margaret Ragland, the former head resident. However, there is no indication that they were ever called into service.[58]

CONCLUSIONS

The coming of World War I has often been associated with the end of the Social Gospel movement and the Progressive Era, and their decline is usually linked to the loss of innocence and optimism that the war occasioned for many individuals and perhaps even nations. However, as will be illustrated in the next chapter, the Social Gospel activities of the Methodist women of New Orleans only increased during the next two decades.

It is true that questions continued about the advisability of the church addressing social problems. As Jane Addams wrote, when denominational organizations such as The Methodist Church began to deal with contemporary social issues, the work necessarily "proceeded slowly . . . for there was inevitably both honest doubt as to its wisdom and downright opposition on the part of those who sincerely believed that the church was going outside its proper field."[59] However, by 1917, the Methodist women of New Orleans had already overcome the most dangerous resistance to their work, when S. H. Werlein replaced J. W. Moore as overseer of the ministries.

Kathryn Kish Sklar has noted the imposition of so-called "maternalist" motives onto settlement workers and has decried the failure to attach sufficient weight to nonsectarian settlement women's religious motives, even by scholars such as Eleanor Stebner who acknowledged the "spiritual" aspects of the Hull House women's motivations.[60] The near total lack of study about the work of unabashedly religious settlement workers, including a nuanced exploration of their motives, has, in my opinion, helped to obscure important distinctions between the Social Gospel and Progressive movements.

One reason for this scholarly lacuna has been the dismissal of the Methodist women's work by social historians as unimportant. A part of it has been that it was women's work, but because nonsectarian settlements also run by women have been studied seriously, it is impossible to link the lack of consideration solely to the deaconesses' gender. In a larger sense, the failure to study Methodist settlements may be part of the phenomenon that Nathan Hatch has called the "scholarly neglect" of American Methodism.[61]

Whatever the reasons, the lack of historical consideration of religious settlement houses like St. Mark's has had a number of effects. One is the inability of still-extant women's groups, such as the United Methodist Women, to recognize fully what their identity has been in the past. Another has been a contribution to misconceptions about the Social Gospel, including an understanding of it as nearly identical to the work of several northern male theologians, three of the most important of whom died at just this point in history. Following the course of Social Gospel praxis into the Depression era through the history of the women of St. Mark's will provide evidence that calls for rethinking our understanding of settlement work and for making important distinctions between the Social Gospel and other manifestations of Progressive reform work.

3

ST. MARK'S COMMUNITY CENTER IN THE POST–WORLD WAR I ERA

Lagging behind the MEC by nearly two decades, the MECS finally approved laity voting rights for women at the General Conference of 1918. The first women delegates to General Conference were seated in 1922.[1] The bishops had adamantly opposed this change and had successfully stymied campaigns by the women for the last several General Conferences. The MECS women of New Orleans, including Elvira Carré and Hattie Parker, had supported suffrage for churchwomen, as had various Louisiana clergymen like S. H. Werlein. Although decades would pass before the percentage of female delegates would even begin to approach the percentage of females among active church members, it was a significant step in claiming legitimacy for women's leadership in southern Methodism, and it came at a critical time, as the church was shaping itself for the post–World War I world.

Although World War I is commonly seen as having brought the Social Gospel movement to a close, it did not signal the end of the Social Gospel in New Orleans. The movement's ending has usually been attributed to a sense of disenchantment caused by recognition of the war's futility. Yet this overlooks the fact that several of the leading theologians/writers of the movement happened to die just at that time. These included Walter Rauschenbusch and Washington Gladden, both of whom died in 1918, and Josiah Strong, who died in 1916.[2] I suggest that these individuals, three of the most important public voices of the movement, stopped publishing Social Gospel materials at the time of World War I not because they became disillusioned, but rather because they died. Death, I submit, is an even more powerful interruptive force to one's writing than disenchantment. Methodist Social Gospelers, on the other hand, continued with their work unabated, including nationally known writers like Harry

Ward, founder of the Methodist Federation for Social Service (later the Methodist Federation for Social Action), and in-the-trenches practitioners of the Social Gospel, such as the deaconesses and woman's society members of New Orleans.

In fact, the decade that followed the war was one of the high points in the history of St. Mark's. The women moved their settlement house into a large, beautifully equipped, new structure that would serve the poorer residents of New Orleans throughout the rest of the twentieth century and into the twenty-first. This chapter examines the women's design for the structure and the work they performed there during the challenging decades of the 1920s and 1930s. It will demonstrate that work inspired by the Social Gospel continued unchecked throughout the prosperous decade of the 1920s and the early years of the Great Depression. When the New Deal was enacted, a number of Methodist women left the employ of the church and worked with the federal government for the duration of the Depression. As Deaconess Helen Mandlebaum, who grew up as a member of the St. Mark's congregation and moved into government service until the Depression ended, put it, "That was where the action was."[3] The federal government's adoption of responsibility for the physical welfare of citizens living in poverty can, in my view, be more accurately regarded as a declining point for the Social Gospel than can World War I.

"SET APART" AS DEACONESSES

As noted in the introduction, the "garb" that early Methodist deaconesses were required to wear was intended in part to offer them the same protection that habits offered "to the Romish Sisters of charity."[4] The reference to "Romish Sisters" was not inappropriate, because the earliest deaconesses looked so much like members of a Catholic order that many people, especially in a Roman Catholic city like New Orleans, confused them with "Protestant nuns." In truth, there were several things the deaconesses did have in common with Catholic sisters. An especially important resemblance was that the deaconesses who were engaged in settlement work, like Roman Catholic sisters, lived together in community. Further, until 1959, the church required that Methodist deaconesses remain single. Although they did not take a vow of celibacy nor promise never to marry, they could no longer be deaconesses if they did wed. Several deaconesses, including Dorothy Lundy, who married local resident Eddie Smira in 1935, had to leave St. Mark's on the occasion of their marriage.[5]

In the MECS, all the women within the denomination who had fulfilled requirements to become deaconesses in a given year were consecrated together in a ritual at which a bishop officiated. Persons facing designation as missionaries were consecrated at the same ceremony. The ritual used the scriptural text from the fourth chapter of the Gospel According to Luke, where Jesus reads from the scroll of the Hebrew prophet Isaiah: "The Spirit of the Lord is upon me, because he hath anointed me to preach the gospel to the poor." The pericope goes on to mention the mandates to preach deliverance to captives and recovering of sight to the blind, to free those who are oppressed, and to proclaim "the acceptable year of the Lord." The wording used in the ritual, "the opening of the prison to those that are bound," is actually from the original passage in the sixty-first chapter of Isaiah, rather than the quoted version in Luke's gospel. This material was then, as it is now, a favorite of those who are committed to social action and justice ministries.[6]

The consecration liturgy also contained an address from the officiating bishop to all the candidates, which included these sentences: "Dearly Beloved, we rejoice with you, that in the good providence of God, a door of usefulness has been opened for you in the service of the Church of Christ. To you are accorded unusual privileges and priceless opportunities for service. Like our Master, you are set apart for a ministry of teaching and preaching and healing."[7]

Interestingly, this liturgy, setting the persons apart for "a ministry of teaching and preaching and healing," was not modified for the deaconesses despite the fact that women were not expected—and indeed, not allowed—to preach in the United States. Some women were allowed to preach as missionaries on the foreign field, although the same women would not have been allowed to preach in this country because of their sex. Scholars usually interpret this as a manifestation of racism that led white Methodist men to believe that although women were scripturally barred from teaching men like themselves, they were nevertheless good enough to be in leadership over foreign men.

Church Connection Hinders
Acceptance for Deaconess Work

The dissemination of the gospel was, as discussed in chapter 2, a focus of controversy in the lives of religious settlement workers. Authorities in the Methodist hierarchy often thought the women were not interested enough in matters of the spirit, while contemporary secular and nonsectarian agencies and later social historians often faulted them for being *too* interested in spiritual conversions among their clientele.

Judith Trolander, author of *Settlement Houses and the Great Depression*, noted that the primary reason that settlements like St. Mark's did not become members of the National Federation of Settlements was that the federation's "strict, nonsectarian requirements for membership" precluded any agency too closely tied to a religion from joining. The litmus test "was the amount of proselytizing in the settlement's program. If a settlement with religious connections did not proselytize too much, it might be a member of a local settlement federation, but it could not be a member of the National Federation." (Oddly, after explaining at length why religious settlements were not eligible to join the National Federation of Settlements, Trolander then said about the Methodist sponsored settlements, "None of these settlements *bothered with* National Federation membership in the 1930s.")[8]

In New Orleans, Kingsley House belonged to the National Federation, while St. Mark's did not.[9] As Trolander noted, settlements that did not meet the National Federation's criteria regarding non-sectarianism often belonged to similar agencies at the local level. When the New Orleans Council of Social Agencies organized in 1921, St. Mark's Hall chose to join. Although it was not listed among the official charter members, the staff had already indicated an intention to affiliate with the new organization by the time of the first meeting, and an unofficial representative from St. Mark's was appointed to the council. Despite the fact that the council "remained an inactive and rather unimportant agency" throughout much of its first two decades, largely because it always lacked funds, the decision of the St. Mark's staff to join the group is a telling indicator that the deaconesses saw their work as compatible with that of the personnel at other social service agencies.[10]

Deaconesses Address Material
and Spiritual Needs

From the earliest days, the social work aspects of the mission had been primarily the bailiwick of the deaconesses assigned to New Orleans, while pastors' reports devoted more attention to conversions and spiritual instruction. In March 1921, one pastor lamented that during his first two months at the Mary Werlein Mission, "[s]o much of our time has been given to material things, that it seems to have almost materialized our message to the people. We are striving to feed the hungry, clothe the naked and minister [to] the sick and needy along all lines, as far as we are able." He had nevertheless preached twenty-six sermons in English and twelve in Spanish and baptized two infants and three adults. He also reported having "visited the sick, comforted the disheartened, and brought consolation to the discouraged, and attention to the dying," a list of functions that sounds similar to the earliest job description for deaconesses.[11]

At St. Mark's Hall, deaconess Berta Ellison replaced Helen Gibson as head resident in mid 1921. Ellison's staff included a nurse, Lydia Rieke, from Minnesota, and two Virginia natives, deaconess Bertie Breeden, consecrated in 1918, and deaconess Ruth Byerly, consecrated in 1920. Ellison's annual report emphasized that not all of the work the women had accomplished was measurable, but the items on which she was able to put a numeric value were included in the form of a table.[12]

The report revealed that the deaconesses had given 243 Bible readings in homes, attended 388 meetings and spoken at seventy-five, and sponsored a banquet and several parties for neighborhood residents. Some of Meekins's work at the Mary Werlein Mission was replicated at St. Mark's Hall, with 516 people taking showers and eighty acquiring some kind of clothing or other goods from the supply store.

Building relationship with the inhabitants of the neighborhood was always both the goal and the primary strategy of the MECS settlements. Hence, the largest numbers were attached to the categories of "visits made" (4,610) and "visits received" (4,050). They had reached a total of 2,010 families during the year.

Recreation and education for young people and adults was an important facet of the work. Ellison reported that sixty-three people were studying woodwork and forty-two were enrolled in a home nursing curriculum. Thirty-one were learning how to raise a kitchen garden, while twenty-five took cooking classes and ninety-seven were learning to sew. The Boy Scout program reached forty-seven youngsters, and 155 played basketball; twenty-five girls participated in Camp Fire programming.

The health clinic had reached 1,674 families that year, treating a total of 4,058 patients. The nurse had given 1,294 treatments, and 345 vaccinations were administered.[13] At the 1922 annual meeting, Ellison delegated the preparation of the report to Byerly, who told delegates that the facility's clinic continued to serve as "the opening wedge which helps to break down opposition and prejudice, and from its work and the follow-up visits of the nurse come by far the largest number of new comers to other departments and to church."[14]

ST. MARK'S OPENS A GRAND NEW SETTLEMENT FACILITY IN 1923

By far the most exciting development at St. Mark's in the early 1920s was designing, building, and preparing to move into a grand new structure on North Rampart Street. Occasioned by the one-hundredth anniversary of the founding of the Methodist Missionary Society, a movement emerged in 1918–19 in both the MEC and MECS to raise large amounts of money for a Centenary Fund, to be used for both home and foreign mission. A centenary celebration (referred to as "a great Methodist World's Fair") was organized in Columbus, Ohio, and this event helped spur enthusiasm for the project. The MECS set a goal of twenty-five million dollars over and above regular giving, and the amount was oversubscribed.[15] Some of the monies were distributed to the woman's section of the board of missions, and part of that was used to construct the new settlement house for St. Mark's. By early 1923, the presiding elder of the New Orleans District could report that the new St. Mark's building, which had cost about $125,000, was expected to open soon and that Worth Tippy, who chaired the Federated Churches of Christ's commission on social service, had declared the structure "to be the equal of any similar plant he has seen in any city."[16]

Three months later, the head resident, Berta Ellison, showed photographs of "the Finest Settlement Building in the States" to the annual meeting of the conference-wide Woman's Missionary Society. Ellison "declared that we are to be the Voice of Protestantism in New Orleans, standing out with other great philanthropic organizations in that great city," and asked the women for help in furnishing the rooms and for prayer.[17]

Fig. 6. Berta Ellison and Mary Lou Barnwell in 1928.
Note that Ellison no longer wears deaconess garb.

In May, Ellison wrote a lengthy piece entitled, "A Dream Come True," for *NOCA.* She recounted that after years of making do in leased quarters, "somebody began to dream of a new building that should belong to the women, a place that was their very own, and a building fund was started." She named several national leaders who had been instrumental in pushing the project, including Belle Bennett, Tochie Williams MacDonell, and Mary Helm; among the "consecrated local women" who had created the ministry, she named only Elvira Carré. Ellison said that at the 1917 Woman's Missionary Council meeting at First Church in New Orleans, someone had put a barrel near the door of the meeting room with a sign on it: "WANTED! A BARREL OF MONEY TO BUILD A NEW ST. MARK'S." But, she continued, "doubtless nobody thought a barrel full would ever be collected."[18]

Noting that her plea at the recent state meeting had led several local societies to contribute toward furnishing the building, Ellison appealed for more money to complete the task and amplified: "On the 29th of March, we moved into our new building. . . . Already some things are evident. One is, people passing by comment very favorably on the appearance of St. Mark's. . . . It is an eye-opener to the people in the community, whether they come or not. But they are coming. Attendance at church services has more than doubled, Sunday school has set a high water mark, the League has taken on new life, and every department of the work is going well. The supply store will soon be open and all the second-hand clothing you can spare is needed. Send it on as fast as you can, plenty of space to put it now."[19]

Then in May 1923, a *NOCA* editorial celebrated that an "informal opening" of the facility had been scheduled for the evening of May 31. Invitations had been issued to all the Methodists of New Orleans to come and see that "St. Mark's constitutes one of the finest plants in this country for social and religious work, and its activities have already been productive of much good in the section of the city where it is located." The new building would house both the deaconess-run settlement house known as St. Mark's Community Center and the worshipping congregation, to be known as St. Mark's Methodist Episcopal Church, South. The editorial listed the staff: "Rev. John F. Foster, American pastor; Rev. Jos. M. Codispoti, Italian pastor; Miss Berta Ellison, head resident; Miss Ruth Byerly, girls' club worker; Miss Myrle Neely, boys' club worker; Miss

Lydia Rieke, nurse; Miss Maude Fall, office secretary." The pastors, both (at that time necessarily) male, were listed first, although most of the building was devoted to the center and most of the settlement work would be accomplished by the women. The continued concern for ministry with Italians is reflected by the designation of Codispoti as the "Italian pastor."[20]

DESIGN REVEALS SOCIAL GOSPEL AGENDA

One of the most valuable artifacts discovered in my research had been framed by Margery Freeman, the woman who recorded oral histories with members of the congregation in 1979. She had thus preserved the original architect's drawings for the new structure located at the corner of Gov. Nicholls and North Rampart streets, drawn by Dougherty & Gardner, Architects, of Nashville (figures 7, 8, and 9), which state the intended use of each room. This provided extremely helpful insight into what the women hoped the facility would allow them to accomplish.

The drawings show that less than 20 percent of the building's space would be devoted to the worshipping congregation of St. Mark's Methodist Episcopal Church, South, where the pastors were in charge. The sanctuary, which would seat more than three hundred people on the main floor and more in a balcony, and which also had a large choir loft and a pipe organ, is labeled on the drawings as the "chapel," nomenclature that probably reflects an understanding on the part of the designers that worship was not the primary function of the building. A room next to the sanctuary is designated as the pastor's study, and a small, enclosed area at the back of the sanctuary is labeled "committee room." However, from the standpoint of assessing relations between the church and the community center, the things missing from the drawings are much more significant. The committee room, the study, and the chapel itself comprise the entire space allotted for the needs of the congregation. (The building did contain a full apartment for the pastor and his family, as noted below.) Even though the records of the congregation during its tenure on Esplanade Avenue indicate that Bible study and religious instruction, including Sunday school, were important parts of its program, there was not a single room primarily designated for this kind of Christian education. Sunday school classes would have

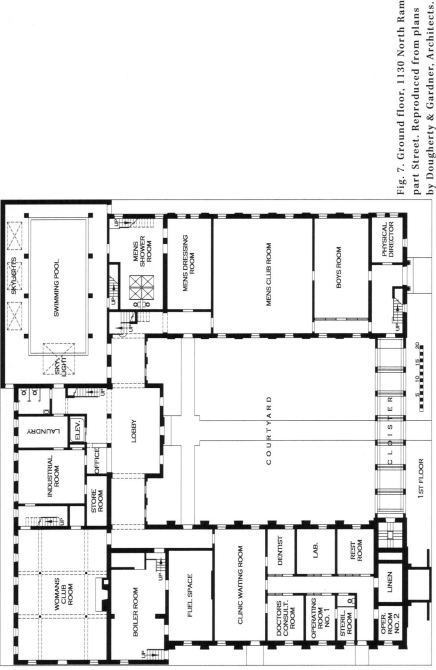

Fig. 7. Ground floor, 1130 North Rampart Street. Reproduced from plans by Dougherty & Gardner, Architects.

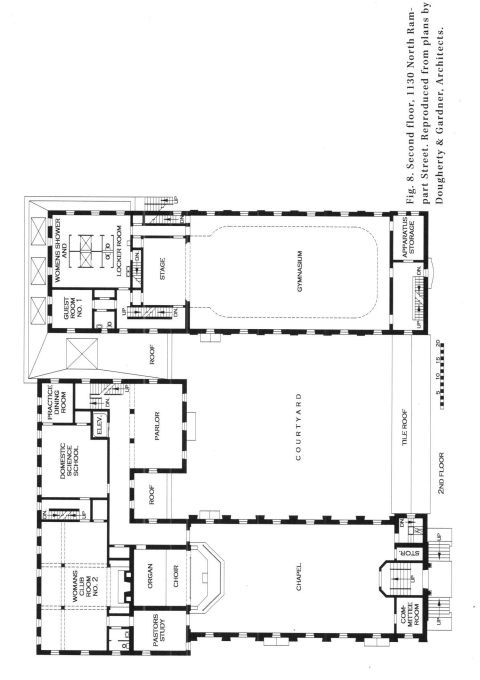

Fig. 8. Second floor, 1130 North Rampart Street. Reproduced from plans by Dougherty & Gardner, Architects.

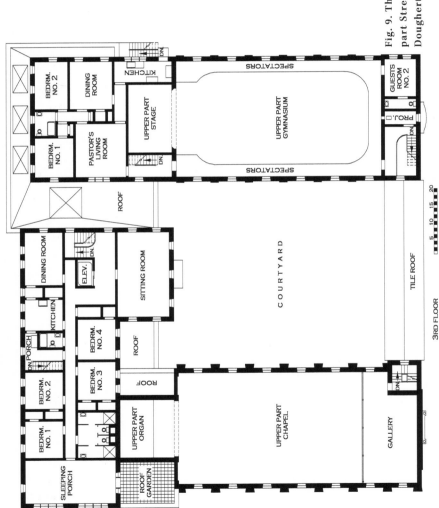

BEDRM.
NO. 2

DINING
ROOM

KITCHEN

DN

UPPER PART
STAGE

SPECTATORS

BEDRM.
NO. 1

PASTOR'S
LIVING
ROOM

UPPER PART
GYMNASIUM

GUESTS
ROOM
NO. 2

ROOF

PROJ.

DN

SPECTATORS

DN

DINING ROOM

DN

ELEV.

KITCHEN

SITTING ROOM

DN. PORCH

BEDRM.
NO. 4

ROOF

COURTYARD

BEDRM.
NO. 2

BEDRM.
NO. 3

ROOF

BEDRM.
NO. 1

UPPER PART
ORGAN

UPPER PART
CHAPEL

TILE ROOF

SLEEPING
PORCH

ROOF
GARDEN

GALLERY

DN

5 10 15 20

3RD FLOOR

Fig. 9. Third floor, 1130 North Rampart Street. Reproduced from plans by
Dougherty & Gardner, Architects.

been secondary users of rooms primarily dedicated to Social Gospel functions of the community center.

At various times throughout the twentieth century, relations between the St. Mark's congregation and the community center were such that this did not present any problem, and it is possible that the women whose dreams the building reflected saw the two as being so deeply linked that the fact that space would be shared did not even need to be articulated. Sherry Smyth, who was involved as a child at St. Mark's Church in the 1960s while a deaconess still ran the center, recalls no conflict over the use of center space by the congregation. "We thought those Sunday school rooms were ours," she said. However, at other times—as when church members arrived one day in the 1970s to discover that a lock to which they had not been given a key had been installed on the door between the center and the sanctuary—the failure to designate education and fellowship space for the church has been an obstacle to the congregation's continued existence.[21]

Overall, the architect's drawings depict a large, three-story building in the shape of a squared-off horseshoe. The space inside the horseshoe is a courtyard, separated from North Rampart Street by a gateway and a partial wall; the courtyard is most often used now, as it was when the building was constructed, as a gathering and play space for children. Most space on the top two floors on the north (lakeside) wing is devoted to the "chapel," described above, while most of the top two floors on the south (riverside) wing is devoted to a gymnasium with a basketball court.

The most striking feature on the first floor was a large indoor swimming pool, thought to be the only one in the city in 1923. The pool was destined to be a major draw for neighborhood children, especially during the steamy New Orleans summers before air-conditioning became common. Along with showers and dressing rooms for men and women (with men's and women's on different floors), a "Men's Club Room" and a "Boy's Room" were located on the first floor, under the gym. There was a stage at the end of the gymnasium itself that would see much use through the years as youngsters performed in plays and pageants. At the opposite end, there was a projection booth so that films could be shown on a screen set up on the stage.

On the second floor, for use in teaching domestic arts and sciences to women, there were a "Domestic Science School" (a kitchen), a "Practice Dining Room" and a "Parlor." Two large "Club Rooms" for women were included on the plans, one not far from the kitchen. It is easy to see how these particular features would double as kitchen, fellowship, and educational space for the worshipping congregation on Sundays.

A health clinic intended to serve the poor occupied the first floor of the lakeside wing, underneath the chapel. Along with a fairly large waiting room, it contained a laboratory, a dentist office, a sterilizing room, and a doctor's consulting room. Two "operating rooms" were used primarily as examining rooms; persons who needed surgery were sent to local hospitals. A nurse deaconess was a member of the center's staff, and the staff and local board members recruited local physicians and dentists to volunteer their services at the clinic.

Three kinds of living space were present in the facility. The first was a single-family, self-contained apartment devoted to the pastor of the St. Mark's congregation. This two-bedroom apartment for the use of the preacher and his family included a full kitchen and a separate dining room. It was located on the third floor in the gymnasium wing.

The second type consisted of two "Guest Rooms," bedrooms that had their own private bathrooms. Tucked away in otherwise unused space—one was next to the projection booth atop the gymnasium—they were clearly intended for visitors. However, the rooms were sometimes used as lodging by students at Tulane Medical School who were expected to help out at the health clinic, in return.

The third, and most important, was the living quarters for the women who worked at St. Mark's. A vital part of the mission of Methodist deaconesses was to live in the neighborhoods they served and become a true part of the community. Therefore, sufficient space to house four deaconesses was included on the third floor. (Though the pastor's apartment was also on the third floor, the deaconess quarters were not accessible from the pastor's apartment except by going down one staircase and up another. Walking through the building itself makes it clear how deliberate a decision this must have been.)

The women's living quarters included four bedrooms, a sitting room, a kitchen, a dining room, a room with showers, and a separate common bathroom. Both a roof garden and a sleeping porch that the women enjoyed using in the summer overlooked Gov. Nicholls Street. The women worked hard and worked long hours downstairs in the community center and throughout the surrounding neighborhood, but the center employed a housekeeper for them, so when they came upstairs, their meals had been prepared. As the convent did for Roman Catholic women, the deaconess quarters provided an alternative space for individuals who did not want to live the traditional life of wife and mother or even that of what would then have been termed a spinster aunt. They were able to do exciting and meaningful work, under the (at least somewhat protective) aegis of the church, and to live with like-minded female companions.

RELATIONS WITH THE ROMAN CATHOLIC CHURCH IN NEW ORLEANS

The overall architectural style of the building made it resemble a Spanish mission. One of the first women to live in its deaconess quarters was Annie Rogers, a Methodist minister's daughter who studied at Scarritt and who was sent to St. Mark's as her first assignment after her commissioning in 1923. She considered the new building beautiful and thought it "compared favorably" with the nearby Catholic churches and convent.[22] Becoming familiar with the Roman Catholic environment of the neighborhood was a major part of Rogers's adjustment to her new surroundings. Several of her friends, on hearing of her appointment, asked her why Protestants were sending missionaries to a Catholic city. She responded that the Methodist women had come to minister "to Protestants who weren't Christians, to Catholics who weren't Christians, and to people who had no church affiliation." It was Rogers's opinion, and the opinion of most, if not all, deaconesses who served at St. Mark's, that Catholics who were practicing their faith had no need for conversion.[23]

It must be admitted that the deaconesses were something of an exception in that regard. The *New Orleans Christian Advocate,* which served as the official organ of the Louisiana Annual Conference and the two Annual Conferences in Mississippi, had summed up its opinion on Catholic-Protestant relations succinctly a few years previously. In an editorial about a controversy that arose between the Vatican and Theodore Roosevelt when the former president visited Rome, *NOCA* said: "The truth is, we have little patience with the view of semi-religious periodicals that the Roman Catholic Church should be accorded the same consideration by Protestant bodies in planning their evangelistic work as they accord one another. From our viewpoint, the Romish Church is heretical in its teaching and corrupt in its practices. Where it has free rein it is the oppressor of the people and the enemy of progress."[24]

With terms such as "heretical," "corrupt" and "oppressor," the editor leaves no room for misjudging the depth of his disrespect for the Roman Catholic Church. There was also local controversy that may have fueled his passion. At that time, along with its primary facility, St. Mark's was also operating an "Italian Mission" at 539 St. Ann Street, on Jackson Square and within sight of the Roman Catholic Church's imposing structure, the St. Louis Cathedral. At an MECS district-wide preachers' meeting the year before, a staff member, Rev. Zito, informed other pastors about his work. *NOCA* said Zito "speaks concerning Jesus and not of the Catholic Church, as do the priests," and reported that "Two priests are visiting Italians and warning them against the Protestant religion. Bro. Zito follows in their tracks to tell the people there is no salvation in church ritual, but in Jesus."[25]

Some of the individual laywomen affiliated with St. Mark's shared his opinion. Mary Werlein, for instance, had "strong feelings about Catholics," according to her grandniece, Leila Werlein Stone, and "no doubt she thought they were headed straight for hell." When Stone was a senior at Newcomb College in New Orleans, she dated a young man who was a Roman Catholic. Not long before Stone graduated in 1937, she and her beau were parked in front of the house where Mary lived. Mary came out to the car and informed him, "No doubt you are a fine young man, but you are *not* for Leila." Stone had no doubt that Werlein's objection resulted solely from the young man's Catholicism.[26]

Roman Catholic priests in the neighborhood of St. Mark's did not share the deaconesses' tolerance, either. In the context of celebrating that there are better relations between Protestants and Catholics now than there were then, Annie Rogers recalled a Vacation Bible School (VBS) session in 1923 when children were gathered on the Rampart Street sidewalk waiting for the doors of the new settlement house to open. A priest came and warned them not to go inside, because what went on in there "was of the Devil." But, she said, "the children knew what was inside, and they came anyway." In fact, Rogers recalled that the

VBS was one of the most successful aspects of the summer program that year. It served approximately two hundred children, representing sixteen different nationalities, during its four-week run. She also recalled a big revival that summer, with an evangelist from Kansas City preaching, where many teenagers and young adults, including a seaman from a ship docked at the wharf, were converted.[27]

As might be expected, the Roman Catholic Church did not simply sit and watch as Italian Catholics were served, and perhaps recruited, by other denominations. St. Mary's Catholic Church, a part of the complex of buildings that includes the Old Ursuline Convent is, like St. Mark's, in that part of the French Quarter then called "Little Palermo."[28] Located at 1116 Chartres Street, it is only five blocks away from the present St. Mark's structure on Rampart Street. In 1921, when St. Mary's received the designation, "St. Mary's Italian Church," the two facilities were even closer to one another, because St. Mark's was still at 908 Esplanade. Because St. Mary's Catholic Church had served various ethnic groups throughout its history, it was natural for it to reflect demographic changes and become an "Italian church." The church made language accommodations and added statues of saints dear to Italians to the sanctuary. At the same time, they established St. Mary's Italian School on the premises of the former convent, and the school remained in existence until 1963.[29]

CREATING "LIFE ABUNDANT" IN THE NEIGHBORHOOD

The beauty of St. Mark's was important to Annie Rogers not just because it allowed the Methodists to "compete" with Roman Catholic facilities. She recalled a poor and elderly lady who was thrilled to be among "nice things" at another center where Rogers later worked. Bringing beauty to an otherwise desolate neighborhood was part of the settlement agenda from Jane Addams onward. The delight on the part of the elderly client, and on the part of Rogers as she remembered it decades later, reflect the settlement workers' intuitive understanding of the effect of physical surroundings on human beings' interior lives.

Assessing her lifetime achievements as a deaconess in a 1976 presentation, Annie Rogers spoke frequently about the concept of "abundant life" that Jesus promised his followers.[30] In her understanding, the settlement workers

Fig. 10. Helen Mandlebaum pictured with Annie Rogers, one of the first women appointed to the new facility on Rampart Street. Helen Mandlebaum grew up to be a deaconess and served the Wesley House settlement in Louisville, Kentucky, for many years.

gained a more abundant life as they tried to give others more abundant life. "That abundant life is not just knowing Christ, but also having what you need, an opportunity to have your children get education, for you to grow physically and spiritually the most you can," she explained.[31]

Her assessment is indicative of a common, and possibly somewhat gender-related, differentiation in how progress at settlements has been measured.

Though some social historians deem settlements houses to have been failures because they did not eliminate poverty and urban problems in their locales, the women who worked in settlements tended to measure success in terms of positive changes in individual lives and use anecdotal evidence to support their claims. Rogers, for instance, talks about encountering years later the father of Mikey, a child with whom she worked, and his telling her that because Mikey got a good start in her preschool, he went on to graduate from college. She also talks about a girl who learned to play basketball at the center, and about the elderly woman whose life was enriched by exposure to beautiful surroundings for at least part of her day.[32]

Along with an attractive environment, the deaconesses tried to offer other opportunities for enrichment of lives. The head resident wrote an article in December 1923 describing the staff's plans for "dispensing Christmas cheer." The Camp Fire Girls, which she referred to as one of the "oldest groups in this institution," were to give a banquet for their mothers. There was also a party for the students of the sewing school, at which, she noted, attendance had increased more than 50 percent during the year. Instruction was provided by volunteers from the Daughters of the American Revolution organization on Saturday afternoons, and then, Ellison said, "the social feature enters in, as these mothers seldom get out of the home for any kind of recreation. They enter into games with the zest of children; so, for that reason, plenty of games will be on the program."[33]

Making Friends of Neighbors

When the women held the dedication ceremony for the new structure on North Rampart Street in 1924, a mysterious power blackout occurred during the proceedings. Delores Prickett, a young woman who became involved with St. Mark's through the Camp Fire Girls program while the mission was still on Esplanade Avenue and who was later employed at the center, recalled the event. When the city sent a worker to try to restore power for the ceremony, he discovered that the electric lines had been deliberately cut. A nearby business owner was found to be the culprit, "and they wanted Miss Allison [sic] to prosecute and she wouldn't do it. She said I'll handle this my way." Although the women's housekeeper normally did the marketing along with the cooking, Ellison began doing the marketing herself. She "goes over and deals with the merchant, never mentioned what happened or anything, and after three months she came back one day all smiles. She said it worked. He's going to give me a discount on what we buy there and he apologized for what he did. And he turned out to be one of our best supporters that we had in the community."[34]

Unfortunately, it is not clear whether the business owner objected to the center because it was a Protestant settlement or because it was serving primarily an immigrant clientele. Whatever his reason, he was apparently won over by Ellison and the other deaconesses, and the women had good relations with the entire neighborhood (except the priests) until the dawn of the civil rights movement.

THE CENTER BECOMES
A COMMUNITY CHEST AGENCY

Another event as significant as the dedication ceremony also occurred in 1924, when a Community Chest was established in the city of New Orleans. It and its successor organizations, the United Fund and the United Way, would be a major funder of St. Mark's Community Center throughout the rest of the twentieth century and into the twenty-first. Because Community Chest policy precluded the contribution of funds to activities sponsored by a single congregation, the community center and the St. Mark's congregation were officially separated into two administrative entities. This was not as jarring as one might suppose, because the pastors who led the congregation had always been affiliated with and appointed by the Louisiana Annual Conference of the MECS and supervised by the presiding elders, while deaconesses had never been formally affiliated with the Annual Conferences in whose boundaries they served, but had always reported to the woman's home mission society. Throughout much of the shared history of the two entities (up until the mid-1960s), the deaconesses continued to belong to the St. Mark's congregation and to play important leadership roles in it, and this did not change because of the administrative separation. Nevertheless, the congregation may have lost some sense of "ownership" of the center as a result of the official separation. Minutes of the congregation's quarterly conference for January 12, 1927, indicate that the nurse deaconess made a report on the activities of the clinic, stating that three persons had recently been added to the center's staff and approximately six thousand pa-tients had received treatment during the past year. However, these are the only extant church minutes from that era containing any mention of community center activities.[35]

In the 1926 *Journal of the Louisiana Annual Conference* and thereafter, there is no mention of the Mary Werlein Mission, and presumably it ceased to exist as a separate entity at that time.[36] It is not clear whether the women's en-ergies were taken up by supporting the expanded work at St. Mark's or whether the people affiliated with the church at the mission were absorbed into other nearby congregations, or both. The Kingsley House settlement continued to operate in the Irish Channel neighborhood, remained operating at the time of Katrina, and has since reopened, and presumably some of the mission's clien-tele may have been absorbed into that facility's work. St. Mark's, however, was expanding its activities and influence on every level as the decade of the 1920s passed the halfway mark.

PART II

Work for Gender and Racial Equality: 1920s–1960

4

"A RESTLESSNESS OF WOMEN"

In the 1920s and 1930s, the deaconesses in New Orleans laid the groundwork that allowed a major incident in the city's civil rights struggle to play out later at St. Mark's. The training that MECS deaconesses underwent, including its theological, spiritual, practical, and economic aspects, prepared them for a profound embodiment of their Christianity. As the MECS women of New Orleans made major advancements in their Social Gospel practice in the decade that followed the First World War, so did their organization at the denominational level, especially with regard to that training. In 1924, Scarritt Bible and Training School moved from Kansas City, Missouri, into spacious new quarters in Nashville, Tennessee, and took the name Scarritt College for Christian Workers. The majority of the deaconesses who served in New Orleans studied at Scarritt College. This chapter examines their training program and demonstrates that the women at St. Mark's were far more radical than female Social Gospel reformers have been thought. This finding offers a much-needed corrective to assertions that all female reformers of the era were intrinsically conservative. A number of white MECS deaconesses joined the National Association for the Advancement of Colored People (NAACP) during their Scarritt training and were, considering their time, place, and cultural backgrounds, truly radical in the area of race relations.

MARY LOU BARNWELL AS CHIEF "LOVING TROUBLE-MAKER"

A Scarritt College faculty member once referred to Methodist deaconesses as "Loving Trouble-Makers."[1] An important moment in the history of St. Mark's

Fig. 11a. Mary Lou Barnwell in the
summer of 1927.

occurred when one of the most outstanding of the "loving trouble-makers,"
Mary Lou Barnwell, came to the community center in 1927. Barnwell shaped
the facility not only during her years as its local director in the 1930s, but also as
a national leader of the deaconess movement for three decades thereafter. As
head of the deaconess program overall, she set policy and influenced the work
of every Methodist deaconess, including those who followed her at St. Mark's.

Born in Georgia in 1903, Barnwell dreamed of going as a missionary to Asia
and did her graduate work at Scarritt toward that end. However, to pass the
physical exam for overseas service, a woman had to weigh at least one hundred
pounds, and she was not able to gain that much weight. So when she graduated, the MECS sent her to New Orleans to work with the St. Mark's program
for boys and to work as receptionist for the health clinic. In 1933, she was relo-

Fig. 11b. Mary Lou Barnwell in
Audubon Park on Easter day, 1929.

cated to the Rosa Valdez Center in Tampa, Florida, but in 1937, she returned to
New Orleans, this time to serve as head resident at St. Mark's for two years.

In 1939, Barnwell was elected to oversee urban work for the women's mission structure in the newly created Methodist church, and she continued to fill
important administrative posts for the rest of her career, including service as
executive secretary of the Commission on Deaconess Work from 1948 to 1964.[2]
Her work in these offices took her all over the world and gave her unparalleled
opportunity to shape the work of deaconesses. Barnwell "chose to live out her
commitment to God through the agencies of churchwomen's organizations"
and "sought racial understanding, crossed economic barriers, helped women
interpret mores of different peoples and, in [the] face of opposition, exercised
strong leadership."[3]

At the time of my interview with her, she was a resident of the Brooks-Howell Home for retired deaconesses in Asheville, North Carolina, and she responded to a question about her understanding of the Social Gospel by saying, "It's just something you live."[4] This deceptively simple-sounding response mirrors exactly the theological underpinnings of the Social Gospel and points to the liberation theology of the mid-twentieth century, with its recognition of theology as a "second order" activity involving reflection on already occurring practice (praxis). It also resounds with the particular Wesleyan emphasis on "social holiness."

Training in Radical Christianity

During the formative period when she studied at Scarritt College, Mary Lou Barnwell did her fieldwork at a Bethlehem House in Nashville. Bethlehem Houses were Methodist settlements that served African American clienteles. The mores of the South at the time dictated that white MECS women were not expected to serve at Bethlehem Houses unless they volunteered to do so. Barnwell said the Scarritt professor who most influenced her overall was her New Testament professor, Dr. Albert Barnett, and he undoubtedly played a role in her decision to work at Bethlehem House.[5]

The focus on New Testament studies, interpreted through the lens provided by a social radical like Barnett, encouraged students like Barnwell to work in countercultural ways toward a society more in keeping with the teachings of Jesus than with current societal norms. "Bible study was of first importance" in all the deaconess training schools, where the "most important objectives were to promote knowledge of the English Bible, provide a high proportion of practical subjects, and expose their students to varied forms of religious work by sending them outside the schools." At Scarritt, the first faculty chair to be endowed was the Belle Harris Bennett Chair of the English Bible.[6]

Albert Barnett began his career as a professor at Scarritt at the age of twenty-nine after receiving his Ph.D. from the University of Chicago. He taught at Scarritt from 1924 until the mid-1940s.[7] As professor of religious life and thought, he "was known throughout the South as a leader in liberal Christian action."[8] He was a prominent white member of the National Association for the Advancement of Colored People (NAACP), and he urged the Scarritt students to become involved in civil rights activism. Deaconess Helen Mandlebaum, who grew up as a member of the St. Mark's congregation, recalled having joined the NAACP during her studies and said that she and other students did so largely because of Barnett's profound influence regarding social justice.[9]

At Emory University, where Barnett later taught, he was known as "a seasoned academician [who] was possessed with a prophetic spirit. . . . He frequently allied himself with the social and economic interests of labor and continually fought for the rights of the underprivileged, especially blacks."[10] When Barnett died in 1961, the dean emeritus wrote: "Dr. Barnett mastered the New Testament and the New Testament mastered him, so Christ became the driving power of his life. . . . He sensed the inclusiveness of the Christian Gospel. The ostracism of any person was repulsive to him. No one, however different from himself, was beyond his interest. . . . Christ's mission was to all and Albert Barnett accepted the authority of Jesus and he consistently acknowledged the dignity and worth of all people."[11]

In the 1950s, Barnett compiled a biography of Andrew Sledd, who had been forced to resign from the Emory College faculty in 1902 because of the furor related to his *Atlantic Monthly* article entitled, "The Negro: Another View." Sledd's viewpoint would hardly be considered progressive today—he began by acknowledging the "fact" that "Negroes" were inferior to whites in the scale of development—but it was nevertheless radical enough in 1902 to get him burned in effigy in the university community where he resided. Many white southerners deeply resented Sledd for criticizing the common "dehumanizing" practice of ignoring or despising blacks and for asserting that their inferiority could be remedied through education if they were treated as "responsible, if humble" members of society. Sledd maintained that black citizens enjoyed "inalienable rights" and condemned segregation in restaurants, hotels, and places of worship.

Barnett knew Sledd personally, and the biography's sources included "letters from Dr. Sledd to me and treasured, personal memories."[12] Originally delivered as a presentation to the Andrew Sledd Study Club, the work was not intended to be objective; it was an unabashed tribute that treated Sledd as a hero who should be a role model for other theologians, scholars, and educators.

To demonstrate Sledd's courage and Christian commitment, Barnett used an anecdote that actually reveals a great deal about Barnett's own character. In 1934, Sledd had recommended Barnett for a faculty position at Southern Methodist University (SMU) in Dallas. The chair of the search committee, Bishop John M. Moore, wrote to Sledd: "Some objection has arisen because of [Barnett's] giving so much time to race relations and other social issues. It is thought that would detract from his enthusiasm for New Testament study." Sledd wrote back: "while [Barnett] has an active interest in race and social questions, I have no idea that that would 'detract from his enthusiasm for New Testament study.' I should rather regard it as *an evidence of that enthusiasm.*"[13] Sledd's linkage of Jesus' New Testament teachings to social action and racial tolerance was plainly reflected in the attitudes of Barnett and also of Barnett's own students, like Mary Lou Barnwell.

Another student of Barnett's, Julia Southard Campbell, came to St. Mark's Community Center in 1935 as clinic receptionist and girls' worker, and she was promoted to head resident when Barnwell left. Campbell worked at St. Mark's until 1943. During her sabbatical, Campbell served as Barnwell's secretary at the national board of missions while attending the New York School of Social Work. Campbell took several classes under Albert Barnett and admired him greatly. "It was no doubt due to Dr. Barnette [*sic*] that we had such a wonderful relationship with [historically black] Fisk University. We exchanged visits all the time. A Fisk University professor, Dr. Charles S. Johnson, taught sociology at Scarritt." Johnson's brother, James Weldon Johnson, who wrote the lyrics for "Lift Every Voice and Sing," read his poem, "Creation," at Scarritt during a reception in his honor. "It was a thrill to hear him," Campbell recalled. She also said, "I was always on the side of good race relationships, thanks to the natural acceptance at Scarritt College, without 'preaching.'"[14]

A prolific writer, Barnett published extensively. His 1955 article, "The Kingdom of God and the Church's Task," lamented that "the Christian doctrine of the kingdom of God," a focus of Social Gospel thought, had "fallen into neglect." He suggested that the extent to which it had been neglected was "perhaps the most accurate gauge of the extent of the responsibility of the church for chaotic conditions in human society, both within nations and among nations." Pointing to the ideas about individual and corporate sin and salvation that were

Fig. 12. Julia Southard Campbell served at
St. Mark's from 1935 to 1943.

hallmarks of the Social Gospel, Barnett speculated that the apostle Paul "would locate the Church's deficiency in its failure to perceive that evangelism must have institutions as well as individuals as its concern." Significantly, Barnett depicted moral deterioration as the result of social disorganization, *not* the other way around. "Economic chaos in Germany and Japan has in our time made the price of a woman's virtue a chocolate bar or a pack of cigarettes. This does not mean that these women were less virtuous than women elsewhere. It simply means that life is a unity and that social disorganization invariably tends to be accompanied by the moral deterioration of individual persons."[15]

The fact that several women of St. Mark's point to Barnett as their most important educational influence is a significant indication of their own radical theology and ideology. For instance, Julia Southard Campbell said that after attending a lecture given by Norman Thomas at Scarritt, "I felt like a Socialist."[16]

A University of Chicago graduate student writing in 1924 on "The Evolution of the Social Consciousness in Methodism" concluded that a "growing minority" of Methodists was discovering that socialism contained "many constructive principles which they believe would result in a wholesome reconstruction of society. Some have even identified socialism with Christianity, believing that both can work together for a Kingdom of God on earth." While acknowledging that "most church literature is still against it," he pointed to the 1912 Board of Bishops statement that decried the ills of unchecked capitalism and acknowledged the need to protect poor people from it. The author cited several official declarations by "the Methodist Bishops and the General Conference, both in the United States and especially in Canada . . . indorsing [*sic*] certain socialistic tendencies, and express[ing] sympathy for it as a movement of the laboring class to better their condition."[17]

Although Methodist bishops have occasionally moved ahead of the laity and local clergy toward liberal social thought, these bishops were not ahead of the deaconesses with regard to economic theory. Along with units imparting skills the women would need to perform social services, and Bible training that pushed them to relate the teachings of Jesus to social action, the deaconess training course published in 1922 included several chapters that dealt directly with underlying economic causes of society's problems. For example, the women were to read Walter Rauschenbusch's *Christianizing the Social Order* and then do their own reflection and writing on economic theory.[18]

The choice of the Baptist Rauschenbusch for the women's training is revealing, because far more conservative writers could have been chosen who would still have been within the Social Gospel stable. Indeed, Rauschenbusch directly critiqued other Social Gospel writers whose proposals were not radical enough. Based on lectures delivered in 1911 and 1912, *Christianizing the Social Order* warned in the strongest possible terms about the evils of corporate greed. Rauschenbusch believed "Socialism is the necessary spiritual product of

Capitalism," and that its spread was inevitable. "God had to raise up Socialism because the organized Church was too blind, or too slow, to realize God's ends." The reason socialism was not already more successful was that socialist leaders had pitted themselves over against the church instead of recognizing the similarities between their agenda and the Gospel's. Rauschenbusch lamented that Christians who saw the good in socialism's economic doctrines were opening themselves to charges of "atheism, free love, and red-handed violence" precisely because many socialists were actually guilty of these things.[19]

Rauschenbusch believed that business was "the unsaved part of the social order." It was the duty of the "saved portions" to "stand together in the consciousness of moral and religious superiority and go after the lost Brother." The church should fight for a program that included: establishing minimum wage boards in every state to see that living wages were paid to all; banning mothers with young children from the workforce but not penalizing them financially for their absence from it; making industrial machinery safer; having industry or the community assume financial responsibility for injured workers; having the aged cared for without sending them to poorhouses; providing proper housing for the poor; regulating drug companies and funeral homes; insisting on safe, clean working conditions in factories; implementing an eight-hour work day and a six-day work week; offering more vocational education; and legalizing collective bargaining.

To pay for these programs, he proposed a startling change in taxation. Every person should have the right to a home and clothing and "any simple savings of his labor," but those who owned rental property should see their taxes increased over a ten-year period until the taxes equaled the rental income. There would be no private ownership of natural resources like oil, natural gas, water, or minerals/ores. He called for socialization of rail transportation and public utilities. "The resocializing of property is an essential part of the christianizing of the social order." He was convinced that the rich would have to be converted and give up their excess wealth. He urged Christians not to miss God as the Jews did when God approached in the person of Christ, his clear implication being that God was now approaching in the guise of socialism.[20]

After reading *Christianizing the Social Order*, the women had to complete an extensive assignment on it. Among the specific questions they were to answer were: "Name some specific ways in which private interests thwart the common good," "State briefly the case of Christianity against capitalism," and "What, in detail, is meant by the rise of the working class?" Finally, the women were to write a thousand-word paper on the topic, "A Christian Social Order," describing in your own words the world as you think it would be if thoroughly Christianized."[21] Coupled with Barnett's Bible teaching, it is not surprising that this training produced deaconesses who were anything but social conservatives who wished to "band-aid" problems so the framework of capitalist society would not be challenged.

The Depression Years at St. Mark's

The 1930s were a time when a hard life got even harder for the residents of the neighborhoods surrounding St. Mark's. Even before the crash of 1929, economic difficulties were affecting the congregation's parishioners. A year earlier, the pastor reported, "In spite of lack of regular employment, and financial hardships experienced by many of our people they have kept faith, and responded admirably when called upon." The men's bible class had an enrollment of twelve "who attend when they do not work."[22]

In 1933, Doris Alford Branton and her family moved into the third-floor pastor's apartment, where they would live for two years during the depths of the Great Depression. Her husband became pastor at St. Mark's when their son Ray, now a retired UMC minister, was three months old. "There were a lot of people coming for help," Doris Branton recalled. "We had a food pantry. We had a clothing closet. There were many who just came in off the street; there were many, many vagrants there during the Depression." Transients were by no means the only ones in need. "The poorest of the poor lived down there in the French Quarter, and we helped a lot of them. Catholic or not, nobody asked when they came to St. Mark's. Many times my husband would go visiting, and in cold weather, he would find them without any heat or any food in the house. And he would come back and carry stuff to them. We had a little Ford roadster, but he mainly walked, because gas was expensive."[23]

She recalled that as she did her midmorning grocery shopping at a nearby store, she regularly saw other customers who "would ask for half a nickel's worth of meal or sugar—that let one know how very, very poor they were—and they would get maybe enough for one meal. Half a nickel's worth of potatoes. ... We were poor, too, but nothing like that, because we had a roof over our heads and a little income every month from the church."

There was close cooperation among her husband and the staff of the center, as they all struggled together to help the needy. All the deaconesses held leadership positions in the congregation and also taught Sunday school classes. They were "good friends, and it was a joy to know them," Branton said. Branton recalled Nettie Stroup, who was head resident at the time, as "a dignified lady, very businesslike, and full of fun. She just loved to laugh. She loved my baby and wanted to get her hands on him every time I went downstairs."[24]

Despite her propensity for fun, Nettie Stroup worked very hard, overseeing a staff of five who lived at the center and a volunteer force of fifteen to twenty workers who kept the center's programming running. Her workday began at

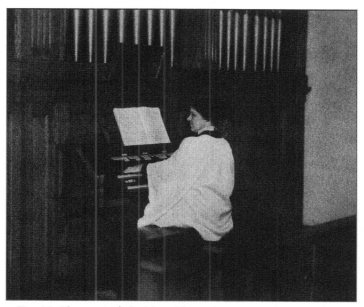

Fig. 13. The center's head resident, deaconess Nettie Stroup, was also the musician for worship at St. Mark's MECS. Deaconesses were strong leaders in the congregation until 1966. Photo from the center's Year Book for 1935.

eight in the morning and ended at ten at night, though she often did an extra hour or two of paperwork after that. Along with the rest of the staff, she made visits to the homes of center's clientele; Stroup said, "We know them all, and often are called on to help with family difficulties."[25]

CREATIVE PROGRAMMING

A trained musician and former music teacher, Stroup was fascinated with religious pageantry and had spent some time in Oberammergau, the site of the famous German passion play, just before she moved to New Orleans. In a long photo essay she prepared for a national Methodist women's magazine in 1935, Stroup talked about working with youth and young adults who "have taken a great deal of interest in dramatic art." The stage at the end of the center's gymnasium offered her an inviting canvas on which to work, and "[s]ome beautiful pageants have been given in connection with the Community Center work and with church services."[26] Stroup told another reporter that she was delighted to see that drama could reach even those who did not speak English well with the Christian message.[27]

After-school programs were important, and Stroup wrote that the library "fairly buzzes" each afternoon with boys and girls "hunting storybooks, browsing through magazines or bound copies of the *National Geographic,* while some are searching for information for school compositions." Young people of both sexes participated in athletic pursuits, and the gym schedule was "always full to overflowing," with five girls' groups and eleven boys' groups using the facility on a weekly basis for sports that included basketball, volleyball, tennis, touch football, boxing, and tumbling. The pool was the site for swimming lessons for many New Orleanians who would otherwise not have learned to swim.[28]

Many adult men and women took classes sponsored by the Era organization, including English lessons for immigrants. "Others who were reared in this country, but have been denied an elementary education, are beginning in the elementary grades. Some are studying cooking, while others are taking music and shorthand."[29]

The center fostered club work for the women of the neighborhood, and the importance of women's club work in the development of women's leadership

Fig. 14. A club room in use as a game room for young people and as a location for teaching boys to use various kinds of tools, as pictured in the St. Mark's Community Center Year Book, 1935.

has been addressed in a number of studies in recent years. In 1935, more than forty women were enrolled in Home Maker's Clubs with programming that included "health problems, book reviews, better movies, cooking, and sewing. Occasionally a visit is made to some factory, bakery, or dairy which broadens their knowledge of other institutions. They sometimes go out of the city for a day's recreation in the country." Stroup was careful to point out the ways that such activities would "enable them to be better wives and mothers. Many hours are spent in discussing topics of interest, or listening to a talk on some phase of home life."[30] What Stroup did not emphasize was that they were also learning leadership skills and, by participating in election of officers and similar activities, preparing themselves for roles in shaping civic life—in short, many of the same things the MECS women who built St. Mark's had learned though their WP&HMS membership.

Fig. 15. The Home Maker's Club as pictured in the St. Mark's Community
Center Year Book, 1935.

Club work met other goals of the deaconesses, as well. For instance, in
the "business girls' club," as in other groups, "world friendship and peace are
stressed. . . . [F]ellowship in the group meetings [has] caused them to think
and plan world peace." The center frequently organized gatherings that allowed
neighborhood people to celebrate their national cuisines and other aspects of
their native cultures. Every other year, the center hosted a major international
art exhibit that involved participation by the foreign consuls present in New
Orleans. "We believe these exhibits mean much in promoting friendship and
fellowship among the nationals living in our midst, and will ultimately contribute something to the cause of peace between nations."[31]

Though the worshipping congregation was no longer called "the Church of
All Nations," its mix of nationalities remained a striking feature when Branton

and Stroup lived at St. Mark's in the 1930s. While Syrian families had "more of a leadership role," Branton said, there were also Spanish, French, and Norwegian members, and "we even had an Eskimo family." Along with an active youth organization, the congregation had a strong woman's society. Branton served as the society's treasurer, because "so many of them couldn't read and write our language, that it fell to me."[32]

Breaking Race Barriers in Health Care

The racially complex population of New Orleans was reflected in the makeup of the center's clientele and the deaconesses' adaptations to it. Julia Southard Campbell, who arrived at St. Mark's in 1935 and stayed until 1943, stated that blacks did not participate in the club activities at the center "unless they 'passed' for white," but that many light-skinned blacks "passed" at St. Mark's with the knowledge and cooperation of the staff. The women "never turned anyone away, nor questioned anyone. We had many who passed."[33]

However, there was no need for blacks to "pass" to receive care in the health clinic. Campbell remembered that St. Mark's "had excellent race relations because of the clinic. If a Negro came first, then the Negro saw the doctor first. Those things mattered not at all at St. Mark's." Theirs was the only clinic in the city "with dental service available to Negroes." At the clinic, "Negroes were treated same as white and used rest rooms."[34]

Nettie Stroup's 1935 article for the national women's publication was straightforward about these racial policies. "The clinic provides our only direct contact with American Negroes. The Negro patients average about one-third of the total number of patients treated." Because roughly three thousand patients were seen each year, some one thousand blacks were among those treated. "The major work done is preventive work," Stroup wrote, and this would rule out the possibility that blacks were seen only in emergency situations. It may be that only people who were raised in the American South in the mid-twentieth century, and who were personally acquainted with the custom of having not just separate waiting rooms for blacks, but also separate treatment rooms and completely separate sets of instruments for medical and dental procedures, can fully appreciate either the significance of the "first come, first served" policy that meant many white people received treatment in the same dental office

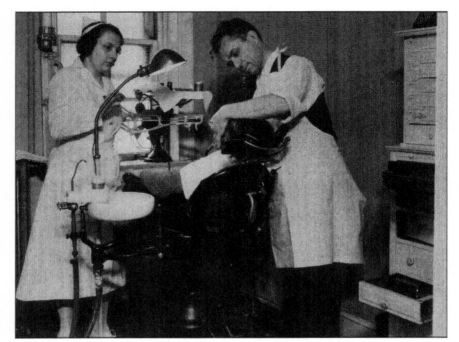

Fig. 16. The center's promotional literature in the 1930s stated that its health clinic served both black and white patients on a first-come, first-served basis. The unidentified dentist would have been a volunteer who gave an afternoon or a morning each week. Until World War II, the women recruited enough doctors and dentists to keep the clinic open six days a week.

or examination room that had just been used by black patients, or the courage required for the deaconesses' and local white MECS laywomen's decision to implement that policy.

Stroup shared the opinion of many other women affiliated with St. Mark's that one of the primary benefits of operating the clinic was the opportunity it provided to build relationships with those who came to the facility simply to use the medical services there. "Out of twenty-two members of St. Mark's Mothers Club, a contract was first made in the clinic with nine of these. Most of the mothers have small children in the pediatrics clinic, and this affords an opportunity to link the health program to the social service program as follow-up work is done in each home."[35]

Fig. 17. Wortley Moorman was a nurse deaconess who worked in the health clinic and
was on call to the center's neighbors.
Margaret Marshall was one of the deaconesses
who became ordained after that career path
opened to Methodist women.

She observed that people who came to the clinic "suffer not only with physical aches, but are often as much in need of love and sympathy as of medicine.
The deaconesses who work in the clinic make some very valuable contacts
with patients while waiting for doctors to come." Doris Branton remembered
that Wortley Moorman, the nurse deaconess who worked in the clinic when
Branton lived at St. Mark's, "was always ready to take people anywhere or do
anything she could for them. She was gentle and kind, and the people loved

her." Moorman was available to the sick day and night, and doctors and dentists volunteered every day at the clinic. "We had two medical students who lived in the building, too; they lived on the second floor," Branton said. "They were such nice boys, and they helped out in the clinic some."[36]

When Julia Campbell arrived at St. Mark's Community Center in the midst of the Depression, the board of directors was composed of members of local Methodist women's societies. In 1937, the center's proposed budget totaled $4,940, including $900 for a janitorial service and $3,500 for all other salaries. Utilities were expected to be about $300, and about $240 was allocated for all programming, including Vacation Bible School.[37]

While this budget devoted little to programming, it allocated no money at all to direct aid for people who were too poor to purchase necessities. Some deaconesses, like New Orleans native Helen Mandlebaum, chose to abandon the church temporarily and work in New Deal agencies in the mid to late 1930s, because they were able to provide more direct financial assistance to people there. "That's where the action really was," Mandlebaum recalled. When economic times became less harsh, she returned to a church-related appointment, as most of the women probably did.[38]

MEC AND MECS REUNITE

The year 1939 finally brought the reuniting of the Methodist Episcopal Church South (MECS), which had broken away in 1844 largely over the issue of slavery, and the Methodist Episcopal Church (MEC). The Methodist Protestant group that broke off from the MEC in 1830, primarily over the issue of rights for laity, was also part of the merger. Though the three became one denomination known as The Methodist Church, the reunion did not eliminate all the differences that had caused the original rifts. Significant disagreements continued within the membership. These included controversies regarding the proper place for women and for people of color in society and more specifically within The Methodist Church itself.

To achieve the long-delayed merger, the church made some most regrettable concessions.[39] Many white clergy, especially (but by no means only) those of the MECS, did not ever want to serve under a black bishop. Therefore, a structure of jurisdictions was created for the new body, with bishops to be elected at the jurisdictional level and to serve within the same jurisdiction that elected them. The United States was divided into five geographical jurisdictions, but a sixth, called the Central Jurisdiction, was also created and was made up of all black-membership churches, no matter to what geographical jurisdictions they would otherwise have belonged. Each Annual Conference had a white version of itself, which belonged to the appropriate geographical jurisdiction, and a black version, which belonged to the Central Jurisdiction. An almost complete segregation of the church at every level below that of General Conference resulted. The shameful compromise that was the Central Jurisdiction continued to exist until the merger of The Methodist Church and the Evangelical United Brethren created the United Methodist Church (UMC) in 1968.

The women's organization of The Methodist Church had great impact in insisting that the Central Jurisdiction be abolished at the time of that merger. However, because this book (other than the brief epilogue) considers events between 1895 and 1965, the merger did not occur within its covered time frame. Alice Knotts has worked specifically with the topic of white Methodist women and race relations in her volume, which is cited below in the discussion of other race-related work in which the women were engaged. Other historians have examined in great depth the issues surrounding the creation and/or dismantling of the Central Jurisdiction. These studies include James S. Thomas's *Methodism's Racial Dilemma: The Story of the Central Jurisdiction* and more recently, Peter Murray's 2004 book, *Methodists and the Crucible of Race, 1930–1975,* and Morris Davis's 2008 volume, *The Methodist Unification.*[40]

WERE FEMALE SOCIAL GOSPEL PRACTITIONERS RACISTS?

Although the existence of the Central Jurisdiction is of immense importance in considering the overall record of The Methodist Church with regard to race, for the white women who worked at St. Mark's, its primary impact would have been related to the fact that St. Mark's was for years the only good location in the city where white and black people could gather together for meetings. Many kinds of organizations used the St. Mark's facility for this purpose.

Individuals across the city who had no other connection with St. Mark's still remember with gratitude the deaconesses' hospitality.

James Bennett's book, *Religion and the Rise of Jim Crow in New Orleans,* looks at the Roman Catholic Church and the MEC in New Orleans in the turn-of-the-century period. Bennett's study focuses on the work of the so-called "northern" Methodists in the city, with little or no attention to the MECS. Further, he includes only a few paragraphs on women's efforts within that organization. The work of the MECS women receives even scanter attention, rating only one-half of one paragraph in the epilogue. Nevertheless, those sentences acknowledge that the white southern women did significant work in race relations. He calls their personal interactions with blacks "intimate if paternalistic" and notes that "the resulting interracial alliances created the cracks that would eventually bring down the wall of legalized segregation."[41]

An examination of the events that led up to the Central Jurisdiction's creation is the focus of Robert Watson Sledge's *Hands on the Ark,* which addresses events in the MECS between 1914 and 1939. Sledge wrote that there were three streams of thought and behavior about race in the MECS. Some members and clergy were extreme white supremacists and some few were true progressives on the race issues, but the majority were neither. The "normative" stance was "paternalism," he said. There was maternalism embedded in the white women's dealings with both black citizens and white immigrants. However, using Sledge's rubric, the MECS women at St. Mark's were not "paternalistic" but rather out on the progressive edge.[42] This is a more accurate description of how they were viewed and how they viewed themselves at the time.

In fact, in view of recent criticism that their agenda was too conservative, it is ironic that in the 1930s, the MECS women were forced to answer frequent charges that they were operating too far to the left. In 1933, Sara Estelle Haskin wrote "Women of the Left Wing" for the *World Outlook* to address the concerns of conservative critics; she did so primarily by agreeing that the women had indeed done everything they were accused of, and more, but insisting that doing so was the Christian course to take. Not unexpectedly, one main "defect" in the "left-wing" women was their openness toward working with people of color.

Although some of the white women's efforts can very legitimately be critiqued for lacking the level of sensitivity and understanding of racial problems that have been achieved in last three-quarters of a century, it is important to remember that in the 1930s, no one was even suggesting desegregation of the settlements for black and white clientele. Harsh criticisms were leveled at MECS women for being so "daring" as to have white women raise funds for establishing Bethlehem Houses—black settlements in black neighborhoods. They were further castigated because a few white women chose to work "among the Negroes" at those settlements.[43]

Compounding their sins against "the southern way of life" were meetings the white Methodist women held with the National Colored Woman's Federation to address racism. One white attendee wrote, "We saw this body of colored women—a great national asset—working with suspicion and distrust of their white sisters, and we realized anew that if the chasm which yawns between shall ever be abridged that the white woman of the South must recognize her own strategic place in its accomplishment and set herself quickly to the task."[44] The white Methodist women prepared study literature for local societies on the topic of race and made other serious efforts to foster improved race relations. Alice Knotts has examined at length the work of white Methodist women and the impact it had on softening what might otherwise have been an even *more* violent response to the civil rights movement in the South, and her 1996 volume, *Fellowship of Love,* made an important contribution to this field.[45]

Summing up the work of the "left wing" women in 1933, Haskin wrote, "While we might wish that the development of interracial work had been more rapid, yet there has been a steady progress." She concluded: "In this recital of interracial work by the women of southern Methodism, credit has not been given to the courage and enthusiasm of thousands of women who have *dared* in the name of their Master. Yet enough has been said to prove that the missionary organization has moved forward, and the leaders of southern Methodist women may well be characterized as 'Left Wingers.'"[46]

On an adjoining page, the president of the Tuskegee Institute, Robert Moton, praised Methodist women for their work toward better race relations, calling Belle Bennett and Mary Helm southern churchwomen who "championed almost single-handed the claims of justice, and even of chivalry, for their sisters in black." Bennett and Helm were among the women that Berta Ellison had listed in 1923 as primarily responsible for establishing St. Mark's. Further, at least two of the women who served at St. Mark's Community Center, Martha Nutt and Margaret Young, and possibly others, also worked at the Bethlehem House in Nashville later in their careers and participated in the cooperative program that helped train Fisk University students in social service. The ethos of the MECS at that time was such that white women who served at black settlements did so because they had volunteered for assignment there. Their choosing appointment at a Bethlehem House is evidence that they were on the cutting edge of interracial cooperation in the South.[47]

I contend that the women who worked in the trenches of the Social Gospel and civil rights movements in the South are more helpful subjects than northern thinkers and writers for studying how racist or non-racist Social Gospel practitioners might have been.

Mary Morrison Takes Role as Congregational Leader

The leaders of the woman's society in New Orleans like Elvira Carré and Hattie Parker, with the aid of male pastors like S. H. Werlein and Nicolas Joyner, had pressed for laity (voting) rights for churchwomen in the early twentieth century, but even after women earned the right to represent congregations at General Conference and Annual Conference gatherings, they were rarely placed in positions of formal authority within local Methodist congregations. Thus, it was an unusual occurrence when Robert Jamieson was appointed pastor of the St. Mark's congregation in the late 1940s and recruited member Mary Morrison to serve on the board of stewards. She thought that serving on the board would be "a right interesting sort of a spiritual thing, I guess. But I didn't think I could do it—I mean first of all where I came from only men were on the Board of Stewards. That sounds funny now, but that was just an expected thing that the Board of Stewards—they were men. In coming up in the Methodist Church I never knew of any board that functioned with women on it." The whole idea seemed to her to be "rather odd" and, lacking confidence that she could do the job, she was "holding back at any rate for whatever reason."[48]

However, that same year, a strong hurricane hit the Mississippi coast. A couple who were close friends of Morrison and her husband were at Long

Fig. 18. Margaret Young, who went on to teach
at Scarritt College.

Beach when the storm made landfall. The Morrisons were not able to determine for several days whether their friends had been killed, until finally a
relative of theirs, Hale Boggs, was able to get into the area via helicopter and
discovered they were safe. During the period of uncertainty, Morrison said, despite injunctions against "making bargains with the Lord," she prayed that if
their friends came safely through the tragedy, she would serve on the board of
stewards. After the hurricane, she kept her end of the bargain. Thus a woman
joined the administrative body of the St. Mark's congregation at a time when

most southern congregations did not put women into formalized leadership positions.[49]

Changes Occasioned by World War II

Despite the contributions of New Deal programs toward that end, it was World War II that finally ended the Depression in the United States. Although it would not be the most significant event of the mid-twentieth century for St. Mark's, the war did occasion changes in the operation of the center. Mary Frances Fairchild Tooke served in New Orleans in 1942 and 1943.[50] As one of the most important ports in the nation, the city was host to many troop ships. Tooke often drove groups of sailors from the docks to St. Mark's, where they participated in worship and in activities planned especially for them.[51] Julia Southard Campbell recalled, "We had something at St. Mark's once a week for the servicemen, and our swimming pool was available to them." The women helped organize what Campbell believed was one of the first USOs in the United States and were very active in that organization. "It was headquartered in one of the other social service agencies, but we were always a part of it. I always took a carload of girls to the USO dances," she said.[52]

Far more significant than the addition of activities for servicemen was closing an important ministry, the health clinic, and replacing it with a day care center. Within six weeks after the attack on Pearl Harbor, a huge demand for doctors and nurses arose in the armed services. "The Army Corps is reported short 1,500 medical officers, and there is a need for 10,000 nurses between the ages of twenty-one and thirty. It is proposed to place on the reserve list nurses who are between thirty and forty, subject to emergency call."[53] The clinic's operation had depended on the successful recruitment of doctors to volunteer their time, and the shortage of civilian medical personnel left in New Orleans forced the health clinic to close. Further, as the war ended, a public health clinic was established on North Rampart Street "near enough to serve our community." This freed St. Mark's from an obligation to reopen the facility, although the dental clinic did continue to operate.[54]

Much of the space devoted to the health clinic was converted to provide day care for children between ages two and five, a program presented as "a long time need in the neighborhood." Even though the war had made it acceptable for women to enter the workforce, a 1948 center publication reflects the quick postwar return to prewar opinions about working women. This societal change has been documented and to a large extent explained in Maureen Honey's remarkable study, *Creating Rosie the Riveter,* which explores the federal government's role in shaping the fiction carried by women's magazines during and after the war. The short stories encouraged women first to find employment in wartime and then to return to the home, making room in the workforce for returning soldiers, as soon as the conflict ended.[55] The 1948 St. Mark's brochure maintained that the women who needed the child care center were working "because of the desertion, death or low wage of the father." Those who chose to read the material that way could have seen an implication that mothers who were working for self-fulfillment might not be so worthy of support. Recalling that it was not until 1959 that married women could hold the office of deaconess helps explain the need to be circumspect about supporting transgression of the custom that only single, childless women should find employment outside the home. There is, not surprisingly, no acknowledgment in the brochure that fathers might need the child care facility.[56]

The brochure promised that mothers who brought children to the center could "know that they are receiving the very best of care and training. A well-balanced meal is served in the middle of the day—and milk or refreshments after a two hour nap in the afternoon." The center opened at 6:30 in the morning and remained open until 6 o'clock in the evening.[57] Child care continued as a part of the center's programming throughout the second half of the century; a program was later added to provide training, supervision, and some financial supplements for women who offered paid child care in their own homes.

Although women who worked at settlements tended to be interested in standards, to set measurable goals for their projects, and to record their accomplishments in numerical terms whenever possible, and Methodist settlement workers were no exception, the center's internal reports and much national documentation has been lost (see appendix A). Further, as head resident Fae Daves explained, the deaconesses at St. Mark's were always more focused on small group work than on "mass activities," because they believed that changing the lives of individuals was the most vital contribution they could make. The women, therefore, have always attached significance to anecdotal evidence in measuring their success. Longtime employee Laura Smith told a story about Daves's last hospitalization before her death. "One of her nurses told [Daves], 'You ladies at St. Mark's made it possible for me to be here. You gave me somewhere safe to put my child so I could go to nursing school.' You always," Smith emphasized, "had these stories."[58]

The switch from providing health care to child care did not adversely affect the support the center received from laywomen across the Louisiana Annual Conference, which continued to be strong and reliable. Despite postwar difficulties in obtaining automobiles, the conference-wide group managed to purchase and donate one to the center, and the head resident wrote, "The new Chevrolet . . . is rendering valuable service. It is a real joy and a big help in carrying on the program."[59]

LAURA SMITH JOINS CENTER STAFF

Smith first came to St. Mark's in 1947 as a volunteer at the community center. She would soon become a key center employee and a valued leader within the congregation. Her twenty years at St. Mark's spanned the middle of the twentieth century and the transition into the modern civil rights movement. When she came to the center, she lacked a high school diploma. When she was first employed, her compensation package included $100 per month in salary and room and board, and her work included (though it was by no means limited to) janitorial duties. When she left in 1967, it was to attend graduate school at Tulane University, where she earned a master's degree in early childhood education.[60]

"Anything good that happened to me in my life happened to me at St. Mark's," Smith said. "I went there as a volunteer, and I met this group of people, and I wanted what they had. They all encouraged me to go to school, because I was working there with people with degrees, and I didn't even get a chance to finish high school." Smith obtained her GED and attended National College, an institution run by the women's division of The Methodist Church that focused on training deaconesses. During her studies, she realized that she did not feel that she ought to be consecrated as a deaconess. Nevertheless, she finished her degree there, receiving the same education as a deaconess, and she continued to work with deaconesses and to immerse herself in what she felt was her own ministry of social work at St. Mark's for years to come.[61]

Women's Ordination Alters Future for Deaconess Program

Even after their consecrations, deaconesses usually continued their educations. Statistical records enumerating how many or what percentage of the women pursued master's degrees in social work or other fields are not available, but anecdotal evidence indicates the majority were intent on both increasing their professional abilities and obtaining certification for having done so. As Sarah Kreutziger has documented, the ground broken by deaconesses and the standards they adhered to led directly to the professionalization of the field of social work, and thus had profound impacts on all of American society.[62] Nevertheless, the professionalization of deaconess work was only one method, and increasingly not the most important one, by which women continued to push for more access to leadership roles in The Methodist Church.

The ban against women in the ordained clergy was the most significant barrier women have faced in seeking power to effect change in Christian denominations. In 1956, The Methodist Church finally approved ordination for women (with membership in full connection with Annual Conferences).[63] However, in many regions, women's service in the pastorate was not immediately embraced (and indeed, it is not met with completely universal acceptance among United Methodists even now). The *Journal of the Louisiana Annual Conference* issues in 1956 and the years following reveal that although some ten women served as lay pastors in the state during that period, no woman was ordained in Louisiana until 1964, when Bonnie Ruth Holley received probationary orders. She was ordained an elder in 1967. The next woman was not ordained in Louisiana until 1970, when Carole Cotton received her probationary orders; she became an elder in 1972.[64]

Opening the route for women to achieve full clergy status weakened the deaconess program, even as it strengthened the position of women in church leadership overall. It became harder to recruit women as deaconesses. The authority to administer the sacraments of Eucharist and baptism, the increased job security, and what might prove to be more power to effect change within the institution of the church attracted many women to ordination. Further, in 1956, deaconesses were still required to be single, a prohibition that did not apply to women clergy. (The church lifted the rule for deaconesses in 1959.)[65] Even some women who were already deaconesses chose to become ordained.[66] Those who remained deaconesses found themselves in a somewhat more uncomfortable middle ground of woman's leadership, as over against their earlier position on the cutting edge of women's professional work in the church.

"A Restlessness of Women"

Throughout the twentieth century, the women who chose to become Methodist deaconesses were by definition outside the mainstream of "typical" female behavior. A mid-1960s pictorial essay about a gathering of deaconesses was entitled, "Salty Methodist Characters at the United Nations." This may have referred to the Bible verse where Jesus tells the disciples they are "the salt of the earth," but it could also have alluded to the deaconesses' reputation for speaking truth to power. The churchwomen's magazine that published the essay quoted from its own 1941 article: "The deaconess movement has always been a salty movement. It was born of a restlessness of women with conditions as they were. From its earliest day it attracted women who were—to put it mildly—characters. In all centers of Methodism there are legends of those characters, and like most legends, they are rooted deep in truth."[67]

Portraying their movement as "born of a restlessness ... with conditions as they were" speaks to the perception of Methodists that the deaconesses were more radical in their assessments of society and more given to activism and agitation in their behavior than women in general. While some of the activities of the New Orleans deaconesses in the 1940s and 1950s fit neatly with those of society around them, others were groundbreaking in their support of women who remained in the workforce after World War II. Nevertheless, the deaconesses were still constrained by the prevalent ideas about the "woman's sphere" and remained prudent about the language they used to describe their work.

5

Addressing Racial Injustice
Before and After *Brown*

The decades following World War II saw significant activity by Methodists in New Orleans seeking gender and racial equality. On a national level, the 1950s were marked by the handing down of the *Brown v. Board of Education* decision in May 1954 and by the first ordination of a woman in The Methodist Church in 1956. Both events had great impact on the history of St. Mark's.

As noted in the previous chapter, opening the route for women to achieve full clergy status weakened the deaconess program, even as it strengthened the position of women in church leadership overall. Now, societal pressure began to bear more heavily on those women on the racial front, as black people agitated more forcefully for full rights as citizens. Deaconesses had always been more radical than the church at large on the issue of racial equality, but their views became more unpopular than ever with many white Methodists in the South as the threat of having to make substantive change in the order of society, including the public schools, became more real.

As New Orleans moved toward the appalling confrontations of the 1960 school desegregation crisis, in which St. Mark's would play as public a role as any organization in the city, Methodist liberals who had been steeped in Social Gospel theology and thought were increasingly unable to avoid choosing sides in the conflict. As one author noted, Methodist women were always affected by "an interplay of religious and cultural factors" as they addressed racial issues.[1] However, I contend that the handing down of the *Brown* decision forced many Methodists in New Orleans to distinguish and finally to make a clear choice between their Christian convictions and their cultural backgrounds. As a result, a pair of individuals with strong ties to the Methodist deaconesses, including a future chair of the board at St. Mark's Community Center, took courageous public stands supporting integration.

"BLACK NEIGHBORS" POSE CHALLENGE FOR WHITE SETTLEMENTS

In the 1950s, as they struggled to deal with ambiguities regarding their own positions within the church, the white women who served at St. Mark's also struggled to adapt the community center to the changing makeup of its neighborhood. As the white immigrant families whom the center had served were assimilated into mainstream culture and became successful, they tended to move to more affluent areas of the city. The percentage of black residents began to increase in the nearby neighborhood of Tremé. The head resident, Fae Daves, monitored census figures diligently in hopes of persuading her board of directors to open the center to black membership, but they remained unconvinced.[2] She made maps of the area that carefully documented changing ethnic and racial makeup, probably similar to the neighborhood maps created at Hull House in Chicago; however, all her maps have been lost, along with the other local records.

Historian Elisabeth Lasch-Quinn insists that any discussion of post-1914 settlement work must view "black neighbors" as the major influence on the movement.[3] Though her study focused on settlements in the Northeast and Midwest, her words echo U. B. Phillips's argument that race (and more specifically, the maintenance of white supremacy) has been the "central theme" of southern history. In 1954, C. Vann Woodward said: "Whether it was the 'central theme' or not, both demagogue and patrician continued to express it in varying degrees of frenzy or quietude. The professors called it 'the maintenance of Caucasian civilization' and the stump speakers called it 'white supremacy.'"[4]

Furthermore, it has never been uncommon for southerners to hear the adjective "God-given" attached to the phrase "southern way of life." Samuel Hill suggested that the phenomenal success of organized Christianity in the region was linked to its use as a tool for sanctifying white supremacy. Now that this aspect of "southernness" is no longer such a prominent cultural feature, Hill has questioned whether it will even be possible for churches to "tie their attractiveness to other features of life than the reinforcement and legitimation of the traditional (white) Southern Way of Life, and thereby preserve . . . [a] role in the society."[5]

Throughout the past century, St. Mark's Community Center and congregation never found themselves completely within or completely outside mainstream Protestant Christianity in the South. A major reason for the discomfort of the larger church with the St. Mark's organization has been the center's relative openness to the marginalized of society, from Italians and other immigrants in the first half of the twentieth century, to blacks in the second half of that century, to gay and lesbian persons at the turn of the twenty-first. Yet despite it appearing liberal enough to cause tension with other segments of the church, St. Mark's was not totally open to the civil rights movement when it arose in the mid-twentieth century. Attempting to explain the failure of settlement women to "redirect" their energies toward their black neighbors, Lasch-Quinn explored the relationship of northeastern and midwestern settlement workers with black individuals who lived nearby. She found that in most locations, settlement residents shared authority with the women of the neighborhoods where they lived, and that some of the reluctance to take radical stands on racial issues may have been more reflective of prejudice on the part of the clientele than of the settlement workers themselves.[6] The ambivalence about integration of the St. Mark's Community Center can be largely attributed to the fact that deaconesses like Fae Daves and other longtime center employees like Laura Smith, whose Christian beliefs impelled them to work toward integration of the center, shared control of the facility with members of the local board of directors who had grown up absorbing typical southern prejudices and/or who were not willing to offend their friends and neighbors by making the unpopular decision to integrate. The courage that earlier laywomen like Elvira Carré and Hattie Parker, who approved and fostered racial equality in the now-closed health clinic, was no longer in evidence.

Whatever its cause, Lasch-Quinn has concluded that the single greatest overall failure of settlement workers was their inadequate response to racial issues in their communities. Noting that not all settlements were equally unresponsive, she does give credit to Methodist women for being more progressive in their race relations work than many others, and she acknowledges

Jacqueline Dowd Hall's inclusion of them in her triumvirate of groups that opened the way for better race relations—black women's club groups, Methodist women's mission societies, and the Young Women's Christian Association. Still, she says, the white Methodist women were ambivalent in their approach toward blacks.[7]

NATIONAL WSCS FIGHTS FOR RIGHTS OF BLACK MEMBERS

In 1939, when the MEC reunited with the MECS and the Methodist Protestants, the women's organizations formed the Woman's Society of Christian Service (WSCS).[8] The first national assembly of the WSCS, set for 1942, was to occur in St. Louis. Planners discovered that black members could not stay in St. Louis hotels and would have to be housed in private homes. Finding this unacceptable, the planners moved to a site farther north, in Columbus, Ohio, but discovered discrimination against black members there, as well. The women conducted negotiations with offending hotels and restaurants "right up to the Assembly's opening morning." They also held their next assembly in Columbus, having gained "firm assurance" that there would be no more discrimination, and on arrival "they found a changed atmosphere." A black leader "was even invited to broadcast a citywide morning radio meditation. . . . The Woman's Division didn't stop there. They pressed the matter with the whole board of missions, arguing for a policy that would forbid the Board from ever meeting again in a city where Blacks were subjected to less than free and equal accommodations. The recommendation was tabled but the women had won their point: the Board met only one more time in a segregated situation."[9]

By 1947, the national WSCS leadership had decided that they must have black members elected to leadership positions in the organization and hired as members of their paid staff. Two early employees included Thelma Stevens, a white southerner known as a pioneer in race relations, and Pauli Murray, a black woman who was given the assignment of writing a report that summarized every state's laws about segregation. The resulting report, which appeared in 1951, was Murray's landmark document, "States' Laws on Race and Color." Considered a definitive work on the topic, it was used by the Supreme Court as they deliberated *Brown.*[10]

In 1952, the first Charter for Racial Justice was submitted by the Woman's Division to the conferences and jurisdictions for ratification. It was adopted and modified in 1962; the text of the 1962 charter is reproduced as appendix B. In 1964, the General Conference adopted it for the whole denomination. In 1978, the United Methodist Women enacted another modified version, which remains the official charter, and the General Conference of 1980 adopted that document.[11]

LOUISIANA'S WSCS RAISES AWARENESS OF RACIAL INJUSTICE

As early as 1917, the white women's society in New Orleans was addressing the issue of race relations. Its social service committee resolved that Methodist women should "learn the needs of the colored people and by sympathy and help strive to create higher ideals and better conditions among them through the organization of Colored Women's Community Clubs."[12] There were, to be sure, matronizing aspects of the white Methodist women's concern for women of color. John Patrick McDowell noted that while many white Americans saw blacks as uneducable, the more enlightened Methodist women saw blacks as capable of being brought to higher levels of civilization through education and exposure to lofty influences. Their culture taught them that the way to expose blacks to lofty influences was to expose them to "broad-minded, large-hearted white men and women." He wrote, "Without arrogance, the leading women of southern Methodism believed that they were such persons."[13] It does speak to that lack of arrogance that the phraseology of the 1917 resolution called for the women to "learn the needs of the colored people," as over against assuming that they already knew what was best for people of color. Further, as noted earlier, when viewed against the backdrop of that era, when the Ku Klux Klan was in powerful resurgence, the women's policies were unarguably progressive.

In the early post–World War II era, Louisiana's white WSCS continued to educate not only their own members but also other Christians about the need for racial tolerance and understanding. In 1946, *NOCA* reported that they were urging every churchwoman to register and vote, and to "study voting restrictions imposed upon minority groups and work for the removal of these restrictions." All members were encouraged to "study Civil Rights Legislation and work for equal citizenship rights for all groups."[14] This was not a resolution of the national group, but rather of the executive committee of the Louisiana Conference of the WSCS. Urging voting rights for black citizens in the late 1940s Deep South was a truly radical position.

Under the work area of "Removing Community Tensions," the women passed a resolution that called for each society to incorporate local study with an already approved national course, "The Christian and Race." The Louisiana Conference WSCS's executive committee asked that the women of each congregation attempt to understand thoroughly the conditions existing among minority groups in their own community and hold workshops to plan for community action that might better those conditions.[15]

Brown Decision Forces Churches to React

Unquestionably, race was the defining issue among New Orleans Methodists in the time frame considered in this chapter, 1939–60. It had far more impact on the history of St. Mark's than World War II, and one might conclude that the 1940s and 1950s served primarily as a significant prelude to the role St. Mark's played in the city's school desegregation crisis in 1960. The handing down of the *Brown* decision on May 17, 1954, was undoubtedly the single most polarizing event of the period for Methodists in New Orleans.

The morning after the decision, the *New Orleans Times-Picayune* quoted both the governor of Louisiana and the president of the New Orleans school board promising that there would be a significant time lag—probably years—before actual change would occur in the city's public schools. Time would prove them correct. Many other state and local officials and dignitaries were also quoted in the *New Orleans Times-Picayune* coverage. The most blatant foreshadowing of what would become the South's campaign of "Massive Resistance" was offered by F. Edward Hebert, who represented the area in the United States House of Representatives. He said, "I am reminded at the moment of what Andrew Jackson told the chief justice of the supreme court, 'You have handed down the decision. Now let's see you enforce it.'"[16]

In the same story, the Very Reverend Monsignor Henry Bezou, superintendent of local Catholic schools, offered a distinctly different response, saying, "This decision is in accordance with what has been expected on the basis of natural justice and the clear intent and purpose of the Constitution of the United States."[17] Ten days later, the archdiocesan school board unanimously adopted a statement approving "fully" of the court's action and deeming it in accord "with Christian social principles affirming the equality of all men and the rights of all men to serve God in this world and to share equally in the blessings of the beatific vision in heaven" and "with the principles of democracy on which our country is based." The board maintained that within its own "religious and educational framework," integration had operated "satisfactorily and peacefully" in several instances. They expressed hope that integration "may prove to be a pattern for better and more enlightened relationships on all sides in the days that lie ahead."[18]

It is therefore ironic that the Catholic system failed to integrate concurrently with the public schools and thereby provided an obvious, satisfactory, all-white alternative for thousands of parents who removed their children from public schools simply to avoid integration. Catholic schools were not finally integrated until 1962, two years later than New Orleans public schools.[19] The action that accompanied, or more accurately, did not accompany the monsignor's rhetoric in 1954 was perhaps foreshadowed by his additional remarks: "For further comment or action, we naturally await the supplementary directives of the US supreme court and also await the reaction of our own state legislators"[20] and the Catholic school board's acknowledgment of "the difficulties involved in the practical application of this decision of the highest tribunal in the land—difficulties of which the members of the court are evidently conscious and which have prompted them to defer the implementing of the decree."[21]

Although much of the response to *Brown* in Louisiana was extremely negative, voices were occasionally raised to approve the move toward integration. A month after the decision, the *Times-Picayune* reported on page one that the New Orleans Council of Churches passed a resolution deeming the ruling "consistent with the spirit and teaching of Jesus Christ." The group nevertheless applauded the court's decision not to call for immediate implementation, but rather to postpone for a matter of "months" the hearings "on the means, methods, and time schedule by which this whole issue of segregation may be resolved." The council asked Louisiana legislators to exercise "clear and calm judgment and Christian good will" so that the matter might be resolved "in accordance with the ideals of our Christian faith."[22]

POLITICAL REACTION FOLLOWS PREDICTABLE LINES

The legislators were clearly not persuaded, or else they had different pictures of what "Christian good will" and "Christian faith" might look like. Governor Robert F. Kennon and most other state, parish, and local officials were extremely vocal and pledged to do everything they could to insure that integration of Louisiana's public schools would never take place. Their rhetoric and the machinations they used to try to prevent integrating Louisiana schools have been well documented.[23]

One tactic the legislature tried was passage of constitutional amendments that would make integration illegal. From time to time, advertisements appeared in the *New Orleans Times-Picayune* urging citizens to pressure their legislators and the governor to resist integration, some headlined with a phrase such as "Uphold Segregation!" One ad that specifically urged the public to vote for the constitutional amendment requiring separate public schools was attributed to the sponsorship of the Louisiana Joint Legislative Committee and its chairman, Senator W. M. Rainach.[24]

IWO OPPOSES LEGAL SEGREGATION

Mary Morrison, arguably the most powerful female member of the St. Mark's congregation, as demonstrated by her formal position on the administrative board and by her informal position as "matriarch," and also a longtime president of the community center's board of directors, was one of the first members of the Independent Women's Organization (IWO). The IWO organized in the mid-1940s to help elect reform candidate DeLesseps "Chep" Morrison as mayor. Mary Morrison's husband, Jacob, was Chep Morrison's half-brother. Chep was first cousin to Corrine "Lindy" Boggs and a law partner of her husband Hale Boggs; Hale and, after his death, Lindy became powerful members of the United States

House of Representatives. Because of its connections with powerful people, and because of its strong stand on reform issues like the use of voting machines, the IWO became a well-known political force in New Orleans.[25]

In 1954, the IWO publicly opposed the constitutional amendment that would have required segregated public schools. Journalistic standards were different from today's, and the *New Orleans Times-Picayune* sometimes printed press releases from well-known groups with no attribution; that is, with no reference at all to any particular member or officer. In the story announcing the IWO's opposition, not a single woman's name was mentioned. Senator Rainach, known as one of the most ardent supporters of white supremacy, struck back. Pointing to the unattributed story, he called IWO a "kangaroo" organization, established to fight anonymously against the amendments he supported.[26] The IWO countered with a strongly worded press release that worked the names of fourteen women into its copy, and that recounted the group's beginnings nearly a decade before. It also pointed to the prominence of the women involved, took exception to Rainach's denigration of them and their aims, and called for a withdrawal of his accusations.[27] It was an extremely courageous stance considering the climate of opposition to integration prevalent in 1950s New Orleans.

According to the author of a history of the IWO's involvement in New Orleans politics, Mary Morrison was self-identified as a conservative, and was convinced that other women in the IWO also fit that label.[28] However, right-wingers like Rainach viewed the women as being far to the left on the political spectrum. It is doubtful that many residents of Louisiana in 1954 would have viewed any white citizen who opposed the constitutional amendment on segregation as "conservative."

ALBERT BARNETT AND JAMES DOMBROWSKI AGITATE FOR INTEGRATION

It is true, however, that some integrationists were perceived as being even farther to the left than others. These included members of the liberal organization called the Southern Conference on Human Welfare (SCHW) and its offshoot, the Southern Conference Educational Fund (SCEF). Albert Barnett, the

New Testament professor at Scarritt who had such profound influence on St. Mark's head residents Mary Lou Barnwell and Julia Southard Campbell, was a member of the board of directors of SCEF. SCEF's executive director was James Dombrowski, a former Methodist minister who had left the pulpit and lived out his commitment to the Social Gospel as director of the Highlander Folk School, and then as executive director of the Southern Conference on Human Welfare (SCHW) and later SCEF. The history of these organizations has been discussed in several sources.[29]

Albert Barnett earned his divinity degree at Emory University in 1921. His studies overlapped with those of Dombrowski, who graduated in 1923, and they may have known one another there.[30] They were friends in later life, and Barnett was one of the more active members of SCEF's board of directors. During Barnett's time on the faculty of Scarritt in Nashville, he worked with Myles Horton, a close associate of Dombrowski's at the Highlander Folk School in Tennessee, and played a key role in supporting several uprisings by coal miners. A historian of white liberalism in the mid-twentieth-century South has characterized Barnett as "left-leaning," and his *Christian Advocate* article discussed in chapter 4 linked socialism with the Gospel.[31]

Dombrowski, whose biographer chose the subtitle *An American Heretic* for his life story, was a Christian socialist. He studied at Union Theological Seminary with socialists Reinhold Niebuhr and Harry F. Ward. Niebuhr had significant differences with Social Gospel theology, but Harry Ward was a prominent Social Gospel thinker (and critic) and a founder of the Methodist Federation for Social Service (later the Methodist Federation for Social Action), the most activist arm of The Methodist Church and one regarded as a classic Social Gospel phenomenon. According to Dombrowski, Ward was a "pivotal influence" on his life. Dombrowski's own 1936 book, *The Early Days of Christian Socialism in America,* examined several influential Christian socialists. He criticized a number of Social Gospel leaders for not taking their economic and social critique far enough, and his work subtly collapses the Social Gospel with Christian socialism.[32] Further, in 1932, he had helped lead a European tour organized by the international secretary of the Young Men's Christian Association (YMCA). The group spent ten days at the Toynbee Hall settlement in London and two weeks or so in the USSR. Dombrowski was detained by customs agents on his return to the United States, because in Moscow he had purchased posters that the agents deemed "seditious." Influenced by Harry Ward and perhaps also by Depression-era conditions at home, Dombrowski was impressed with the USSR and thought it demonstrated that socialization of resources offered hope for humankind.[33]

Senator Eastland Attacks Dombrowski and SCEF

In 1954, coverage of race-related events shared newspaper space with the decline of Joseph McCarthy's influence in the United States Senate. However, McCarthy's personal political demise by no means ended the Red Scare and McCarthy's legacy of distrust and suspicion. The House Un-American Activities Committee (HUAC) and its partner, the Senate's Internal Security Subcommittee, used the threat of Communism to further their own agendas. Opponents of civil rights capitalized on the Red Scare, and Senator James Eastland of Mississippi was a master of this tactic. "Supporting both McCarthyism and the Citizens' Councils, Eastland used his position on the Senate Internal Security Subcommittee of the Judiciary Committee to exacerbate the fears of white southerners by investigating alleged subversives."[34] As a man who had called for an investigation into alleged Communist influence on the Supreme Court regarding *Brown,* Eastland found Dombrowski, with his avowed belief in Christian socialism and his trip to the USSR as evidence, a perfect target.

In March 1954, Eastland personally conducted hearings in New Orleans on Dombrowski and SCHW and SCEF supporters such as Clifford and Virginia Durr. (Virginia Durr's relationship to her brother-in-law, Supreme Court Justice Hugo Black, may have been one underlying cause of Eastland's crusade.) Protests to the head of the Senate Judiciary Committee, including one signed by Eleanor Roosevelt, Mary McLeod Bethune, and Harry F. Ward, were unsuccessful at stopping Eastland's witch hunt, and SCEF was branded as a subversive, Communist-leaning group.[35] Noting the lengths to which the senator went to paint integrationists as Communist supporters, one witness concluded that "Eastland saw a Red behind every black."[36] He was hardly the only southern politician willing to use any tactic that worked to prevent or delay integration.[37]

Accusations of supporting Communism continued to limit SCEF's achievements. In 1963, Dombrowski was arrested by New Orleans police, and his and the organization's papers were seized. He filed a lawsuit and eventually saw the

United States Supreme Court issue the 1965 *Dombrowski v. Pfister* ruling that the Louisiana Subversive Activities Criminal Control Act was unconstitutional, because it had a "chilling effect" on free speech.[38] In March 1954, however, no such ruling existed to lessen the damage the Eastland hearings inflicted on SCEF and on the lives of the individuals who were investigated.

THE CITIZENS FORUM ON INTEGRATION

Less than two months after the Eastland hearings, the *Brown* decision was handed down. Dombrowski and Rabbi Julian Feibelman of Temple Sinai immediately began to organize a group to support integration in New Orleans public schools. Though Feibelman admired Dombrowski, he limited his association with him because everything Dombrowski or SCEF "touched was doomed at once to failure." He attributed this not to the charges of Communism, but rather to SCEF's being "completely identified with integration."[39]

Feibelman was correct about the public's perception of SCEF. In response to the newspaper advertisements urging citizens to support segregation, Dombrowski placed a three-column by thirteen-inch ad in the *Times-Picayune.* The design was similar to the segregationists' ads, but its headline was "Uphold Integration!" It quoted statements on *Brown* issued by the Archdiocesan School Board, the New Orleans Council of Churches, and the Rabbinical Council of New Orleans. Styled as an appeal to Governor Kennon and state legislators "to uphold the law of the land and the laws of God and of conscience," the ad contained a coupon-like form that could be sent to the governor or a state senator, asking that the official "take steps to comply with the ruling of the Supreme Court concerning segregation in public schools." Small print at the bottom stated that the ad was sponsored by the "Southern Conference Educational Fund, Inc., Aubrey Williams, President; Dr. James A. Dombrowski, Director, 822 Perdido Street, New Orleans, Louisiana."[40] Because Williams did not live in Louisiana, Dombrowski was the sole target of local reaction.

Dombrowski's willingness to place the advertisement so soon after enduring the traumatic Eastland hearings is a tribute to his commitment and courage. However, recognizing that a group less identified with integration might prove more effective at swaying public opinion, he and Feibelman organized the Citizens Forum on Integration (CFI). Feibelman was also publicly associated with the cause, and they decided it would be beneficial to have a chairperson who did not already have a high profile in the city. They chose a Methodist clergyman, the Reverend Mr. John Winn, who would two decades later serve as chair of the board of St. Mark's Community Center.[41]

FUTURE CHAIR OF THE ST. MARK'S BOARD LEADS CFI

Winn had grown up as a member of the Algiers Methodist Church in New Orleans, but had frequently been involved in activities at St. Mark's Community Center. Winn participated in basketball tournaments and swim meets, but athletics were only part of his exposure to the center's programming. Because a pastor at the Algiers church was "unusually mission-minded," he saw to it that the young people were well acquainted with the work of the St. Mark's deaconesses. The head resident, Fae Daves, a classic Social Gospel reformer who was consecrated a deaconess in 1924, had a great influence on Winn. He was also introduced to the work of, and deeply influenced by, a deaconess who worked among Native Americans at Dulac, Louisiana. After graduating from Tulane University, Winn attended seminary at Southern Methodist University in Dallas. He was ordained in 1953, and in June 1954, appointed pastor of Felicity Methodist Church in New Orleans.[42]

Winn's grounding in Christianity had led him to believe that segregation was not in keeping with the faith. He was recruited to participate in the CFI by Feibelman. Because he had moved back to New Orleans in June, he was not aware of the Eastland hearings, which had occurred in March. By the time he realized exactly how much controversy his actions would stir, he had become deeply involved and so admired Dombrowski that he did not withdraw from the CFI, nor from SCEF, where he had become a member of the board of directors.

"[Dombrowski] was a person who was regularly vilified, but he was the politest, kindest person you'd ever want to meet. He was a real example of Christian nobility, and I can't recall anything he was coercive about. When I realized what hot water I could get into, the fact that he was such a genuine person made me want to stand with him," Winn said.[43]

Various histories of that period, such as Liva Baker's *The Second Battle of New Orleans,* make references to "a group of Methodist ministers" who agitated for integration, but names of individuals are never mentioned.[44] That group was the CFI, and the names of participants were deliberately not mentioned in conjunction with many of its activities. Winn likens the group to "an underground movement," noting, in understatement, that "it was not popular" for white citizens to be associated with the drive for integration.[45] The group was not composed solely of Methodist clergy; along with the rabbi, it included the pastor at First Unitarian Church and several nonclergy members of the social work faculty at Tulane.[46] However, two Methodist clergymen, John Winn and Clarence Snelling, served as its first and second chairpersons, and because only the leaders' names were revealed, it must have appeared to many that the group consisted primarily of Methodist ministers.

Because of the ever-present threat of HUAC harassment, and because support for integration was so unpopular, the group had no membership roster. Snelling said this was deliberate, in case the FBI or some other agency should demand to see the list of members. A list that did not exist could not be produced. Each time a business meeting was held to plan a public event, a piece of paper was circulated, and those persons who were willing to be listed publicly as individual sponsors of that particular event would sign the paper.[47]

One of the first CFI projects was a petition urging the New Orleans School Board to make immediate plans for integrating the schools. Dombrowski circulated it and garnered around 180 signatures. Winn went with the group that presented it at a school board meeting on September 12, 1955, and his name appeared in the front-page newspaper story about it. Feibelman and local activist Rosa Keller spoke for the petition. Keller told a historian, "They practically threw us out of the place, and such howling and screaming you never heard. . . . This is *very* unsettling when grown people behave like that. It was very frightening." Feibelman received threatening calls and letters. Keller was castigated by acquaintances, and even her friends ostracized her for some time thereafter.[48]

Winn was interviewed on television about other CFI activities, and because his family did not yet own a set, he went to a parishioner's home to watch the coverage. Almost fifty years later, he still felt gratitude, relief, and even some surprise that he was not asked to leave the Felicity congregation.[49] The other CFI-sponsored events in 1955 and 1956 were more consequential than the petition. "The point of the Citizens Forum" was to take advantage of experience other cities had gained in implementing school integration. Winn explained their rationale: "It's just a matter of time. Nobody knows what 'deliberate speed' means, but it's coming, so we would be crazy if we didn't find where there's a laboratory of experience in the country. What other cities have peacefully and successfully made the transition from separate to integrated schools?"[50]

The first speaker the CFI brought to New Orleans was the Reverend Mr. Allen Hackett of Pilgrim Congregational Church in St. Louis. "This guy was one of the most articulate people that I had ever heard," Winn recalled. The CFI wanted the meetings to occur in a public school building "for symbolic purposes," and permission had to come from the school board. "The board refused, so we threatened a lawsuit and they acquiesced," Winn said.[51] Hackett spoke on December 15, 1955, at Rabouin School on Camp Street.[52] Despite the obstacles, Winn said, "This first Citizens' Forum made a big splash.... [Hackett] was interviewed on television and we had a large crowd at the school. Most of them were people who were opposed to what we were doing, and most of them were loud and abusive, and there was a lot of press coverage, which to be honest with you, was exactly what we wanted, because we wanted to keep the public eye on, and have the newspaper report on, what other communities had done peacefully to bring this about. And we brought a succession of speakers, but none of the men was nearly the rousing success that the first one was. The television time became less available, but they were always covered in the papers."[53]

Deaconess's Son Becomes Second CFI Chairperson

The *Times-Picayune* story on the first forum was accompanied by a photograph of Hackett at the podium, flanked by a panel of persons who offered questions after his presentation. One of the panelists shown was the Reverend Mr. Clarence Snelling, pastor of the Methodist student center, the Wesley Foundation, at Tulane. Snelling became the CFI chair after Winn was assigned to start a new church in Metairie, a New Orleans suburb, and urged to curtail his involvement with SCEF by church higher-ups who feared it would hinder the new congregation being planted in a white-flight community. Snelling recalled that the district superintendent at that time was "not a bad man" but was nevertheless "a political animal, and the bishop and the cabinet did not want preachers to get involved in race relations. They were being very, very cautious, and so John had to make a decision—either he was going to build the church, or he was going to be in SCEF."[54]

Snelling, the son of a Methodist deaconess, spent much of his career as a professor at Iliff School of Theology in Colorado. In 1951, the young pastor, who had received his seminary degree only two years earlier, received appointment to the Eighth Street Methodist Church, located at 8th and Laurel streets in New Orleans. By coincidence, it was only a few blocks from the Memorial Mercy Home-Hospital for unmarried mothers, where his family had worked for years. Snelling's mother, then a deaconess named Virgia Mae Hahn, was sent to work at the home that his grandparents ran; she met Snelling's father there. Snelling's grandmother, Susan Elizabeth Murph Snelling, had been a driving force behind the establishment of the facility.[55]

Snelling said that when the infamous red-light district known as Storyville, where prostitution was legalized and regulated, was closed down by order of the military during World War I, there were "unanticipated effects." Along with precipitating the movement of newly unemployed jazz musicians to Memphis and Chicago, the closure "interrupted a social system that had formed in the South. If a girl got pregnant, she was given a one-way bus ticket to New Orleans by her family. If she was going to be sinful, she could go to that sin-soaked city." Madams would meet girls at the bus station and provide them room and board during their pregnancy. When the time came to deliver, they were taken to Charity Hospital, and the babies were put up for adoption. Then the girls were given employment as prostitutes. "It was really a form of white slave trade," Snelling said.[56]

When Storyville was closed, this network that absorbed young pregnant women was displaced. Four local women, two Presbyterians and two Methodists, became appalled at the increased numbers of young women begging on the streets. One woman owned a Model T and would take the girls to the large house that another owned. After the births, Snelling's grandmother helped the women find jobs. She eventually obtained training that let her teach young women the skills necessary to become licensed practical nurses. Snelling said she also wrote the first law regarding adoption passed in Louisiana and lobbied the legislature for its enactment in the 1920s.[57] This project to help unmarried mothers was adopted by the MECS and placed for a time in the 1920s under the auspices of the Mary Werlein Mission. Snelling's grandfather was a Methodist minister who asked "to be part of the work with the women" at the Methodist Home-Hospital for unmarried pregnant women and was assigned to a nearby church. The mission board assigned the deaconess who would become Snelling's mother to that congregation and also to the Home-Hospital as a counselor.[58]

Because he lived with his grandparents while he attended Tulane University, Snelling views them as "a strong influence" on his life. His grandmother's commitment to racial justice had made her resign from the Daughters of the American Revolution in the 1930s over the group's refusal to let singer Marian Anderson, who was black, perform at their venue in Washington, D.C.[59] In the 1950s, Snelling was among a group of white persons in New Orleans who decided to join the NAACP to express solidarity with black citizens (just as many of the white deaconesses had joined the NAACP at Scarritt). However, at the time, the NAACP discouraged white people from joining. Dr. Prince Taylor, then editor of the version of the *Christian Advocate* published in New Orleans by the all-black membership Central Jurisdiction, served as a "wonderful advisor" for the CFI. It was Taylor who explained to Snelling that "[w]ith the FBI and southern conservatives maligning every integration organization that came along as being a communist front, the Urban League and NAACP wanted to be very cautious not to get real practicing communists into their groups. They knew how to screen blacks. They didn't have the network to screen whites, and therefore, they did not want white members during that period."[60]

The intention of the NAACP to distance itself from Communism is evident in its press releases and announcements from the period. At the 1954 annual meeting, the statewide NAACP adopted a resolution condemning communism and calling on local branches "to be constantly on the alert for attempts of communists and their sympathizers or supporters of any totalitarian system to infiltrate and gain control of any units of our organization."[61] In keeping with that goal, the NAACP returned Jim Dombrowski's dues, which he faithfully sent for many years, refusing ever to accept him as a member.[62]

White liberals were thus forced to stand alone, without even the unqualified support of the mainline black organizations that worked for integration. Not surprisingly, because there were so few white people willing to expose themselves to the dangers involved, Snelling and Dombrowski became close friends.[63] Like Winn, Snelling joined the SCEF board of directors. He recalled one particular SCEF/CFI project, a petition to the mayor asking that city government appropriate funds to provide race relations training for police officers and public service employees like bus drivers and streetcar conductors. It also called for a major education effort targeted at the entire population, preparing New Orleans for integration "instead of spending all our taxpayers' money on lawyers to fight the inevitable."[64]

Four men presented that petition: Dr. Samuel Gandy, the chaplain at Methodist-related and historically black Dillard University, who later became dean of the Howard University School of Theology; Rabbi Feibelman; the Episcopalian chaplain at Tulane University; and Snelling. They went to the mayor's office about two o'clock, hoping they had waited late enough so that the story would not be carried in the afternoon paper. "But lo and behold, they put a box on the front page that said, 'Group Presents Petition on School and Bus Integration.' The last line said, 'The group included the Rev. Clarence H. Snelling, Jr. (continued on page so and so).' The rest of the story and the other three names were buried somewhere inside, and mine was on the front page." Snelling's father owned an insurance agency in Denham Springs, and the Ku Klux Klan "attacked his office" and burned a cross in front of his house that night. "Every time my name was in the paper that happened, and he lost a few customers," Snelling said.[65]

Snelling was the minister at Tulane's Wesley Foundation, where he felt that he was somewhat insulated from negative reactions to his activism. "My board was 'second-hand'—it had ministers, students, graduate students, and a number of laypeople, but the majority were members of the WSCS, and you could nearly always count on the women. So I was protected, and I thought I had an obligation to be active." Even on campus, however, he was not immune to repercussions. Each spring his board met to consider asking the conference for Snelling's reappointment. "Every spring," he recalled, "the conversation took a little longer." When it took an hour in 1958 for the board to decide to keep him, he "got disgusted waiting in my office for them to decide I should still have a job."[66]

Snelling had an application for a fellowship on his desk, and while he waited, he filled it out. He was awarded a Danforth grant and went to Drew University in New Jersey for a doctoral degree. Snelling had to resign from the SCEF board, because only residents of the South could serve, but they still used him "for fund-raising in the East. Jim [Dombrowski] would come up and take me to some party in Connecticut, and I'd make a speech about what SCEF was doing in the South, and people would write checks." He spoke at a fundraising party at the Waldorf each year, meeting Eleanor Roosevelt and other luminaries; twice he was master of ceremonies. He "made a pitch for money," led folk songs like "If I Had a Hammer," and introduced Martin Luther King Jr. as the speaker one year and Fred Shuttlesworth the next. "We raised a bunch of money," Snelling said.[67]

His departure from Louisiana signaled the end of the CFI. "It went out of existence after the year and half I chaired it. We had at least six, maybe ten, of these public forums, and Jim really felt that we had done what we had intended to do."[68] In one sense, the CFI had not stood alone. Considering that its editorial stance clearly favored maintaining segregation, the *Times-Picayune* was fairly conscientious about printing press releases issued by groups who held the opposite viewpoint. There is no way to determine how many releases they did not use, but they did print pro-integration statements from religious organizations such as the *Episcopal Church News,* the Rabbinical Council of New Orleans, the Presbyterian Synod of Virginia, the national convention of the Disciples of Christ denomination, and a working group of the World Council of Churches.[69] Nevertheless, most of these groups were not local, and the white Methodists in New Orleans whose theological beliefs led them to speak publicly in favor of integration in the 1940s and 1950s were taking a stance that their cultural backgrounds alone would never have led them to take.

CONCLUSIONS

John Patrick McDowell's acknowledgment that southern Methodist women were motivated by a mix of religious and cultural factors is a much more profound observation than it might first appear, and its relevance to this study deserves elaboration.[70] Many anthropologists and other social scientists regard religion as a primary source of the "glue" that holds societies and cultures together. For one thing, shared understandings of how the universe functions tend to create shared values for living. Partly as a result of these genuinely held values (and partly as a result of the desire of individuals with power to retain that power), ostracizing or otherwise meting out social punishment to individuals who step outside the boundaries of socially accepted behavior is tolerated by many religious authorities, and oftentimes even considered to be their particular responsibility and privilege. Consequently, there has been an undeniable tendency on the part of the church, at least since the early fourth century, to maintain the status quo and to discourage, if not punish, those who agitate for change. (The Roman Catholic practice of excommunication for non-conformists is the ultimate form of this phenomenon, because the supposed result for the offender is being denied inclusion with her group even after her death. However, it can be used for purposes other than support of a community's mores and practices, as when arch-segregationist Leander Perez was excommunicated for his extreme racist views and actions by Archbishop Joseph Rummel in 1962.)[71]

Samuel Hill's assertions that Protestant churches in the South were vital to the maintenance of segregation, and that their support of segregation was a crucial factor in their success, are no doubt accurate.[72] Yet during the civil rights movement, a significant minority of individuals within those Protestant churches were committed to racial justice. In New Orleans, that minority was closely linked to the earlier Social Gospel movement.

For instance, at St. Mark's Methodist Church in June of 1958, the board of Christian education voted not to allow a woman who had volunteered to teach the junior department of the Sunday school to do so. As those who have been responsible for Sunday school programs are aware, volunteers are always needed and are rarely turned away. The board's reasons for refusing to let this woman teach, as recorded in the minutes of their meeting, included her membership on the White Citizens Council, one of the best-known organizations that ardently opposed integration. The makeup of the St. Mark's board that denied her permission to teach the youngsters included deaconess Fae Daves; the deaconess college–educated center employee Laura Smith; Mary Ethel Mandlebaum, the mother of deaconess Helen Mandlebaum; the newly assigned pastor, the Reverend Lloyd Anderson Foreman, one of the main actors in the events surrounding the school desegregation crisis recorded in chapter 6; and four other Methodist laywomen.[73] The strong impact of the deaconesses on the anti-segregation stance of the congregation is clear.

The presence of the deaconesses' professor, Albert Barnett, on the board of directors of SCEF, which organized the CFI's activities in New Orleans related in this chapter, and the leadership provided by male clergy who were connected to powerful Methodist women who worked and lived from a deep grounding in the Social Gospel, demonstrate that assertions that the Social Gospel was a uniquely racist phenomenon need corrective.[74] Regarding the post-*Brown* era as a whole, John Winn, who assumed leadership of the CFI despite the professional risks associated with the position, said, "Those were exciting days—there was no lack of definition, if you were interested in being defined." Discussing some of the apparent failures of nerve on the part of "liberals," such as the one that kept Archbishop Rummel from integrating the Catholic schools when he had said that he would, despite his apparently genuine belief in racial equality, Winn explained: "What saved the liberal conscience in that day . . . is that they agreed in principle with the concept of integration, and it was almost like, that's what we can contribute. If we can get the better part of society or a local community to agree in principle that it's right, then those other doors will open. And so that was the position that [liberals] were always taking, they were agreeing in principle."[75] Despite his conclusion that those who participated in the events described in this chapter and the next were "liberal," many of the women described (or would have described) themselves as "conservative."[76]

The difficulties that historiographers have tried to address in determining whether the Progressive Era and the Social Gospel movement and, for that matter, other phenomena like the New Deal were liberal or conservative in nature are mirrored by the difficulties in deciding how to characterize the individuals who participated in them.[77] In seeking definitions or labels for the Methodist women who supported the activities documented in this chapter and the next, it is necessary to remember that all religions, including Christianity, are systems of thought constructed by human beings, and they necessarily reflect the cultures of the people who are doing the constructing. Christians like Daves and Smith, along with the scores of Methodist women who volunteered at and supported St. Mark's throughout its history, were steeped in religious instruction and grounded in the Social Gospel, but they responded to racial issues and problems out of personal influences that were as mixed in origin as the religion they practiced. This helps to explain why the community center itself was not integrated until 1965 (see chapter 7), despite the desire of some of the women to do so earlier. Although Christianity has a long history of preserving the status quo, it also has a history of serving as a major catalyst *for* positive social change. Although some Methodist women were as prejudiced as other members of southern society, many of the southern Methodist women who belonged to the missionary society and had thus been trained in Social Gospel thought were catalysts who helped bring about significant change in society in New Orleans. To try to assign "conservative" or "liberal" labels to these women is to overlook the multidimensionality of their motives. It may well be that terms like "salty" and "restless with conditions as they were" will, in the last analysis, prove more helpful than more common, but also more generally misunderstood, labels like "liberal" or "conservative."

PART III

Crises in Church,
Center, and City:
1960–1965

6

ST. MARK'S IN CRISIS,
1960–1965

The first half of the 1960s was a time of trauma for St. Mark's. Both the congregation and the community center were struggling to meet the ethical challenges of the civil rights movement and the reality of integration in New Orleans. The still-recent granting of clergy rights to women in The Methodist Church and the much broader burgeoning movement for women's liberation presented additional challenges. The deaconess movement, which had served scores of women well in their attempts to reconcile their calls to ministry with the cultural taboos against leaving the proper "women's sphere," underwent a decline. Deaconesses all over the nation strove to reidentify their roles in the church and in urban ministry more clearly, and they embarked on a major recruiting drive designed to prevent the complete disappearance of the office of deaconess.

For those women who worked at St. Mark's Community Center, the process of role redefinition was immensely complicated by the actions of the pastor of St. Mark's Methodist Church during the school desegregation crisis of 1960. Because of his decision to leave his daughter in school with the first black child assigned to William Frantz Elementary School, an act that required defiance of a well-organized white boycott of the school, St. Mark's itself was vandalized, and there were so many threats of violence that the pastor and his family were forced to go into hiding. The women who continued to live in the St. Mark's building were called upon to exhibit extraordinary courage. Further, they were not just prominent leaders in the congregation from an administrative standpoint. They were also the primary spiritual shapers of the group, because many, if not most, of the members joined the congregation and/or maintained their membership there because of their deep connection with the deaconesses of the community center. The women were therefore not just responsible for leadership in matters such as the administrative board's vote to support the pastor, which was taken during the height of the crisis, but they were also ultimately responsible for having created the spiritual ethos of a group that tolerated its pastor having stepped completely outside the bounds of culturally acceptable behavior for white southerners. In other words, while it was the pastor of the St. Mark's congregation who defied the white boycott of William Frantz Elementary School in the dramatic events described later in this chapter, it was the women of the community center who were the primary shapers of the congregation's reaction to his decision. It is important to recognize that every aspect of the women's work at St. Mark's and every event that occurred there in the 1960s was affected by the prophetic stand of the pastor and congregation of the church in 1960. It is also important to note that the women were classic products of the Social Gospel era.

During the time frame covered by this chapter, the deaconesses were also pushing for the integration of the center itself, an effort blocked repeatedly by the members of the center's local board of directors. In 1965, pressure from a major funding agency, the city's United Fund, finally forced the board to capitulate, and the first black children joined the community center as official members.

THE STAGE IS SET FOR SCHOOL DESEGREGATION

Despite the work of the Citizens Forum on Integration and continued litigation on the part of the NAACP, the public schools in New Orleans remained completely segregated for more than six years after the 1954 *Brown* decision. Finally, on November 14, 1960, the last barriers imposed by Louisiana's version of "Massive Resistance" cracked, and the first two public schools were integrated, or more accurately, received their first black students. True integration was not achieved that day. Although the parents' organizations of two white schools in the Uptown section of New Orleans had volunteered their children's schools to be the site of the first integrated facility, the school board chose two schools in an area populated with poorer families—William Frantz Elementary and McDonough 19.[1]

The parsonage owned by the St. Mark's congregation and occupied by the minister, the Reverend Mr. Lloyd Anderson "Andy" Foreman, and his family was located on Alvar Street and zoned for William Frantz. When St. Mark's moved to 1130 North Rampart Street in 1923, pastors of the congregation and their families lived there in the apartment intended for their use. However, in the 1950s, pastors began to object to living in the third-floor, two-bedroom apartment, and the church purchased a house to use as a parsonage. Because the house they bought on Alvar Street was some distance from the church, in the late 1950s the congregation tried to purchase a home closer to St. Mark's. They found one on Gov. Nicholls Street in Tremé, a neighborhood adjacent to the French Quarter. The move would have been in part for the pastor's convenience, but was also prompted by the church's desire to have him become more entrenched in the community that surrounded St. Mark's. "When you're the church, you go where the people are—that's the way I felt," said center employee and congregational leader Laura Smith. However, the church hierarchy refused them the needed permission to acquire the property, because it was in a "questionable" neighborhood (a phrase those at St. Mark's interpreted to mean "racially mixed").[2] It is ironic that had the Annual Conference's hierarchy let St. Mark's purchase the parsonage they wanted, the Foremans would not have been living in the William Frantz Elementary School zone when desegregation occurred.

Foreman himself had also made an attempt to alter the living arrangements, with his location of choice being an apartment building owned by and adjacent to Redeemer Methodist Church, at the corner of Chartres Street and Esplanade Avenue. Redeemer Methodist Church was on a circuit with St. Mark's Methodist Church at the time, meaning that Foreman also served that church as pastor, so using their building would have made great sense. However, the Redeemer congregation was renting it and using the income, so they did not want the Foremans to move in.[3]

THE CIVIL RIGHTS MOVEMENT ARRIVES ON THE FOREMAN DOORSTEP

So it was that in November 1960, on the day that the black first-grader Ruby Bridges made her way into William Frantz Elementary, she entered the school where Foreman's five-year-old daughter, Pamela, was attending kindergarten.[4]

The residents of New Orleans had known that integration was coming, but the exact schools to be integrated had been kept a closely guarded secret. Foreman and his wife, Nyra, found out that William Frantz had been chosen when a neighbor who often walked Pamela to school brought her home unexpectedly. Foreman, who had been taking a day off, stepped out on the porch in pajamas and robe and saw the neighborhood full of police cars and activity. Word had spread quickly that a black child had arrived at the school, and white parents were rushing to take their children out. Their neighbor assumed that the Foremans would want Pamela taken out along with the other children, and so she brought her home. Although they left Pamela at home for the rest of that day, Foreman determined right away that if Pamela wanted to go back to school the next day, she should do so. Pamela did want to go, and so the next morning, Foreman took her.[5]

With more than six years having passed since the *Brown* decision, and with various lower court orders and decrees having been issued, it had become clear to Foreman that school desegregation in New Orleans was inevitable. He said that "during the weeks and months leading up to this . . . I had been trying to get the people of St. Mark's to understand that this was the right thing to do and that we as a church should be not only praying for the success of the program, but working in whatever ways we could." On the Sunday before integration began, the identity of the schools chosen to receive the first black students remained secret. Foreman said from the pulpit, "If this thing breaks tomorrow, and I think it will, I will be in the middle of it." His members later accused him of having had knowledge that William Frantz was one of the schools that would be integrated, but in fact, he did not know.[6]

THE "CHEERLEADERS" BEGIN THEIR HARASSMENT

For several days, Foreman was able to escape notice as he took Pamela to school. However, he said, "By the end of the first week . . . they knew that I was doing what I was doing . . . and so the Monday following the first week, they were ready for us when we started to school." The white women who gathered to intimidate Ruby Bridges as she entered the building were doubly incensed because a white student was breaking the boycott, and they unleashed even more anger on the Foremans than on Bridges. Groups of these women stood outside William Frantz every morning for the rest of the school year, screaming threats and invective. Photographs of Foreman and his daughter walking through the gauntlet of cursing women who came to be known as the "Cheerleaders" appeared in newspapers all over the United States and in several foreign countries. Film of their walks was run on national television news, and photographs appeared in national periodicals, including *Life* magazine, where they were shown in the weekly photo essay, "A Look at the World's Week," with the subtitle, "A Child's View of New Orleans' Angry Mothers' Mob."[7]

On the first morning that they were accosted, a Roman Catholic priest came to Foreman's door and asked him if he would like company on his walk. Foreman was happy to say yes. "So he was walking on her left, and I was on the right, and I had my right hand in my pocket," Foreman said, when the Cheerleaders blocked their path: "One of the ringleaders, who was bordering on being out of her mind, began pushing on my chest. I knew it would be deadly to hit her or to make some move toward her, so I caught her eye, and I screamed at her, 'Don't you touch me. You can talk to me, but don't you touch me.' So she stepped back, and then the police moved in and opened the way for us."[8]

The priest who joined Foreman on the walk that morning was Father Jerome Drolet, an activist who had received a national award in 1954 from the Workers Defense League for "outstanding contributions to the cause of labor." The league described itself as a "nonpolitical and anti-Communist organization." Drolet, who was born in 1908 and ordained in 1936, and who had a pastorate in Thibodaux at the time of the award, was honored as "a militant worker for Louisiana sugar cane field workers in their strike last year" and for having testified before a congressional committee "about the close kinship of organized crime to anti-union forces in Louisiana." Drolet said that instead of claiming individual credit, he wanted to point to "the glorious labors for Christian social justice by countless members of both clergy and laity from coast to coast."[9] Although various volunteers drove the Foremans to school from time to time, risking and sometimes sustaining damage to their automobiles, he was the only person who ever made the walks with Andy and Pamela.

At that time, John Steinbeck, the novelist who would win the Nobel Prize for literature in 1962, was completing the tour around America on which he based his book, *Travels with Charley.* Drawn by national news coverage of the

Cheerleaders, Steinbeck made his way to New Orleans and watched Bridges as she made her way into school, surrounded by federal marshals. He wrote:

> The papers had printed that the jibes and jeers were cruel and sometimes obscene, and so they were, but this was not the big show. The crowd was waiting for the white man who dared to bring his white child to school. And here he came along the guarded walk, a tall man dressed in light gray, leading his frightened child by the hand.... His body was tensed ... his face was grave and gray ... a man afraid who by his will held his fears in check as a great rider directs a panicked horse.
>
> A shrill, grating voice rang out. The yelling was not in chorus. Each took a turn and at the end of each the crowd broke into howls and roars and whistles of applause. This is what they had come to see and hear.
>
> No newspaper had printed the words these women shouted. It was indicated that they were indelicate, some even said obscene. On television the sound track was made to blur or had crowd noises cut in to cover. But now I heard the words, bestial and filthy and degenerate.[10]

Steinbeck said that in the "unprotected life" he had lived, he had been exposed before to the "vomiting of demoniac humans," but never to screams that filled him with such a "shocked and sickened sorrow." He was so depressed by what he witnessed in New Orleans that he cut his trip short and made his way directly home.[11]

Margaret Conner, one of the white parents who soon put their children back in William Frantz Elementary but who did not receive as much publicity as Foreman, revealed in an interview published in 1985 that she was utterly dismayed at the "unwomanly" behavior of the Cheerleaders. They frequently cursed her in person and in anonymous telephone calls. She was pregnant with her ninth child at the time, and one woman demanded to know whether the child would be black or white. The women would sometimes stand in front of her house, shake "their backsides" at her, and do "all kinds of nasty movements."[12] Her recollections provide a marked counterpoint to the claim of one of the Cheerleaders' organizers, Una Gaillot. In *A House Divided,* a film on school desegregation in New Orleans produced by Xavier University, Gaillot maintained that all the women who protested were "ladies" and that they unfailingly conducted themselves in a ladylike manner.[13] Gaillot's assertion does not match the perception of the photojournalists and reporters who covered the story, nor that of Steinbeck, nor that of the Foremans and their friends.

Daves's and Smith's Home Is Targeted

While Foreman was involved in the drama at William Frantz only because he lived some distance from St. Mark's, settlement houses bore that name because the workers settled in the communities they hoped to serve, and thus both Fae Daves and Laura Smith lived on the third floor inside the St. Mark's building. Smith opened the mail at St. Mark's, and in the weeks after Steinbeck watched the Foremans walk to school, she dealt with sack after sack of hate mail, often filled with threats toward the building where she and Daves resided. Vandals climbed onto the roof one night when a group of young girls was present for a sleepover and threw tar or creosote onto the front of the sanctuary.[14]

Another individual who would later become a United Methodist minister in the New Orleans District has a vivid memory of that vandalism. He was involved in the demonstrations at the school, but on the opposite side of the issue from Foreman. The Reverend Mr. Gene M. Faurie was eleven years old in 1960, and his family lived in the 5400 block of North Rampart Street. "We were going to McDonough 19 when they integrated the school," he recalled. "I'll never forget that—the hatred in people's faces when those little kids were going into the school. Kids standing along with parents and yelling." Although the majority of the demonstrators were female, Faurie's father went along to the school with the rest of his family, because he worked the night shift. "We went in the mornings. I don't remember the children always coming on time; they came at different times, sometimes mid-morning, ten or so, they'd show. Once the black kids got inside, we'd leave; it was just to aggravate them going in." As soon as it became clear that the black students were not going to abandon McDonough 19, Faurie's parents sent him to a school in St. Bernard Parish, where he attended until he went to junior high.[15]

Faurie recalled passing by St. Mark's after it had been vandalized "and seeing all the black paint and stuff thrown on the building." When they saw the damaged sanctuary, his parents "made approving remarks, saying 'That's good enough for them,' and stuff like that. I remember taking some joy in that myself, because it was the 'nigger-loving' church. It was the church involved in integration, and it was to be scorned. It brought joy to see it defaced. It didn't matter what they thought or what they must feel."[16] Faurie later underwent a complete conversion in his attitude toward racial issues and actively sought forgiveness from black colleagues for his past racism, but in 1960, for him, as for most white New Orleanians, anyone associated with St. Mark's was a legitimate target for hate. Unquestionably, Fae Daves and Laura Smith were included among the targets of the community's resentment and desire for revenge.

DEATH THREATS DRIVE THE FOREMANS FROM THEIR HOME

The parsonage on Alvar Street was also repeatedly vandalized, more frequently and more seriously than the church itself, and death threats became so frequent that the Foremans had to go into hiding. At first, the Foremans stayed with their friends, the Reverend Mr. Ed Barksdale, and his wife, Mattie. Barksdale was pastoring St. Paul's Methodist Church in Harahan, a small, incorporated city bounded on three sides by Metairie, the largest suburb of New Orleans, and on the fourth side by the east bank of the Mississippi River.

Barksdale said that he and his wife invited the Foremans to stay with them, "because I was frightened for them—[people] doing such things to their home, throwing paint on it, standing there shouting obscenities." Because Harahan is an almost all-white, very conservative community, Barksdale was worried that the people of St. Paul's would be angry because he had invited the Foremans to stay in their parsonage. However, he said, "To my happy surprise, the church was very much behind me and Andy, and they thought this was not right, for them to be persecuted."[17] Foreman's personal collection of documents from that time includes letters he received from the administrative board of St. Paul's and from the adult Sunday school class expressing their support for his stand. Soon, though, the Foremans' whereabouts became more widely known, and then, Barksdale said, they received numerous threatening telephone calls. Eventually, the Foremans moved again, and stayed for a while with parishioners.

In his mid-eighties, Barksdale denied having acted because he was personally a liberal, stating, "I was more conservative than liberal." He had found his seminary studies at Emory University "rather shocking," and even felt some concern that students might "lose their faith" there. Nevertheless, he said, he felt that what the Foremans were doing was right. "I might have thought it wasn't fair to the child, but apparently the daughter was courageous enough to not get upset about it."[18]

OTHER LOCAL METHODISTS PROVIDE SUPPORT FOR FOREMAN

The Reverend Mr. Donice W. Alverson, who was appointed to the Napoleon Avenue Methodist Church, and his wife, Julie, were also close friends with the Foremans and the Barksdales, and maintained "close contact" with them during that period. The Napoleon Avenue congregation had been founded as an outpost of the Methodist Episcopal Church (MEC) during the period when the Methodist Episcopal Church, South (MECS) had broken off from it over the issue of slavery. When several black individuals attended a service there in 1966, he recalled, there was "no reaction whatsoever; people spoke to them."[19]

Alverson grew up in north Alabama and did his seminary work at Emory University. He believed his exposure to new ideas in seminary changed his own thinking on the topic of race. In 1960, he was among the signers of a newspaper advertisement the Greater New Orleans Federation of Churches published while Pamela Foreman was attending school with Ruby Bridges. The ad was "not as strong as it could have been," he said, merely offering a "general message" against violence and urging cooperation. He believes that all the Methodist ministers in the New Orleans district except one affixed their signatures.[20] Alverson said that after the advertisement appeared, "Our house was egged once," and one day, a man telephoned around five o'clock in the morning, said,

"I see you have joined the gang," and hung up. "That was the only repercussion that I recall, that and the egging. There was no voice in the [Napoleon Avenue] church ever against us."[21]

Despite the relatively minor nature of the vandalism actually carried out against their home, his wife, Julie, recalled, "It was a very frightening time for all of us, because I was home with Meg—she was a baby—and Don was off attending these meetings, and we were very much afraid that someone would attack our own homes because our husbands were participating." Her primary memory of the time is "thinking that Don should not participate, because I had a new baby at home, and I couldn't handle it." She also noted that "while everybody was feeling supportive of Andy, none of us were out there with him walking to school. I don't feel that we jeopardized ourselves for him. While we supported him in theory, he pretty much did this alone."[22]

POLITICAL LEADERS FAIL TO
UNDERMINE THE CHEERLEADERS

During the second week of integration, a "Day-By-Day Summary of Events" in a local newspaper noted that on Thursday, "Angry women demonstrators at Frantz school set upon bystanders, manhandling a university student, an elderly New Orleans attorney, cameramen and a local newspaper reporter," and that a police cordon was put up "around the house of a Protestant minister who has been the special target of demonstrators for accompanying his daughter to the Frantz kindergarten." The paper noted that while the white boycott of McDonough 19 remained complete for a fifth straight day, "four more white children attend[ed] Frantz, joining the original two."[23]

A caption accompanying a United Press International photograph noted that a hostile crowd had gathered at Foreman's house "shortly after the minister returned from accompanying several white pupils into William Frantz school." An effigy of Mayor Chep Morrison was burned in front of the parsonage.[24] As deeply in love with politics as his first cousin, Lindy Boggs, and her husband, Hale, New Orleans Mayor DeLesseps "Chep" Morrison yearned to be elected governor of Louisiana, and he tailored most of his work as mayor toward that end. Although there are many indications that he was personally a moderate on race issues, Morrison believed that he could not be elected to statewide office if he offended the white voters of the state, the majority of whom were segregationists. In his desire to avoid becoming tainted as an integrationist, he failed to restrain the Cheerleaders, whose activities were almost certainly orchestrated by notorious segregationist Leander Perez of Plaquemines Parish. They could easily have been kept back a little distance by police, so that Andy and Pamela Foreman did not have to walk within inches of the screaming women, but Morrison failed to have the police chief take that action. The photographs and film footage of the gauntlets the women formed were so compelling that they were printed and shown all over the world, which "sullied the city's reputation in the national eye." What Edward Haas calls Morrison's "studied caution" resulted in the almost ubiquitous perception that he failed to provide any strong leadership during the crisis. Thus, he was left without a strong constituency on any side of the issue.[25]

PROMISED INTEGRATION OF ROMAN CATHOLIC SCHOOLS IS DELAYED

A study on how political leadership contributed to the school desegregation crisis revealed that as soon as the Roman Catholic school board announced that it would desegregate its schools, "reaction was immediate and effective." Catholic laypeople from south Louisiana, "including arch-segregationist Leander H. Perez, Sr.," made a trip to the Vatican to try to obtain "papal blessings" for their viewpoint. "Although these individuals were rebuffed, a short time later Archbishop Rummel of New Orleans announced that parochial school desegregation would be delayed because of 'administrative difficulties.'"[26] The archbishop, who had been outspoken about the appropriateness of integration when the *Brown* decision was handed down back in 1954 and who had originally indicated that Catholic schools would integrate no later than the public facilities, and possibly before them, did not open the Catholic schools to black students until two years after public schools were integrated; he excommunicated Perez and a handful of other virulent racists at that time.[27]

Interfaith Support for Foreman Begins to Materialize

Persons of other faiths also continued their involvement in the struggle. Rabbi Leo Bergman called an interfaith meeting at Touro Synagogue on St. Charles Avenue to address the situation. "The house was filled with clergymen," Foreman recalled. The rabbi wanted to organize a march to show solidarity with Foreman's actions, but Foreman was afraid that some members of the clergy might lose their jobs if they marched. He knew that many of the Protestant clergymen present were not United Methodists, but were rather from self-governing congregations. If pastors in a denomination where congregations are self-governing displease their congregations, they can simply be fired by the local group, and they must then set about locating another job on their own. United Methodist ministers operate under a system called "itinerancy" that involves appointment by a bishop. Once Methodist ministers become elders—a status roughly equivalent to achieving tenure on a faculty—they are guaranteed an appointment of some kind unless they are formally ruled "unappointable" for gross misconduct or for refusing to accept the appointments they are offered. Foreman had achieved elder status in 1954, and thus knew that he could not be fired by the St. Mark's congregation, and that even if they persuaded the bishop to move him at the next Annual Conference, he would definitely be given full-time employment somewhere else in the state. Because he also knew that many of the other ministers present did not enjoy that job security, he asked them not to stage a march that might endanger careers and possibly even lives, and merely asked them to pray and to offer to drive him and Pamela to school if necessary.[28]

The need for drivers was occasioned by the fact that after the first week or two of the Cheerleader demonstrations, federal marshals were assigned to accompany the Foremans to school. Further, because they were no longer able to stay at the parsonage, the Foremans needed transportation because where they were staying was often distant from the school. One task taken on by the Save Our Schools (S.O.S.) organization, founded to help prevent the closing of public schools, was recruiting volunteers to drive the Foremans and other white children to William Frantz. S.O.S. had three clergymen, one Jewish, one Roman

Catholic, and one Protestant as its chairpersons, and many of the laity in leadership positions were also religiously motivated. Ann Dlugos, the group's secretary, who was born in 1927, told an interviewer in the early 1990s that the Social Gospel preaching in her church, along with a family history of involvement in Progressive reforms, had led her to act as she did in 1960. Other persons interviewed at that time also said their religious convictions were a motivating factor.[29]

INDEPENDENT WOMEN'S ORGANIZATION TAKES A STAND

Other groups outside the organized church were also adding their voices to the public debate, including some groups established by women to work for progressive reforms. For instance, the League of Women Voters supported the school board's decision to proceed with integration and issued public calls for peace and calmness. The Independent Women's Organization (IWO), the group to which St. Mark's member Mary Morrison belonged, issued a number of press releases. One attacked Governor Jimmie Davis's plan to fund segregated school systems with an additional sales tax: "Anyone who can add one and one can see that, in order to operate two school systems, one public and one private, the state will need twice as much money." They said the proposed tax would not only "cripple business," but also "work a cruel injustice on every citizen each time he buys a loaf of bread or a quart of milk." The women demanded to know, "Where is the peace, harmony and economy promised by Gov. Davis again and again during the last year's campaign?" They refused to interpret the mere silencing of opposition as peace, insisting, "There is no peace and no harmony when law-abiding citizens are intimidated in their own homes, and when people are afraid to speak for law and order for fear of drastic reprisals.[30]

At about that same time, the IWO sent a "message of confidence" to members of the Orleans Parish School Board and urged that they resist public pressure to resign. They noted that an entirely new board would have no more chance of operating a second, segregated system successfully than the sitting board had, and that those who were calling for the current board members' resignations knew that. Furious that state officials had tried to shut down the Orleans Parish School Board by instructing banks not to honor their employee paychecks and by erecting other financial barriers, the women assured the board members of their own continuing political support.[31]

ELECTED OFFICIALS FOLLOW PUBLIC OPINION

It may be supposed that the school board members were delighted to receive anyone's support at that point, especially that of a prominent women's political organization like the IWO, considering that they were undergoing some of the same harassment that the Foreman family was facing. The *New York Times* reported that one school board member would not let his family leave the house until he had ensured that their car had not been "booby-trapped," and that the board's president, Lloyd J. Rittiner, would no longer allow his daughter to answer their home telephone because they had received so many obscene calls.[32]

Further, many other political figures were actively attempting to solidify their own positions at the expense of the school board's. A paid advertisement in a December edition of the *New Orleans States-Item* reproduces in its entirety a concurrent resolution passed by both houses of the Louisiana legislature. Signed by the lieutenant governor and president of the Senate, C. C. Aycock, and by the speaker of the House of Representatives, J. Thomas Jewell, the resolution commended the white parents who had removed their children from William Frantz and McDonough 19 for their "courageous step . . . to maintain our customs and our traditions and our way of life" and for their stand "against the forces of integration and those who seek to destroy all that we hold near and dear." The resolution urged parents and children to continue the boycott and promised that the legislature would do all it could "to assist them in their brave fight." The ad stated that the clerk of the House had been directed to have the resolution printed in every New Orleans newspaper for three consecutive days; that the ad was to occupy at least a quarter-page space in each paper; and that the House of Representatives would bear the expense.[33] Governor Jimmie Davis mentioned interposition—a state's refusal to obey a national law with which it does not agree—as a "last resort" before secession. These politicians may have been motivated in part by a poll revealing that 83 percent of white citizens would prefer to have the schools closed than to integrate them.[34]

Segregationists Insist that God Is on Their Side

The Save Our Schools (S.O.S.) collection at Tulane's Amistad Research Center abounds with evidence that many protesters felt the standards of the southern community regarding segregation, and their own actions in particular, were endorsed by God. The boxes are full of letters to S.O.S., copies of letters to the editor, and various other kinds of documentation that all contain the message that the writers considered it their "God-given duty to preserve the southern way of life." Typical of the content is a letter to the editor of the *New Orleans States-Item* signed by Mrs. E. Weiss and printed on December 20, 1960:

> In answer to the letter written by Mrs. Dorothy Barden (Dec. 13) asking "What would Jesus do about our school integration problem?" He would do the will of His Father, God Almighty. Jesus would do as God did in the beginning—segregate the races.
>
> We have only to read our Bible which tells us that God made everything after its kind. The beasts in the jungle live segregated lives. . . .
>
> Therefore, when you integrate the races you are breaking God's law and replacing it with the law of some greedy, ambitious politicians who are using the Negro people as a pawn to get power and wealth, and the Negro is using his vote as a weapon to break God's law.[35]

Another clipping details a resolution passed by the official board of a Methodist congregation in Denham Springs, Louisiana. It called upon "[a]ny member of our Methodist churches including our laymen, clergymen and other high officials that might be thinking of, or attempting to do something to comfort the cause of integration" to "cease such action at once." The district superintendent in that area told the newspaper that he had not yet seen the resolution and therefore could not comment, but the pastor of the church, the Reverend Mr. William J. Reid, said that he had opposed the resolution "and his district superintendent backed him up."[36] Presumably, a congregation that passed such a resolution as an action of its official board must have had some confidence that what they were doing was not totally offensive to God, even if their "misguided" clergy thought it might be.

The film *A House Divided* includes footage of Cheerleaders carrying signs that proclaimed, "God Keep Us Cool, Calm and Segregated" and "God Curses All Integrators."[37] A January 31, 1961, clipping in the Save Our Schools (S.O.S.) collection refers to Mrs. B. J. Gaillot Jr. as the president of Save Our Nation (an obvious parallel to the Save Our Schools organization). In the clipping, Gaillot addressed Jack Nelson, who was cited as a Catholic layperson who had helped orchestrate a "call for peace in New Orleans" issued by the national Catholic Conference for Interracial Justice. She challenged Nelson to come to an open forum and debate her on the ethics of segregation. The reporter wrote: "Mrs. Gaillot cited the Holy Bible as her reference. She said that several members of the Catholic hierarchy, including Pope Urban VIII, believed in segregation."[38]

FOREMAN RESPONDS TO A DIFFERENT VIEW OF THE GOSPEL

Despite the common conception that Foreman was in the wrong not only socially but also theologically, and despite the abuse he and his family and his church members suffered and the traumatic nature of the experience, Foreman doggedly persevered in defying the boycott and serving as pastor at St. Mark's. He had been appointed to a pulpit in New Orleans because his research project for a Th.D. degree in practical theology, with a specialization in evangelism, that he had been pursuing at Boston University had not worked out. He had received appointment as an associate pastor at a Nebraska church where the senior pastor had achieved a phenomenal growth in membership. Foreman was to study this minister's methodology and write his findings as his dissertation. However, he and the senior pastor could not work together, and Foreman left that appointment and sought one in his home conference, Louisiana, instead.[39]

In 1960, he and his major advisor at Boston University, the Reverend Dr. Allan Knight Chalmers, still hoped that Foreman could eventually complete a different project; thus, Chalmers considered Foreman, and Foreman still considered himself, as a potential recipient of the doctoral degree when the events of 1960 occurred. In a 1998 interview, Foreman began his answer to a question about how he came to take his stand on school integration by mentioning his association with Dr. Chalmers at Boston University, an institution Foreman characterized as "the seat of liberalism" at that time. "Allan was a great help in facing these things," he remarked.[40]

After graduating from Centenary College in 1948, Foreman intended to pursue his seminary studies in a manner that would expose him to as many different theological points of view as possible. He planned to study for a year at Asbury Theological Seminary in Wilmore, Kentucky, which is known as an extremely conservative school; to study the second year at Emory University's Candler School of Theology, which could be classed as theologically moderate; and to finish his work at and graduate from Boston University, a liberal institution. In fact, he attended Asbury for two years and then graduated from Emory. Next, he earned a master's degree in theology at Temple University in Philadelphia, and then returned to the pastorate in Louisiana for two years for the purpose of obtaining his permanent (elder's) orders. A few months after his ordination, he left for Boston University to pursue the Th.D.[41]

He soon discovered that his major advisor, Allan Knight Chalmers, had two primary interests, prison reform and the eradication of racial discrimination. Therefore, Chalmers's major concern "was dealing with methods of changing social attitudes. How do you change the social attitudes of people that you come in contact with?"

Chalmers was a member of an important NAACP committee that dedicated finances and effort toward achieving equal justice under the law. Just as the women of St. Mark's Community Center had been influenced by Albert Barnett, their professor at Scarritt, Andy Foreman, the pastor of the St. Mark's congregation, was profoundly influenced by Chalmers. Further, Barnett and Chalmers were both members of the same NAACP committee. As theologians teaching at Methodist schools, and as two white members of a national NAACP committee in the mid-twentieth century, it seems unlikely in the extreme that they were not acquainted with one another. Both were well known as white radicals; Barnett's status in that regard has already been discussed, and Chalmers had gained fame as a primary figure in obtaining the release of the Scottsboro Boys, as documented in his book, *They Shall Be Free*.[42]

Chalmers told Foreman about a professional risk he had taken when he was pastoring a large congregation in New York City. One morning, a very upset Sunday school teacher came into his office and reported to him that "a colored child" was attending Sunday school. Chalmers encouraged the teacher to let the child stay because a black child was, after all, still a human being. Foreman said that because of this incident, Chalmers avoided losing his job with that congregation by a margin of only one vote.[43]

Another white Methodist clergyman who was a civil rights activist in Mississippi, Ed King, was also a student of Chalmers. Ed King's biographer, Charles Marsh, noted that Chalmers's homiletics and social ethics courses were "deeply informed" by Chalmers's political activities, and that he told students about and sometimes took them along on "weekend trips to New York, to Washington, and to the deep South in the cause of social justice."[44] Chalmers had also taught Martin Luther King Jr., who graduated from Boston University the year before Foreman arrived.

During the 1960 crisis in New Orleans, Chalmers came to New Orleans to offer assistance to Foreman, who insisted that the two meet "under cover of darkness," because he did not wish anyone to know that he was connected with an NAACP member.[45] Chalmers came not only to see whether funds might be needed to assist persons who had lost their jobs because of their involvement in integration activities, but also because he was concerned about Foreman on a personal level. Chalmers assured him that if he needed or wanted to leave Louisiana, Chalmers would do all he could to help him relocate. "This was the thing that so many of our men faced—not because they wanted to leave, but because they had to leave—in Mississippi and other places," Foreman said.[46]

Chalmers wanted Foreman to write up his experiences with school desegregation as his dissertation. The professor approached other faculty at Boston University about the possibility, but they would not agree to it. After the experiences of 1960, Foreman wanted to stay at St. Mark's, and eventually he put his doctoral work "further on the back burner and for all practical purposes, abandoned it."[47]

Along with the influence of Chalmers and his studies at Boston University, Foreman also credited his childhood background for helping him make the decision to keep his daughter in William Frantz Elementary. He mentioned his upbringing in Kaplan, a small, French-influenced, south Louisiana town, amid a family that did not instill any racial prejudice in him. Although there was no formal instruction or discussion of racial tolerance in his home, his parents "set the example; Dad always treated people as though they were equals." In short, he said, "I felt that everybody was a child of God and that I was no better than anyone else."[48]

Foreman also recounted a formative incident that occurred during his studies at the Methodist-affiliated Centenary College in Shreveport, Louisiana. Serving as a student pastor in a nearby small community, Foreman regularly took the bus to his assignment. On one occasion, when the station was particularly crowded, the driver tried to leave despite the fact that his bus was pressing individuals against another bus. One young black man shouted at the driver, "Stop that damn bus!" The driver and "five burly guys" charged off the bus to confront the black man who had dared to speak so insolently to a white man, and Foreman followed. When the whites encircled the black man, intending, Foreman felt, to "stomp him," Foreman shouted at the group and caught their attention, allowing the black man to crawl under a bus and escape. When the driver admonished Foreman for his role in the incident, Foreman responded, "Did you think I was going to let you stomp that man? You have another thought coming." Thus, he pointed out, school desegregation was not the first time that he had ever had to take a stand based on his convictions about every person's status "as a child of God."[49]

Psychiatrist Robert Coles, M.D., now retired from the medical school faculty at Harvard University, wrote *Children of Crisis* based on interviews with parents and students who defied the New Orleans school boycott, including Ruby Bridges. Coles was intrigued not just with the effects this episode would have on the children involved, but also with the motives that led the parents to take their courageous stands. The book contains lengthy reflections based on conversations with white parents who kept their children in William Frantz. Mention of Foreman, however, is extremely brief; Coles simply states that one parent was a Methodist minister who acted from religious motives.[50] Foreman did not recall meeting or even knowing of Coles, but Coles remembered having interviewed Foreman, though his memories of details had faded over the years.[51] (As discussed later on, his bishop instructed Foreman not to grant interviews and, by and large, he did not.)

Negative Responses within the Congregation

Many of the St. Mark's congregation who retained their church membership during the 1960 crisis had moved away from the French Quarter and were driving back into the neighborhood to worship there. Their reasons for maintaining contact with St. Mark's despite Foreman's defiance of the boycott did not always include genuine support for the stand Foreman had taken regarding integration. A few members stated that they supported Foreman primarily because they thought that what he did was not a genuine reflection of what he believed. They said Foreman told them the church hierarchy forced him into keeping Pamela in William Frantz Elementary.

Among the most prominent members of the congregation were the members of a Syrian family. Two of the women remained at St. Mark's for some time after the events of 1960, but they were not at all happy about Foreman's actions during school desegregation. One told an interviewer in 1979 that the district superintendent had forced Foreman to leave his daughter at William Frantz. She said that when Foreman took her to school himself, "they almost killed him," so the district superintendent came and personally took the child to school.[52] Such an incident never happened.

The woman said that she accepted the inevitaly of integration, and that the family had stood by Foreman, though many of the congregation left. When they tried to persuade others to stay, she said, "They thought we were crazy."[53] However, when the community center integrated, the family did leave the congregation and joined an all-white church. Another family member told the interviewer that the family had donated a marble baptismal font to St. Mark's in memory of a deceased family member. "When all of this happened, the Center was all Negroes, there was no cooperation between the two, people had left St. Mark's, our congregation had gone down to hardly nothing, so we decided why leave that baptismal fount [sic] there. We were afraid it would be stolen." They removed the marble font from the St. Mark's sanctuary and gave it to St. Luke's Methodist Church. St. Luke's is located on Canal Boulevard in Lakeshore, an area that was all white, and a number of those who left St. Mark's joined St. Luke's instead. The extreme action of taking back a dedicated baptismal font and moving it to an all-white congregation is a powerful witness to the depth of the family's feeling about integration.[54]

Perhaps because they felt a need to justify their decision to stay as long as they did despite their convictions about racial issues, these church members attempted to absolve Foreman of responsibility for his actions. Their memory of Foreman's motives is not consistent with the memory of other individuals involved in the events, but the attribution of "blame" to the church hierarchy rather than to Foreman himself is consistent with the information provided by another individual who kept her membership at St. Mark's.

That longtime parishioner was a first-generation American; both parents were born in Mexico. Her remarks in a 1999 interview made it clear that she considered the presence of blacks to be a detriment to the center and church. She, too, absolved Foreman for his actions, saying that the bishop required him to act as he did. Her memory was that Foreman said that because the government had mandated it, he had to support integration or lose his job, and he could not afford to lose his job because he had a family. After the center was integrated, this member was angry "because blacks were destroying the center." She said that they broke pianos and broke chairs and threw them into the alley. She felt that the congregation's membership dissipated after integration, and her memory was that "only three or four" families stayed. She did not leave, she said, "because it was *my* church." In 1965, the same year the center integrated, her family moved to the largely white suburb of Arabi, in St. Bernard Parish, but she continued to attend at St. Mark's until she became a shut-in. She died in the year 2000 at almost one hundred years of age, still a member at St. Mark's.[55]

CONCLUSIONS

It seems unlikely that Foreman lied to these members about whose decision his actions were based upon, and more likely that they chose to adapt their understandings and/or their memories of the events to ensure their continued attendance at their beloved church (even temporarily, in the case of the first family). However, Foreman did publicly insist in 1960 that his actions were not linked to racial issues, but rather to the right of taxpayers to have their children attend public schools. For instance, in a 1960 *Chicago Sun-Times* story, based on what the author maintained was "the longest interview [Foreman] has granted to date," the pastor stated that "personal conscience and Christian tenets were the guidelines" he had followed, but that his primary purpose in defying the boycott was simply to defend his daughter's right to attend public schools. "I want my daughter in school," he was quoted as saying. "I want the right to have her in school; if other people want to keep their children at home, that is their privilege."[56]

Colleagues among the clergy also remember Foreman's insistence that it was not a racial issue in which he was involved. John Winn recalled Foreman saying that "it was about public education, not race." Winn also stated that the clergy of his acquaintance were "all so surprised when he did this, because theologically, Andy was more conservative than the rest of us. It was a joyful surprise that he chose to do this." Clarence Snelling also noted, "For many years, Andy claimed that he wasn't involved in race relations; he was just a supporter of public schools and taxpayers." Snelling noted that Foreman's conservatism made other clergy in Louisiana surprised that he went for his doctoral studies to Boston University, a liberal institution where he would study with Chalmers, instead of the more moderate Emory University or an even more conservative school.[57]

When the Urban Ministry Board of the New Orleans District of the United Methodist Church presented Foreman with an award at a session of the Louisiana Annual Conference in the late 1990s, in very belated recognition of his courageous stand in 1960, it occasioned resentment on the part of some black members of the clergy. They believed Foreman to be a racist, because of derogatory racial comments they had heard him make throughout the ensuing years. At the time of Foreman's first interview for this study, his language was still decades behind accepted usage; for instance, he frequently used the word "colored" to refer to black individuals, not in the current usage, "people of color," but in what would have been the polite terminology in the 1950s—"colored." He also commented, "They had set this up to where this one little nigra girl would be the focal point of the integration process." "Nigra" was, decades ago, one of the most polite ways that white southerners referred to black individuals.[58]

In 1996, Foreman and his daughter, Pamela, appeared on the *Oprah* television show as part of a segment entitled "35 Years Later: Black & White Student Reunions."[59] Pamela and Ruby Bridges met for the first time on the show. Oprah Winfrey asked Andy Foreman only one question: "Did you feel brave or courageous at the time?" His response included his assertion that he was doing "the thing that I had been committed to do because I believe that every child has a right to go to the school of his or her choice, regardless of the color of their skin, and my decision to take Pam was made out of—out of a prior commitment that I had made years before to the Christian ministry."[60] When he discussed that appearance during the initial interview for this study, he expressed frustration over the fact that when he talked with Winfrey backstage, he had not been able "to make her understand" that in the New Orleans school desegregation crisis, "it was a white-against-white thing," and that "blacks had nothing to do with it."[61] It hardly seems surprising that Winfrey remained unpersuaded that blacks "had nothing to do with" school desegregation. However, it also seems understandable that Foreman, who had very limited contact with black individuals at the time, and who was the victim of hate crimes perpetrated by whites on him and his family, remembered that period of his life being populated only with white characters. The political structure and the cultural structure he challenged were white structures; the persons who held power over and stalled his career in the church were white men; the women who screamed at him and his daughter each morning were white women. Indeed, the villains of the story were all white, but Foreman's belief that the entire struggle was a white struggle overlooked the fact that all the heroes were not.

As John Patrick McDowell noted about MECS women, both cultural conditionings and religious convictions were part of their makeup. Foreman's traumatic experiences at the hands of whites, his white male privilege and cultural conditioning that tended to make blacks invisible, and the fact that the race-based Central Jurisdiction's existence ensured that his interactions with the larger church occurred almost exclusively with whites were all no doubt factors in his later interpretation of events, along with the theological convictions underpinning his countercultural stand. What is irrefutable in Foreman's story is that he and his family took truly heroic risks to break the white boycott at William Frantz Elementary and thus contributed greatly to the death of legal segregation in New Orleans public schools.

7

ASSESSING ST. MARK'S IN THE SIXTIES

As member Mary Morrison later wrote, Foreman's stand "under these danger-ous and trying conditions focused national attention on him and his church," and "led to turbulent days" for St. Mark's.[1] Subjective opinions offered by per-sons who were members of the congregation at the time range from "hardly anyone left as a result of what happened,"[2] to "the congregation was de-stroyed—all but three or four families left."[3] A more nearly objective assessment was offered by Morrison, who had access to membership rosters and figures for a short history she prepared in 1971. According to her, "[W]e lost, all told, about two dozen members which at the time constituted less than ten percent of our membership."[4]

Furthermore, the official position taken by the congregation was support for Foreman's stance. Morrison recalled, "Sometime between January 1961 and May of that year the official board passed a resolution at its monthly meeting that 'any Negro attending St. Mark's would be seated and any Negro presenting himself for membership would be accepted.'"[5] Despite the fact that that no Af-rican Americans did join at that time, the congregation became known among local segregationists as "nigger-lovers" and/or "the nigger church." Even though they had been looking for a different parsonage in November 1960, the church did not sell its parsonage immediately after the school desegregation crisis, but rented it out instead. They felt that if they put a "For Sale" sign out front, it "would look as though we were walking on our convictions."[6] They did buy a new parsonage that was, ironically, even farther from St. Mark's. A year later, the church finally sold the house on Alvar Street.

CENTER-AFFILIATED WOMEN
SUPPORT INTEGRATION

Sherry Gordon Smyth grew up in the St. Mark's congregation, and in 1960 she was an actively involved eleven-year-old. She had begun attending church there when she was six or seven years old and her family lived at 1400 Esplanade Avenue. She remained an active member at St. Mark's until about 1972, even though her family moved several times, each time farther away from the facility. Smyth's perception was that the congregation in 1960 was very supportive of Foreman. Although she remembers one family that stopped attending because the father was afraid there could be additional attacks against the building while his children were in it, her belief is that the membership remained essentially stable after the crisis. Among the persons she recalled as being especially "supportive or understanding or tolerant" were Fae Daves, Laura Smith, Mary Ethel Mandlebaum (deaconess Helen Mandlebaum's mother), and Mary Morrison. At age eleven, Smyth did not perceive this as greater support from the center's paid staff and its longtime president of the board of directors than from the congregation as a whole, because at that point, she had never processed any real difference between the community center and the church, a fact that speaks to how intertwined the two entities were at that time.[7]

When Foreman made his stand against segregation in 1960, deaconess Fae Daves had been the head resident of the center since 1948. Daves was consecrated a deaconess in the early 1920s, and thus had received her spiritual formation and training in the Social Gospel era. Before arriving at St. Mark's, she had been affiliated with the Moody Bible Institute of Chicago, an early advocate of integrated Sunday schools, and with a community center located on Chicago's South Side.[8]

Foreman said that after his appointment to St. Mark's Methodist Church, he and Daves worked together well, with each supporting the work of both the congregation and the community center as much as possible. He felt that both Fae Daves and Laura Smith played very supportive roles during the school desegregation crisis, because both women "were committed to the program [of integration] and to doing the right thing." In 1960, most members of his congregation did not live in the French Quarter, but were rather individuals who "had been influenced by the Community Center when they were young, and they came back" to St. Mark's to worship.[9] Thus, the makeup of the group was heavily weighted toward persons who had been exposed for years to the teachings of deaconesses like Julia Southard Campbell, Mary Lou Barnwell, Nettie Stroup, and Fae Daves, who believed in racial equality. Despite the resistance toward integration on the part of a few persons, the congregation's leadership voted to support Foreman's stand and to welcome blacks into attendance at Sunday worship, a truly radical stance for a white southern congregation in 1960. The women of St. Mark's deserve much of the credit for the congregation's publicly positive stand behind Foreman.

DIRE PROFESSIONAL CONSEQUENCES FOR INTEGRATION SUPPORTERS

The paucity of information about Foreman in *Children of Crisis,* Robert Coles's book about the motivations of people involved in the school desegregation crisis, is the result of Foreman's having refused to participate in an extended series of interviews like the ones Coles conducted with many persons involved. This was in keeping with Foreman's instructions from his bishop, Aubrey Walton. Foreman explained that Walton told him to "keep doing what you're doing," but that if any statements were to be made about Foreman's position, he, Walton, would make them.[10] Both the bishop and the district superintendent, Benedict Galloway, were out of town at the time Ruby Bridges entered Frantz Elementary, so Foreman could not immediately meet with either of them. When they returned the next week, Foreman was summoned to the bishop's office for a consultation. Walton, who had been pastor of a large Methodist church in Little Rock, Arkansas, during the armed confrontation over the city's school integration in the mid-1950s, told Foreman that he was doing the right thing. He and Galloway both attended a service at St. Mark's to demonstrate solidarity with Foreman. However, Walton forbade Foreman to speak to any of the dozens of media representatives who waited outside the church that morning. Foreman was taken out the back door to avoid them.[11]

Although the presiding bishop thus nominally supported Foreman, he did not offer as much support as he could have, and as Foreman's clergy colleague John Winn noted, Foreman's appointments after St. Mark's were widely perceived by other clergy as "punishment" appointments.[12] In a published interview with

Margaret Conner, another white parent who later brought a white child back to William Frantz, one historian addressed professional repercussions suffered by the parents involved in integration. Conner's husband was employed by Lykes Brothers Shipbuilding, one of the first businesses in New Orleans to integrate its workforce, and its management assured Conner that although they were not completely in agreement with the family's stance, he would not lose his job because of it. Along with discussing the firing of Ruby Bridges's father from his job at a gas station and a white parent having been harassed on his job as a city employee, the author mentioned Foreman: "Finally, the Reverend Foreman has been transferred numerous times in the last twenty years and is now on leave of absence from the Methodist church."[13]

The historian seemed not to understand that being transferred is not necessarily a sign of problems for a Methodist minister, because the Methodist system of appointment, called "itinerancy," would normally result in several moves over a twenty-year period. Being transferred several times could easily demonstrate success, as long as each move was to a larger church with a larger salary. In fact, Foreman's problem was precisely that he had not transferred from the congregation in Luling, Louisiana, where he was appointed when he left St. Mark's in 1965 after seven years in that pulpit. He was left at the Luling church for eight years, and this was an exceptionally long appointment in a low-level position. Methodist leaders are now making efforts to lengthen appointments, so this would have been even more unusual in the mid-1960s.

Finally, in 1973, undoubtedly frustrated with the Annual Conference's appointment-making system and the unwillingness of the bishop and district superintendents to arrange a positive move for him, Foreman took a position as "conference evangelist." This job did not guarantee any income, and Foreman was not paid unless individual churches decided to hire him to preach revivals. It did, however, remove him from the total control of the appointment system and signaled a movement away from dependence on the Annual Conference structure for his employment. In 1979, he took an official leave of absence. Foreman spent at least part of the next five years working for a company that catered for offshore drilling rigs. In 1984, during the conference year, he was appointed to fill an unexpected opening at Matthews-Bayou Blue, a small, rural circuit near Houma, Louisiana. In 1992, the church sent Foreman to Algiers

United Methodist Church in the West Bank section of New Orleans, where he stayed until he retired in 1997. Foreman himself merely said that there is "no doubt" that the events of 1960 "hurt my ministry in the course of time" with regard to the appointments he received.[14]

Professional consequences for clergy who openly supported Foreman could also be dire. Clarence Snelling said that after he left New Orleans to attend graduate school in 1958, another Methodist clergyman, the Reverend Mr. Spencer Wren, became active in "a variety of integration activities in the city." In 1960, Wren supported Foreman. Wren served a church in the New Orleans suburb of Kenner, and when it was time for him to move, the bishop attempted to send him to a church "up in the delta country, in the Monroe district." At the Annual Conference gathering held just a week or so before Wren was to move, a lay leader from his new congregation "told him that if he came, the Klan would meet him at the edge of town and keep him from moving in, that he shouldn't accept the appointment, they didn't want him," Snelling said. Wren told the bishop and asked not to be sent to that church, but "the bishop said 'You're going.' So he took a leave." Snelling helped Wren obtain a church-related post with a community organization in Colorado, where Wren eventually returned to parish ministry. "In short, he was so active in race relations work in New Orleans that the laity up in Monroe knew about it and were very upset, and the bishop knew about it and was punishing him and sent him out of New Orleans on purpose," Snelling said.[15]

"THE DEACONESS HAS A NEW IMAGE"

Fae Daves and Laura Smith were employed not by the Louisiana Annual Conference or by the local congregation, but rather by the Woman's Division of Christian Service of The Methodist Church, which had long publicly favored integration; the "Charter of Racial Policies" reproduced as appendix B was approved in 1962, but an even earlier version had been approved by conference and jurisdictional women's societies a decade before. The 1962 document pledged, "We will open the facilities and services of all Woman's Division institutions without restriction based on race and make such policies clearly known." Therefore, though the two women's support for Foreman presented various kinds of physical risk to them, they incurred no risk of losing their employment as a result. Indeed, they would have been seen by the Woman's Division as fulfilling their proper professional role through their actions.

In 1962, the *Methodist Woman* discussed the status of the office of deaconess within the Methodist structure. "Today's Methodist deaconess has been relieved of many inconveniences endured by those of the early days." Working conditions were usually "adequate," and it was "no longer necessary for a deaconess to exist on a subsistence salary." However, serious new difficulties did exist: "she may serve under pressures somewhat different from those of her earlier sister. The deaconess serving in areas of racial tension may be called upon to stand firmly for unpopular principles she feels are right in the face of possible violent actions."[16] The women at St. Mark's must have been in the forefront of the author's thoughts, because less than two years before the article appeared, the facility in which they lived had been vandalized and threatened with worse destruction as a result of the church's stand on school desegregation.

Although she did not know it in 1960, Fae Daves would prove to be the last deaconess appointed to St. Mark's in the twentieth century. (Another was appointed to the reorganized center after Hurricane Katrina.) As discussed in chapter 5, when The Methodist Church began ordaining women in 1956, the opening of that professional route made the pursuit of consecration as a deaconess seem less attractive than it previously had to many young women. Leaders of the national deaconess program, under the direction of the former St. Mark's head resident, Mary Lou Barnwell, recognized that the office of deaconess would have to be made more attractive if the program were to survive.

Because the first deaconesses had been consecrated in the MEC in 1888, the year 1963 was deemed the seventy-fifth anniversary of the movement. The Woman's Division organized a major push for new deaconesses and set a goal of consecrating seventy-five women to celebrate the seventy-fifth anniversary. In June 1961, a national Methodist women's periodical published an article written by Barnwell and entitled, "Deaconesses Are Needed, Too: Seventy-five New Deaconesses by 1963!"[17] Inclusion of the word "too" in the title seems an acknowledgment on the part of either Barnwell or the editor—either way, an influential Methodist woman—that ordination was sapping the deaconess program.

In this article, Barnwell focused on how examples of the deaconesses' work could prove important and meaningful. One of her examples sounds much like what was happening at St. Mark's Community Center: "Deaconesses are needed in inner-city situations, where fear and unrest are undermining thousands of families; where employment of mothers leaves many children without adequate care; where older people have developed a sense of uselessness and loneliness; where juvenile delinquency has taken on new dimensions. Some of these areas have been deserted by the church. In others, there is a vision of the possibilities and responsibilities, but qualified workers are not available to render the needed services."[18] Her observation that "some of the areas have been deserted by the church" points to the fact that deaconess work could take women into arenas of service where pastoral ministry would be most unlikely to send them. The problems she listed were those that persons who received their compensation from a local church were unlikely to have time to deal with, even if they possessed the needed skills to do so. She also detailed the need for social welfare workers, especially in homes for children who had suffered "from the effects of broken homes and rejection," and "where the 'shape of the cure must fit the contour of the hurt.'"[19] Her use of the language about fitting "the contour of the hurt" emphasized that deaconesses were usually freer to adapt to the community they served than pastors of established congregations, a factor that might have been especially important to socially conscious young women in the early 1960s. Barnwell repeatedly used the phrase "qualified workers" in her writing, which one can interpret both as a comment that ministerial training did not often equip pastors to address effectively the kinds of social difficulties she mentions and as an acknowledgment of the increasing professionalization of the deaconess office.

Fae Daves wrote a comprehensive report on the center at St. Mark's in 1965. She discussed the importance of professional employees and the problems she experienced in obtaining them. She needed a staff "in sufficient number, adequately trained, who are not only Christian and dedicated, but who are mature, enabling persons, able to help people attain the fuller life desired for all." Barriers included the "mundane level" of salary; she said it was almost impossible to attract the kind of staff she had described at the levels of pay then offered. Daves noted that when she arrived at the center in 1948, salaries for women in church agencies were still "pitiful. We were just emerging from an era when deaconesses and home missionaries worked for an allowance plus room and board. (I started for $50 a month before the Great Depression of the 30s. During those days some joined our staff at Marcy Center Chicago, for as little as $35 a month.)" She said that despite a "gradual" rise in the salary scale since World War II, there had been "a decided drop in the number of candidates for church related vocations." St. Mark's was experiencing a particular problem in recruiting people with graduate degrees in social work, and the board had recently instituted a scholarship in that field, hoping to "train our own" employees.[20]

As part of Barnwell's national push for seventy-five new deaconesses, three deaconesses were assigned to full-time recruiting of new candidates, with one working on college campuses; a second recruiting among already employed, "professionally qualified workers"; and a third attending conference, district, and local church meetings. All three women recruited across the nation. They realized the need to package the office in more modern terms, and when Barnwell appeared at the annual meeting of the Commission on Deaconess Work in Detroit, she announced that, "The deaconess has a new image," one that contrasted "with the solemnity and the dark garb of the past." She likened Methodist deaconesses to "a domestic peace corps" and said substantive changes such as better salaries and a placement service had "helped upgrade the deaconesses."[21]

These strategies resulted in an achievement of the recruitment goal. Between 1960 and 1963, eighty-three candidates were accepted into the program, and during the anniversary year, twenty-five women were consecrated, "a record number."[22] To celebrate the anniversary and the record-breaking number of consecrations, Barnwell wrote an article about the traditional contributions of women to the church throughout the centuries, beginning with Phoebe, a woman described in Paul's New Testament letter to the Romans as a deacon (diakonos).[23] She cited a presentation by an editor of the Methodist Publishing House, who "called upon deaconesses to be nonconformists in a conformist society. This, too, has been a traditional role of women." Barnwell offered models of women who had been outstanding leaders in "effecting social reforms," including temperance leaders Frances Willard and Carrie Nation. Nation, in particular, was a "courageous woman" who "defied social customs to enter and break up saloons!"[24]

Using language about nonconformity and defiance of social customs was appropriate for women who were attempting to redefine their place in society during the early years of rising consciousness about women's rights issues. Susan Hill Lindley and, following her, Jean Miller Schmidt have discussed Methodist women's reliance on "soft feminism"—a strategy in which women neither unquestioningly accept assignment to the "women's sphere" nor openly defy its existence, but rather operate within the sphere all the while constantly endeavoring to enlarge it from within.[25]

For instance, Barnwell told the Commission on Deaconess Work in 1963 that deaconesses were "greatly concerned" about the status of women worldwide, "even without desiring to become a feminist movement." She observed that while women in "new nations" were gaining "leadership opportunities," she was seeing in the United States "a decline in use of women in policy and administrative situations." Specifically, she observed that in The Methodist Church, "where membership is predominantly women, fewer are chosen to represent the church in denominational and interdenominational considerations."[26] Concern for having appropriate representation in leadership for the female sex sounds like part of the feminist project, and her simultaneous assurance that deaconesses did not desire "to become a feminist movement" seems to be an example of couching a desire for an enlargement of the proper women's sphere in a deliberately nonthreatening way.

Later that year, she wrote of the deaconess program as "a spiritual movement" that could be traced back to the biblical figure of Phoebe and reminded readers that early Methodist deaconesses had established "hospitals, mission schools, homes, community centers and reached out to strengthen the life of the church in rural areas." She equated the story of the deaconess movement with "the story of the development of the social service program of The Methodist Church" and stated that it involved "leadership training and the reconciling love of Jesus Christ reaching out through his servants to his children. Looking to the future, we see boundless opportunities limited only by the measure of our obedience to his call."[27] This statement can easily be read as an attempt to provide reassurance that even while deaconesses might endeavor to become leaders, they would remain "obedient" servants—at least to Jesus.

In her position as national director of the program, Barnwell worked hard to prepare deaconesses to take on the kinds of national and international leadership roles that she desired to see Methodist women fill. She and her office staff in New York City constantly designed and offered training workshops that afforded deaconesses opportunities for enrichment and for learning about national and international issues. Along with her desire to prepare them for leadership, Barnwell thought it vital to give deaconesses in the field the ammunition they needed to combat the kind of ultraconservative opinions sometimes expressed in local churches, both for the purpose of defending programs she felt needed defending and for the purpose of helping the individual women feel more self-confident and less vulnerable to criticism. For example, when the United Nations Children's Fund (UNICEF) program came under attack in the 1960s because some of the funds were sent to children in Communist nations, some local churches stopped letting children collect for UNICEF on Halloween. In 1962, Barnwell arranged a workshop at the United Nations for thirty-four women. She said that because the group sat in on a meeting of the UNICEF Committee, they could no longer be told that UNICEF was "'of no value,' that it is 'wasting our money,' that it 'should be abandoned.'" The women were so moved by what they heard "that they spontaneously took an offering (true Methodist fashion) and made a contribution to UNICEF." She also arranged for them to have briefings by representatives of the National Council of Churches and the World Council of Churches, two organizations that conservatives often attacked. After their time in New York, the women journeyed to Washington, D.C., where they watched a session of Congress, sat in on a congressional committee meeting, met with their own members of Congress, and attended briefings by the staff of The Methodist Church's Board of Christian Social Concerns. Barnwell featured this workshop in an article for the *Methodist Woman* with comments from letters written by participants, including one who said, "I am reading the newspaper with more intelligent understanding." At such events, deaconesses were encouraged to take their newfound knowledge back to the Woman's Society of Christian Service (WSCS) and Wesleyan Service Guild groups in their communities and to their local congregations. Barnwell wrote: "On the Sunday following her return from the workshop in 1961, one deaconess wrote that the entire class period in church school had been devoted to criticism of United Nations, National Council of Churches, and World Council of Churches. Her fresh experience in the workshop enabled her to reply appropriately to the attacks and she was well fortified with interpretative literature which she distributed. In those few days she had gained competence and confidence to deal with such attacks."[28]

LEADERSHIP DEVELOPMENT FOR GIRLS

The programming that Barnwell and the other deaconesses had developed at St. Mark's was so well regarded nationally that the WSCS in the North Central Jurisdiction chose to study the facility as part of their 1961–62 focus on "Churches for New Times." A national Methodist women's publication noted that the purpose of the St. Mark's Community Center was "to provide a warm, friendly climate in which youth, with all their problems of insecurity today, can take root and develop, broaden their horizons, and find fulfillment for some of their basic needs."[29] In Fae Daves's opinion, fostering leadership among young women was "a strong point" of the overall St. Mark's program. The center offered a formal leadership training course, and she was happy to report in 1965 that several high school girls who were alumnae of the course would work at the center in the summer and that two of them were "thinking of social group work as a career because of their association with St. Mark's."[30]

Daves put great emphasis on the fact that while she was director of St. Mark's (from 1948 to 1966), "we considered ourselves a group work agency." This meant they were "more interested" in working with smaller groups than in trying to effect change in a large segment of the community. She saw their work as "a developmental program" rather than "rehabilitation." The goal, she said, "was really to help our young people grow so that they would be able to fill a responsible place in society."[31] As an illustration, she said that at a center where she worked before coming to St. Mark's, she was once away for six weeks. She came home to discover that a college student who was working at the center part-time and who had been assigned to work with a group of neighborhood girls had been elected chair of the group. She was dismayed that the young woman had not understood that the primary purpose of the endeavor was to let the participants learn to manage their own activities, and she had the young woman resign the post immediately.[32]

Personal Development for
St. Mark's Women

Since the beginning of the twentieth century, when the "Cult of True Woman-hood" was still firmly in place in American society and its religious institutions, women associated with settlements had been on the cutting edge of social action. They were powerful individuals who achieved great good for marginalized groups in society. It is not coincidental that the authors of a history of women in the Progressive Era attributed the accomplishments of such a powerful woman as Eleanor Roosevelt in part to her association with Florence Kelley and her training in settlement house work in New York City.[33]

St. Mark's also served as a training ground where individual women grew and flourished as denominational leaders, like Mary Lou Barnwell, and as community leaders, like Mary Morrison. Morrison was the longtime president of the community center's board of directors and the first female member of the St. Mark's congregation's board of stewards. One woman who grew up in the St. Mark's congregation remembered Morrison as a woman who "knew stuff, she knew how to get stuff done. She was active. She was a leader."[34]

Staff women, too, found their individual development deeply tied to their work at St. Mark's. Like the young women among their clientele who were urged toward spiritual and personal development, the staff members themselves were encouraged to grow. Laura Smith, who came to the center as a volunteer in 1947 and who was a paid employee from 1953 until 1966, filling at one time or another literally every position from janitor to director, is an excellent example. When she came to St. Mark's, she had not completed her high school education. Working with the women on the staff and living with them in the deaconess quarters, she was inspired to complete her GED and to attend college at a deaconess training facility in Kansas City. When she resigned from the center in 1966, it was to attend Tulane University, where she earned a master's degree in early childhood education. She was motivated to do so by the realization that she could not prepare for retirement on the salary she was earning at St. Mark's. Despite the necessity for leaving, she continued to love and support the facility and to feel grateful for the opportunities she had there. "Everything good in my life that ever happened to me, happened because of St. Mark's," she said.[35]

WOMEN SEEK INTEGRATION OF THE CENTER

It is ironic that the employees of the center were more ardent supporters of school desegregation in 1960 than some others in the congregation, because the center itself did not integrate until 1965. However, the tardiness of the facility's integration owed solely to continued resistance from the local board of directors, who faced pressure from the congregations of which they were a part. It was eventually the threat of losing United Fund monies (as over against pure religious conviction) that made the local board members change their minds.[36]

At Smith's instigation, the center had begun an extension program in 1963 for low-income persons who occupied the Iberville housing development, which was fairly near the center but separated from it by railroad tracks that were difficult for the children to cross. The development's managers donated an apartment for the community center's use, and Smith conducted many sorts of educational and religious projects for the residents there. At that time, all the residents of the project were white, including many Spanish-speaking Cuban immigrants.[37]

The Methodist news service reported that in the twelve months prior to May 20, 1964, the center had served "635 individuals, age range 4 to 90, from many racial backgrounds, several economic levels, from low to moderate income, on a nonsectarian basis." About half of them lived within walking distance, and "the others come from all the downtown area north to the lake and east to Chalmette.... Almost 700 individuals participated in the 1964 program of the center, which was the biggest ever."[38] The report said that when St. Mark's opened in 1909, its purpose was "to help new immigrants from southern Europe find their way to fuller life and productive citizenship in the new country of their adoption," and maintained that during the ensuing half-century, "the purpose has changed according to the needs of the people of the area."[39] In fact, however, the purpose and activities of the center had not changed as much as they had remained the same.

In her 1965 report to the Louisiana Annual Conference, Daves wrote that St. Mark's was founded as "the Church at work in the inner city—the Church reaching out that second mile without regard to race or creed to serve people." However, she placed an asterisk after the word "race," and at the bottom of the report, after her signature, added this note: "Actually we are not yet serving Negroes although they are a part of our neighborhood. As a Church Agency it seems too bad that we have not taken the initiative in this direction. Now it seems we will be forced to take this action if we are to continue as a participating member of the United Fund of New Orleans."[40]

Because more than two-fifths of the center's funding—41.7 percent—came from the United Fund (the predecessor organization of United Way), its financial influence over the board was powerful.[41] Daves's observation—"it seems too bad"—understated how sorrowful she felt because the church was being led to take what she deemed the Christian course of action as a result of coercion by a secular agency, and because the prospect of losing funds was more important to the board than the ethical high ground they lost by refusing integration.

She recalled for an interviewer in 1978 that she and her staff "were ready to integrate long before we could—but the board wasn't." She did point out that in some respects, St. Mark's had always been integrated, because it was the one place that racially mixed church and civic groups could come to hold meetings. Nevertheless, membership in the center was denied to black children and adults, which precluded their using the pool or gymnasium or joining any of the clubs. Architecture featuring very large windows, designed to catch any breeze, is common in New Orleans, and the St. Mark's building had a number of these large windows that opened out onto the street. The workers recalled small black children coming to the windows and asking permission to come into the center. They found it heart-breaking to try to explain to the children that one day they would be able to become members—but not yet.[42]

When she was asked by an interviewer in 1978 whether she personally had been trying to convince the board, Daves responded, "Oh, yes! For years." Her philosophy was that a community center should not have the right to call itself that if it denied services to a part of its community. Nevertheless, she said, "It just takes a long time to change. If you had seen the change in some of those people over the years. But it takes years to get that change." Daves employed many tactics in her efforts to get the board to alter its policy, including the regular compilation of demographic data. "I always kept the census figures and mapped our neighborhood to see what was there. . . . [W]e made one every time we had a census to see how much more our neighborhood was becoming black. Of course it would change a lot in other ways, too."[43]

A few board members were in agreement with Daves's and Smith's position; Daves pointed especially to Carmel Tackaberry, a former president of the board who had died in March 1962, and said, "Now she was the kind of a board member you look for . . . she would never have held up integration."[44] Yet the majority of the board resisted, in part because they believed that the white members would leave the center if blacks were admitted. In some respects, this pessimism was justified, because within two years of the first black members joining St. Mark's Community Center, the membership was entirely black.

A comprehensive report that Daves wrote just before her retirement in 1966 celebrated the establishment of the work at the Iberville housing development that had "opened doors" to Cuban families, and the fact that the center was now swinging open its doors "to the Negroes of our area." She wrote: "We have often felt concern for this group, and sometimes guilt for not extending our service sooner. It has been a difficult step to take because of the feeling of our members but now I believe they see the handwriting on the wall. Serving the whole neighborhood seems not only the logical but the only Christian thing to do."[45]

CROSS BURNING AT THE ST. MARK'S CAMP

The workers had also instituted a camping program to expose city children to life in the country. Although St. Mark's later acquired a camp of its own, at that time they were using a camp owned by the Salvation Army and located near Covington, north of Lake Pontchartrain. Laura Smith's service at St. Mark's included ten years as supervisor of the camping program. It was she who took the first group of black youngsters to the camp in 1966, soon after the center was integrated in September 1965. A cross was burned at the entrance to the property the night they arrived. Although no one was hurt physically during the incident, Smith said, it hurt "in other ways."[46]

DAVES, SMITH LEAVE THE CENTER

In 1965 and 1966, there was an almost complete turnover of community center personnel. When Daves retired in April 1966, Laura Smith was the only remaining member of the staff who had been there as long as one year, and she left the next year to attend graduate school at Tulane University.[47] Daves's replacement, Louise Sharp, a graduate of Scarritt College, had some experience in community center work, but she was not a deaconess. She did not share the deaconess position about living in the community she served. She resided in the living quarters in the building for only a short time before moving into a home on the west bank of the Mississippi River, some distance from St. Mark's.[48]

By the time of her 1979 interview, Daves had concluded that in reality, the center never truly integrated, but rather simply converted from an all-white clientele to an all-black one. "That first year while Laura was still there, she managed to keep the membership kind of even . . . Negro and white. But you see what happened was that just gradually . . . the white dropped out!"[49] The question remains unanswered as to how many of those who stopped attending would have done so if they had not already moved some distance away (often as a result of white flight) and had not been driving back into the St. Mark's neighborhood to participate.

WERE INTEGRATIONISTS "INEFFECTIVE"?

In their history of public education in New Orleans, Donald Devore and Joseph Logsdon wrote: "Desegregation failed to produce immediate widespread change within the New Orleans public school system, but the presence, during the 1960–61 school year, of four black students at two formerly all-white schools contained the seeds of change."[50] It contained those seeds precisely because the St. Mark's pastor, Andy Foreman, broke the white boycott, thus allowing integration efforts just enough success to thwart the belief of white segregationists that they could prevent integration forever.

Nevertheless, Devore and Logsdon maintained that the work of integrationists was ineffective and that even moderates achieved limited effectiveness in bringing about the change. The authors admit that in the years after *Brown,* as the state's attempts to maintain segregation became more futile, "The few proponents of desegregation who did exist in the white community increased their numbers somewhat." Despite this, they said, "The few courageous white integrationists such as James Dombrowski of the SCEF had little influence of any kind." They also assessed that moderates, "to the extent that they mobilized," were faced with a total absence of leadership from elected officials, and that because they had to rely on people in business and the professions instead, they were unable to have much influence in the struggle to desegregate. "And the number of moderates always remained small," Devore and Logsdon added. "For example, when a group organized by SCEF presented the school board a petition supporting desegregation with 179 signatures, the segregationists countered with a petition signed by thousands."[51]

Devore and Logsdon stated that only the threat of the closure of public schools prompted "white integrationists and moderates" to act, and that the action they took was the organization of Save Our Schools (S.O.S.). "[B]ecause the moderates greatly outnumbered the integrationists, S.O.S. refused to endorse desegregation on its merits. They made it clear they only wanted to keep the schools open, even at the cost of limited desegregation." Rather than stressing the ethical implications of racism, they tried to appeal to the self-interest of the community, hammering home the idea that school closure would "inevitably" lead to a rise in juvenile delinquency and a decline in the city's economic condition, for "new industries refuse to move into an area in which the public schools have been closed."[52] Historians Edward L. Pinney and Robert S. Friedman, whose monograph considers *Political Leadership and the School Desegregation Crisis in Louisiana,* also maintain that integrationists had "no effect at all" on the situation in New Orleans. They use the fact that the S.O.S. organization had to portray themselves as simply interested in keeping schools open as evidence that those who favored integration were ineffective advocates for their cause.[53]

Historical assessments such as these that conclude the work of liberals and, to a lesser extent, moderates in support of integration was "ineffective" seem to overlook a crucial part of the historical picture—namely, that integration was achieved. To contend that the legal system alone implemented integration is to reveal a naiveté about how much force a law can bring to bear on a society if almost no one agrees with it. It is by no means insignificant that the *New Orleans Times-Picayune* quote from United States Representative F. Edward Hebert in the story printed the day after the *Brown* decision was handed down (as discussed in chapter 5) referred to President Andrew Jackson's defiance of the Supreme Court in the early 1830s regarding the removal of Native

Americans from Georgia. Jackson stated publicly that if Chief Justice John Marshall and the Supreme Court did not want the Native Americans removed from Georgia, they should send their army to prevent it. In fact, the Court did not command an army, and therefore the Court's decision was, for all intents and purposes, nullified as the Cherokee people were forcibly removed along the Trail of Tears.[54]

Both interposition and secession were mentioned by elected statewide officials as possible courses of action for the state of Louisiana to prevent school integration in 1960, but something, somewhere changed just enough hearts and minds to make the white southerners who opposed integration give up their battle. The first chairperson of the SCEF-sponsored Citizens Forum on Integration, John Winn, observed that white southern liberals believed that what they could contribute in the civil rights movement was to make more people "agree in principle" that integration was the right thing to do. To dismiss the work of changing people's minds and hearts as useless is to ignore important dimensions of the civil rights movement. The question that preoccupied Foreman's academic advisor, Allan Knight Chalmers—"How do you change the social attitudes of people?"—is still worth asking, and to dismiss out of hand the work of people who agitate for change, especially when that change is actually accomplished, takes an amazingly short-range view of historical process.[55]

Further, the assertion that it was only "moderates" rather than "integrationists" who had any impact at all in the New Orleans situation—that is, that those who concealed their approval for integration as an ethical course of action and instead pretended to be interested only in pragmatic issues of keeping public schools open or staving off federal intervention were the only effective agents for social change—needs examination. If voices that seem extreme are not raised in public discussion, then "moderates" are no longer moderate in comparison, and the fact that this may sound simplistic does not make it any less true. The voices of those who believed integration to be the ethical course of action were fewer in number and lower in volume than the voices that demanded the continuance of segregation, but this does not lead to the inevitable conclusion that those fewer voices did not make a meaningful contribution to public discourse on the issue.

Assertions about aspects of race relations larger than school integration in one city can also be viewed through the lens of the century-long history of

St. Mark's. The argument of one scholar that the Social Gospel is by definition a racist movement was simply not born out in the real world of St. Mark's. The deaconesses of St. Mark's were steeped in classic Social Gospel training and were part of a movement deeply rooted in Social Gospel principles and methodology. It was largely the work of Fae Daves, Julia Southard Campbell, Nettie Stroup, Mary Lou Barnwell, and the other deaconesses who served at St. Mark's and who were committed to racial equality that created a congregation that would publicly support Foreman as he took his radical action in 1960. To assert that if a person is not a racist, then he or she cannot possibly be operating from the Social Gospel mindset is to skew the definition of the Social Gospel movement so profoundly as to make it meaningless. However, the work of Ralph Luker, who attempted to prove that the Social Gospel was *not* racist, also began from a flawed definition of the movement—one that omitted the practitioners of the Social Gospel who were female and southern from consideration—and I contend that it is precisely this omission that left his work without the weight of evidence it should, and could, have had.[56]

This is not to deny that the Methodist women of New Orleans, including the laity who made up the women's societies and the deaconesses who were appointed to the St. Mark's Community Center, did not approach their work with persons from other races and cultures with the same level of sensitivity that would be considered appropriate today. Yet it is irresponsible for historians to judge women who lived in the Deep South in the early 1960s by the standards of the early twenty-first century, and the stands that the women's societies were taking then and had taken as far back as 1917 in pursuit of better race relations can legitimately be called liberal, if not radical, for that day.

Overall, the school desegregation crisis in New Orleans revealed great paradoxes in the ideologies, statements, and behaviors of those involved. As detailed in chapter 5, in May 1954, officials of the Roman Catholic Church immediately spoke out in approval of the *Brown* decision and made courageous public statements about the correctness of integration, but when the time came in 1960 to fulfill their pledge to integrate Catholic schools at the same time public schools were integrated, they failed to do so. This failure on their part totally disrupted the integration of public schools by giving white parents a good, segregated alternative for their children. On the other hand, the socially and theologically conservative Andy Foreman, whose public statements were anything but ardent appeals for racial tolerance, is the person whose actions broke the white boycott and forced integrated public schools in New Orleans into existence, at literal risk of his and his family's lives. Despite the various indications of extreme conservatism on Foreman's part, few, if any, white Methodist pastors in the Louisiana Annual Conference have taken equal risks, either professional or personal, to support radical social change. Foreman maintained, "My involvement in the school integration program was primarily my own initiative," and his explanation for his actions was simple: "I simply wanted the people to know that as their pastor, I did this because I believed that it was what God wanted done, and that I understood that many of them had mixed feelings. . . . I wanted the church to make a witness to the community that we believed that we're all God's children, and we all have a right to do what others do. I made a decision on the basis of a Christian conviction that this is what it's all about—this is what God's trying to get us to see."[57]

It is also important to recognize that in 1960 New Orleans, people who fell into any category that would be recognized today as "racially progressive" were few and far between. Rabbi Julian Feibelman of Temple Sinai, who helped organize the Citizens Forum on Integration and who made courageous public stands, such as reading to the school board the petition that called for conforming to the *Brown* decision, was following in the tradition of many other southern rabbis, including his predecessor at Temple Sinai, Max Heller, when he took liberal racial stands. He maintained, "I have always thought of myself as a liberal." Nevertheless, in his 1980 autobiography, Feibelman discussed at length the negative aspects of integration: "Jim Crow is buried, but the grave is desecrated by the lowering standards in school and college to admit all on a false consideration of color rather than merit," he wrote. Regarding the *Brown* decision, his opinion was that although he supported the court's decision as a matter of principle, based "on many Biblical texts, on the dire effect of disfranchisement, and on the ultimate horror of complete denial that had come to its peak in the Hitlerian and Nazi edicts," he had since come to believe that blacks were "not ready" to receive educational freedom. "Often, we are not ready for the rights we may feel we have attained. The decision came too quickly, and neither the whites nor the Negroes were prepared for it." He also made disparaging comments about labor unions and other causes that most people who self-identify as "liberals" would be likely to support.[58]

Just as Methodist deaconesses, now labeled "conservatives," were forced in the 1920s and 1930s to answer frequent charges that they were operating too far to the left because of their openness toward working with people of color, in the 1950s, accusations of being Communist dogged Methodists like James Dombrowski, whose hearing in New Orleans is discussed in chapter 5 (and on a national level, Bishop G. Bromley Oxnam and the Methodist Federation for Social Action, a Social Gospel era action arm of the church), primarily because of their support for integration. It is difficult to understand today exactly how risky it was to speak out in favor of rights for black citizens in the mid-twentieth-century South. The decisions of Fae Daves and Laura Smith to continue to live in the St. Mark's building at risk of their lives and to continue to press the board of directors to integrate the community center, at the risk of damaging their personal relationships and their standing in the community, were truly courageous in that place and time.

CONCLUSIONS

On the occasion of the seventy-fifth anniversary of the deaconess movement in 1963, Eleanor Clarkson recounted the history of the movement for readers of the Methodist women's mission magazine *World Outlook.* Clarkson maintained that Methodist deaconesses had coped with the "tremendous" changes during the past seventy-five years by cultivating a stance of "intelligent flexibility." This flexibility had allowed them to abandon the requirement for the deaconess "garb" in 1927 so that women could assert their own individuality; to change the pattern of "congregating together in a deaconess home" as it became more acceptable for single women to live in their own apartments; and to become less tied to immovable structures that were not always able to meet changing needs of changing neighborhoods, relying more on the women themselves, who were free to move when the need arose. Further, as colleges and universities became more open to the presence of female students, and as the professionalization of the work of the deaconesses increased, "the specialized deaconess training school has given way," and "[a] broader training secured in an academic setting has become necessary." Alluding perhaps to the fact that deaconesses were no longer automatically expected to leave the office when they married, the author spoke of a decrease in need "for the parish deaconess" and an increasing need "for directors of Christian education with a lifetime attitude toward their work," which had led more deaconesses to enter the field of religious education.[59]

Another part of the political backdrop of the 1960s was the presidencies of John F. Kennedy and Lyndon B. Johnson, with their emphasis on governmental care for the poor and disadvantaged. Clarkson also stated that because of the increased services provided by hospitals and the wider availability of public assistance, few deaconesses were needed in 1963 to give home care to ill poor people. "In fact," she wrote, "many of the social services performed by deaconesses in the early days of the movement have been taken over by the state. Thus, referral to a public agency has become not only more feasible but desirable in order that the deaconess of today can give more of her time to filling needs only the church can meet."[60]

This represents an interesting turnaround from the challenges of 1911–12, when the women had to fight those who believed that social service was not an appropriate activity for the church. The 1960s forced redefinition of the deaconess movement as government took on more aspects of social service, as the women's movement and women's ordination both broadened and narrowed opportunities for deaconess leadership within the church, and as the civil rights movement forced them to take the kinds of unpopular stands that earlier, universally well-regarded Methodist women, such as Lillie Meekins, had never been forced to take.

Overall, I maintain that trying to attach labels to the Social Gospel practitioners in the South can be a mistaken practice, but this is particularly true if the historian doing the labeling does not take seriously enough the religious motivations of Methodist women. Women whose cultural upbringings and natural political leanings might easily fit the description of "conservative" nevertheless acted in ways that helped subvert the established, segregated order of things. Southern Methodist deaconesses were not primarily occupied with maintaining the status quo; rather, they were primarily occupied with the idea of doing what they could to help bring in the Kingdom—the Reign of God—which they envisioned as a place where all would be equal. The deaconesses were often radical, Winn and Snelling were self-proclaimed liberals, and Foreman was a theological and political conservative who proved to be as radical in his stand against racism as any of the group. One primary historical lesson from the events of 1960 may be that Christian practice, as embodied by Christians, is far too nuanced and too complicated to benefit from simplistic attempts to apply secular political or ideological labels to it.

Andy Foreman's greatest disappointment surrounding his years at St. Mark's was that the congregation itself did not become integrated. Despite its resolution to open the doors to black worshippers and members, there was "no influx of blacks walking through our open doors," he said. A few black individuals did visit worship services from time to time, mostly, he thought, from curiosity, but none stayed to become an active member. He also regretted that he followed the instructions of his bishop and severely limited his speaking engagements, turning down almost all of the many invitations he received to talk about his experiences. The only major body he addressed was The Methodist Church's General Board of Social Concerns in Washington, D.C. He gave almost no interviews to the press, refusing even television network newspeople who tried to speak with him. "The bishop had put a quietus on those things, so I didn't."[61]

In later life, though, Foreman believed that was not the best way to have proceeded. "If I had it to do over again, in retrospect, I would do it differently," he said. "I feel that the church failed to make its imprint in the racial crisis in a way that would have brought people together. We were more on the defensive rather than the offensive. We did not move to take the positive note that had been sounded and help it work." He thought the church at large, and particularly The Methodist Church in Louisiana and in New Orleans, was willing to go along with integration only so far as it could "without getting penalized—[getting] funds cut off and so forth. I really think that we had not faced up to the issue of integration of the public schools and made up our minds that the church was to take the lead in the process."[62]

Despite the fact that Andy Foreman's career path after he defied the white boycott at William Frantz Elementary in 1960 was not a positive one, it is significant, if not amazing, that he was able to remain as pastor of the St. Mark's congregation for another five years. This speaks volumes about the nature of the worshippers there. Although the itinerancy system in Methodism removes authority from local congregations over who will serve as their pastor, the fact remains that if members complain sufficiently, the hierarchy will move a pastor.

The willingness of the St. Mark's congregation to retain Foreman as their leader and to pass a resolution officially supporting his stand says that despite the exceptions presented by a few members, the group as a whole was far more tolerant of integration than most other New Orleans congregations at that time.

The term used for the title of the 1965 article that deemed the former head resident at St. Mark's, Mary Lou Barnwell, "the length and shadow" of the deaconess movement—"Loving Trouble-Makers"—is a wonderfully descriptive and apt designation for most deaconesses.[63] So far as deaconesses were concerned, success did not necessarily require a sea change in their communities, but could rather be perceived in the lives of individuals. By 1960, the women of St. Mark's had lovingly influenced enough individuals to create a place for Foreman to stand on the school integration issue.

PART IV

Post-1965
and Conclusions

8

SINCE 1965

This chapter, covering the time between 1965 and the landfall of Hurricane Katrina, is an epilogue to the story of St. Mark's that this book has recounted. It discusses a few selected events from that period, focusing in part on the years immediately after the last deaconess retired. Programming in the decade immediately preceding Katrina's landfall is also examined briefly for the purpose of facilitating the next chapter's comparison of activities at the center at the beginning of the twentieth century with activities at the beginning of the twenty-first.

After 1965, one more name change took place for the St. Mark's congregation. When The Methodist Church merged with the Evangelical United Brethren to create the United Methodist Church (UMC) in 1968, the worshipping congregation at 1130 North Rampart Street became St. Mark's United Methodist Church, which it remains today. As noted earlier, the community center was reorganized after Katrina, and it is now known as North Rampart Community Center.

POST-DEACONESS LEADERSHIP

In 1965, Lloyd Anderson "Andy" Foreman left St. Mark's Methodist Church. The next year, Fae Daves, the last Methodist deaconess appointed to St. Mark's Community Center until after Katrina, retired, and the longtime center employee, deaconess-school-trained Laura Smith, left to attend graduate school.

Louise Sharp, who was never a deaconess and who had not previously served on the staff at St. Mark's, became director when Daves retired. Like many of the deaconesses, Sharp was a graduate of Scarritt College. However, before coming to St. Mark's, she had not been engaged in community work, but rather served as director of Christian education at Rayne Memorial Methodist Church, a white-membership congregation located on St. Charles Avenue, just a few miles but also worlds away from St. Mark's. The St. Mark's newsletter described her as someone who had "much experience in [the] Louisiana conference in youth work and camping."[1] However, Methodist youth camps were at that time completely segregated by race, and it is most unlikely that working at Rayne would have given her much opportunity to get to know young African American people like those who lived in Tremé.

Sharp is a part of this chapter's discussion because seven years later, an article in the national Methodist women's publication, *Response,* portrayed Sharp as a kind of savior-figure for the center. There is so little published material about St. Mark's in the 1960s that it seems important to correct a false picture presented in a nationally distributed publication. Entitled "Community Centers Are No Longer Child's Play," the *Response* piece made the point that Methodist facilities had become increasingly responsive to modern urban problems. The author wrote that "sources around the Center" considered Sharp's arrival at St. Mark's to have occasioned a "watershed" year: "For example, before she came, the St. Mark's Board of Directors was made up mainly of middle-class housewives who, while earnest and diligent, found it difficult to relate closely to the community residents. Today, the Board is made up of one-third United Methodists . . . , one-third neighborhood people, and one-third qualified and interested residents at large. Five years ago, there was a single token black on the board; today, over half the board is black."[2]

However, all my interviewees who expressed an opinion felt that her tenure actually represented a setback for race relations. They saw Fae Daves and Laura Smith as much more deeply committed to integration. Several individuals mentioned that Sharp was the first director who ever moved her living quarters out of the building, a step they believed she took because she was fearful of residing in the racially mixed neighborhood. One longtime employee who is black believed her to be less comfortable working with black people than previous directors.[3]

Furthermore, the move toward inclusion of persons other than middle-class females on the board of directors actually began during Daves's administration, when it was becoming clear that they would lose United Way funds if the center did not integrate. In the early 1960s, the board was composed of representatives from each of the women's societies in the district, but Daves recruited several men to serve, as well. Some had legal or financial expertise and would, Daves believed, be more willing to face the reality of what losing United Way sponsorship would mean and therefore much more apt to vote to integrate.[4] Among those she recruited was the Reverend Mr. John Winn, who had been influenced as a youth by the deaconesses at St. Mark's. Winn's work after the *Brown* decision with the Citizens Forum on Integration (CFI) was explored in chapter 5, and his public stances about school desegregation would have made it evident that he would not be averse to integrating the center. In fact, Winn said he was serving as chair of the board later on when David Billings, a very strong activist against racism, was hired as director.

Though all previous head residents and/or directors of the community center had also been members and active in lay leadership of the St. Mark's congregation, Sharp never joined St. Mark's Methodist Church and did not attend worship there. The deaconesses had not worked within the congregation housed in the same building where they lived because it was part of their responsibilities as employees of the center—it was not—but rather because they saw the activities of the center and the congregation as organically linked, and because it was the most natural place for them to worship and to receive spiritual nourishment and to offer their own spiritual leadership as laywomen. After Fae Daves retired, the relationship between the community center and the worshipping congregation that had shared its building since 1923 began to decline.

When she moved out of the building, Sharp apparently removed all the center's records from the center to her home on the west bank of the river.[5] She resigned in 1974, moved back to Mississippi, and is now deceased. She apparently never returned the records to the center, and their current whereabouts, if they even still exist, remains a mystery.

APPOINTMENT OF FIRST BLACK PASTOR

In January 1965, St. Mark's Methodist Church had 245 adult and youth members, with "another 50 to 100 children, youth and adults . . . a part of our constituency."[6] By 1972, the congregation had dwindled to an average of eighteen in attendance at worship, and their average age was sixty-four. The membership prepared a resolution to dissolve the congregation, and it was presented at a May 21 meeting of the administrative board. The district superintendent, the Reverend Dr. Robert F. Harrington, persuaded the group to delay acting on the resolution for one week, and the one week has stretched into almost four decades.

Harrington probably did not have to be very persuasive, because the group had already prepared another document to accompany the resolution for dissolution; it was a list of suggestions for how the Annual Conference might keep the congregation alive. These included financial subsidies for pastoral support and the appointment of "a dynamic black preacher" to "bring blacks back into the realm of Christ" and a white assistant pastor who could minister to hippies inhabiting the French Quarter.[7]

In June 1972, a black clergyman, the Reverend Mr. Edward Albert Kennedy Jr., was appointed to St. Mark's. Kennedy was well educated; he was about to receive a doctoral degree and had served in administrative and/or teaching positions at several universities. Mary Morrison wrote a press release for the *Vieux Carré Courier* about Kennedy's appointment, in which she recalled the 1960 incidents involving the Foremans and William Frantz Elementary School, including the vandalism at the parsonage and the church. She said, "Though the incident seems long ago it was the beginning of a public stand on the part of St. Marks' [*sic*] parishioners with regard to race relations that his [*sic*] continued to this day and has culminated in another 'first' in this field." She provided a copy of the release for the 1979 oral history project on St. Mark's and attached a note saying she had sent it to the weekly newspaper published in the French Quarter "because it not only seemed to be news, but good news, and I guess that is why they never published it. If the congregation had developed a schism over Dr. Kennedy's appointment or if some of the members had picketed the church in protest, we'd have been on the front page of every paper in New Orleans."[8]

BILLINGS LEADS CENTER AND CONGREGATION

When Sharp resigned as director in 1974, David Billings, who had been employed in the center's business office for two years, took the position. Some twenty-five years later, he believed that Daves, Smith, and Sharp did as well as they could have given the circumstances, but he nevertheless viewed the integration process at the center as having been handled with what would, judged with twenty-first-century standards and understandings, be considered a "paternalistic approach."[9] In 1977, Billings was also appointed as pastor of the St. Mark's Methodist Church when the previous pastor left in mid-year. The St. Mark's pastorate was a position he "had longed for but never voiced," Billings said. As the first person to hold simultaneously the official leadership of both the congregation and the center, he was able to heal some of the rifts that had occurred in the decade just past.

During his tenure, the center's staff tended to focus on community activism, sharing many of the same emphases as secular institutions in similar urban settings. They did meet some resistance from more conservative elements of the United Methodist Church, which mirrored the resistance that all political leftists were meeting from conservatives during the 1970s, an era of polarization marked by conflict over U.S. involvement in Vietnam, the Watergate scandal, and other social crises.[10]

Billings was not ordained at that time, because he had not graduated from seminary, and so he left both the directorship of the center and the pastorate at St. Mark's in 1981 to attend a new program in urban ministry at New York Theological Seminary. He also worked for the UMC's General Board of Missions during his studies there. He is now ordained and appointed to a social service agency devoted to combating racism. He is married to Margery Freeman, who conducted the 1979 oral history project on St. Mark's funded by the General Commission on Archives and History.[11]

ST. MARK'S CONTINUES TO FOSTER WOMEN'S LEADERSHIP

Margery Freeman and another longtime member of St. Mark's, Judy Watts, were among the early second-wave feminists in New Orleans. Thus St. Mark's became a cradle for the mid-twentieth-century women's movement, a development that would no doubt have excited Methodist suffragists like Elvira Beach Carré and Hattie Parker, who brought St. Mark's into being and nurtured it a half-century before.[12]

As noted earlier, the achievement of ordination for women, a right for which the work of Carré, Parker, and other laywomen laid the groundwork, had a negative impact on the deaconess program. Although the office still existed, only a few women were consecrated as deaconesses in the early decades after ordination became a possibility for women. However, in recent years there has been resurgence in interest in a professional yet lay position, and the number of new deaconesses is increasing.

The number of ordained women in the UMC also continues to grow. In 2008, slightly more than one-half of students in mainline seminaries, including those sponsored by the UMC, were female. Barriers to women's professional advancement in the church—which Susie Stanley has termed "the stained glass ceiling"—are very slowly being removed.[13] Several women have served in the pulpit of the St. Mark's congregation since ordination for women was approved, including the Reverend Ms. Marta Sanfiel, the Reverend Dr. Millicent Feske, the Reverend Ms. Marva Mitchell, the Reverend Ms. Roshan Kalantar, and the Reverend Ms. Anita Dinwiddie.

HOMOSEXUALITY BECOMES THE NEW "CUTTING EDGE" ISSUE

Since the 1990s, much of the debate within the United Methodist Church and other mainstream Protestant denominations has centered on the issue of homosexuality, and again St. Mark's has found itself at the forefront of controversy. The congregation is a member of the Reconciling Congregations movement, which provides UMC congregations with a method of publicly declaring themselves open to membership and lay leadership of gay and lesbian individuals. As of 2010, St. Mark's was the only United Methodist Church in Louisiana that had officially identified itself as "Reconciling."[14]

A sign outside the sanctuary declares that St. Mark's United Methodist Church is "A Reconciling Faith Community" that meets for worship at 10 o'clock on Sunday mornings. Lest anyone miss the subtext of the sign, as many easily might, an additional self-descriptive message was added to the outside wall around 2004 stating that St. Mark's is a "church fellowship which recognizes and seeks to embody the truth that all people are the children of God regardless of race, sexual orientation, life history, education, place of birth, age. . . . God's love is not only for all but God's Spirit seeks to create us into a community filled with genuine care and love for one another."

In decades past, congregational leaders have taken other public stands on the issue. The files of St. Mark's UMC contain a letter from Margery Freeman, the congregation's representative to the board of the Greater New Orleans Federation of Churches, tendering her resignation from the federation. She resigned because it had refused admission to the local congregation of the Metropolitan Community Church, a denomination especially open to gay and lesbian persons, not only as members but also as ordained clergy.[15]

However, the act that many New Orleanians are most familiar with is the congregation's permitting memorial services to be conducted at St. Mark's for the gay men killed in the 1973 arson-caused fire at the Upstairs Bar in the French Quarter. Several other local churches had refused to allow services to be held in their sanctuaries. Among those killed in the blaze were the pastor and several members of the Metropolitan Community Church.[16] The year 2008 marked the thirty-fifth anniversary of the fire, and several national organizations honored St. Mark's for its role after the tragedy.[17] The 2008–9 Prospect 1 art installations around the city included a display at the Contemporary Arts Center that focused on the fire, and the memorial service at St. Mark's was featured as a part of that installation constructed by artist Skylar Fein.

However, this position of openness regarding homosexuality has not been taken without the cost of internal conflict. When the St. Mark's pastor, the Reverend Mr. Jerry James, wrote a letter to the editor of the *New Orleans Times-Picayune* in 1977 expressing the view that homosexuality was not, in and of itself, sinful, member Mary Morrison wrote a follow-up letter vehemently denying that he spoke for the congregation and expressing her own disagreement with his stand.[18] Although she officially remained a member of St. Mark's until her death, Morrison stopped attending services there, and some members thought the reason for her (and some other members') exodus was the congregation's stance on homosexuality. (Nevertheless, historian Pamela Tyler, who interviewed Morrison for her book on the Independent Women's Organization, believed that Morrison would have been tolerant toward homosexuals, because as a French Quarter preservationist, she was accepting of their residing in the Quarter.)[19]

Threats of Vandalism and Violence over Racial Openness

Homosexuality was not the only source of controversy surrounding St. Mark's at the end of the twentieth century. In 1999, Murphy J. "Mike" Foster was running for reelection as governor of Louisiana. It came to light that he had once paid white supremacist David Duke for a copy of Duke's mailing list. The former grand wizard of the Ku Klux Klan, Duke had been elected to the state House of Representatives, and he had made the runoff in both a United States Senate race and a gubernatorial race in the early 1990s. Because Foster did not actually use the list, many Louisianans considered the money to have been, in reality, a payoff to keep Duke from entering the race and to garner his support for Foster. A number of individuals who believed that Foster's connections with Duke should have received more attention during the campaign formed an organization called Mobilization to End Racism in Government Everywhere (M.E.R.G.E.).

In one of its meetings held at St. Mark's UMC, the group decided to send a petition to Foster urging him to either publicly renounce Duke (something he had already indicated he was not going to do) or to resign. M.E.R.G.E. garnered some media coverage, and one Sunday morning before church, the Reverend Mr. Gregor Dike, who was serving as both pastor at St. Mark's UMC and director of the community center, found a letter in the St. Mark's mailbox. The letter, signed, "United Klans of the Crescent City Chapter 30," was directed to Suzanne Bundy, a spokeswoman for M.E.R.G.E. It began with a statement of what the group wanted: "Here are our simple demand; you will announce that your organization was wrong in its prosecution of Governor Foster and Mr. Duke and withdraw the petition. This will be done before July 30th."[20]

Rife with spelling, punctuation, and grammatical errors, the letter continued with a series of obscenity-laden threats about what would happen if M.E.R.G.E. did not capitulate to its demands. "First, we will blow to hell that nigger church your using (plastic undetectable explosives have already been placed inside and can be detonated at any chosen time!)" Then, the letter said, they would "eliminate" all the members of M.E.R.G.E. "through very violent methods" and then "go after liberal, nigger loving whites that sign your petition." The writer said the group was "really disappointed in you Ms. Bundy, we would've thought that a sociologist would know that whites are superior to niggers and other minorities." They urged her to "take a walk around the neighborhood next to that nigger church on Rampart and, if you survive, you can write a report on nigger 'equality.'"

They boasted that their membership had tripled since M.E.R.G.E. announced the petition drive. "You claim to have 60 members, we now have 157 members and growing!" They professed to have been "stockpiling ammunition and arms for a long time, we would love nothing better than to be able to use them against niggers and communists." The letter concluded with a personal threat to Bundy—"sleep well tonight because we know where you live"—and a last obscene insult aimed at her.[21] The content makes clear the group's opinion of St. Mark's, which it refers to twice as "that nigger church." The phrase is an echo of the terminology that the Reverend Mr. Gene Faurie recalled being commonly used about St. Mark's back at the time of the school desegregation crisis.[22]

In a July 30 *New Orleans Times-Picayune* article, Dike was quoted as saying he made copies of the letter as soon as he found it and distributed them to people arriving for worship that morning, so that they could decide for themselves whether they wished to stay for the service. No one left. Once the service was over, he contacted the police and the FBI. An employee at the Southern Poverty Law Center's Klanwatch section told the *Times-Picayune* that their records did not list any New Orleans group called "United Klans of the Crescent City," but that this did not mean such a group did not exist. Contacted for a response to the incident, David Duke said he thought the letter was "bogus." He told the reporter: "I've never heard of any such group and I do not think such an organization exists. I think it is a hoax put on by M.E.R.G.E. to give them publicity. This has happened in other parts of the country."[23]

The community center staff had to notify the parents of five hundred young people enrolled in the center's programs about the threat. They hired a security guard to monitor the premises, but it is doubtful that anyone believed the guard could prevent an attack, particularly a detonation of already planted explosives. A key employee of the center, Alexis Brent, said Dike wanted M.E.R.G.E. to stop meeting at St. Mark's because he felt it was not the members of the group, but rather the children and staff members who spent extensive amounts of time in the building who were truly at risk. However, prominent members of the congregation who were active in M.E.R.G.E. were intent on it meeting there, and they cited the long St. Mark's heritage of activism on social issues.[24] Although the polity of the United Methodist Church gives the pastor of a congregation authority to decide what meetings can and cannot be held in its buildings, Dike was unwilling to impose his will on the group, and they continued to meet in the sanctuary. The police continued to investigate, but no one was ever arrested for making the threat, and the problem died away after Foster was reelected handily.[25]

TURN OF THE TWENTY-FIRST CENTURY PROGRAMMING

In the year 2000, St. Mark's offered some programming that would be expected at any similar community center, including basic education and literacy classes and tutoring for adults, and an after-school program that included training in computer literacy, tutoring, art, music, swimming lessons, and a variety of organized sports. However, the center was also engaged in innovative urban ministries held up as models in nationwide church publications.[26] For instance, the cover of a 1999 issue of the United Methodist magazine, *Interpreter,* pictured two students at work at the center's Tremé Corner Café; the "teaser" promoting the story inside read: "From ex-con to gourmet cook." The café, located just a few blocks from the center, was staffed by high-school dropouts who learned "every part of the restaurant business from dishwashing to bookkeeping to cooking." To work there, youth were required to be enrolled in a general equivalency diploma (GED) program and they received tutoring for the GED at the café in the afternoons. Twenty students per year were placed in New Orleans restaurants after working at the café.[27]

The *Interpreter* article also featured a success story from the CUBEY program—Caregivers United for Better Educated Youth—which offered training for certification in early childhood development for child-care providers. In 2000, 130 providers who were serving approximately 650 children were enrolled. The center provided nutritional monitoring and reimbursement for meals for children in the trainees' care. Off-site, the center sponsored the Carver Day Care Program, which supplied free on-site child care, parenting classes, and health care for up to fifty teenage mothers at a local junior-senior high school.[28]

Perhaps the center's most ambitious undertaking was the Street Academy, an alternative school for seventh to tenth graders designated as being at risk of failure in traditional educational settings. The school had 110 students in the 2000–2001 academic year, and there were plans to expand it to a full middle and high school with approximately two hundred students by the year 2003.[29]

Proving to be a surprisingly good motivator for the students, the center's jazz program was an especially appropriate effort for young New Orleanians. Its creators took inspiration from studies that linked music education to improved academic performance. Free lessons were available to students who performed well in school, and the program furnished musical instruments to those who needed them. The project received the ultimate compliment in 1998, when the center's band was invited to perform at JazzFest (otherwise known as the New Orleans Jazz and Heritage Festival). The *New Orleans Times-Picayune* featured the St. Mark's Tremé Jazz Ensemble, noting that "As the opening act in the Kids' Tent, the group will perform five jazz pieces written . . . especially for the fest."[30]

Interpreter recognized the jazz program as a model urban ministry. The magazine ran a sidebar, "How To Make Your Church A Community Center," next to the piece on the St. Mark's ministries. Acknowledging that most churches could not approach the level of community involvement that St. Mark's had achieved, they ran a list of suggestions for small projects that a local congregation could undertake. Many, such as the establishment of food or clothes banks, would have fit perfectly into a Social Gospel–era congregation.[31]

It is revealing to see how many of the St. Mark's activities that were held up as models of urban ministry in the first decade of the twenty-first century parallel what Methodist deaconesses were doing in the first decades of the twentieth. Although the practice of having staff live in the building to allow them to associate with persons who would not normally be part of their everyday world ended in the mid-1960s, the idea of offering neighborhood residents a safe, clean, and stimulating place to visit and the opportunity to spend time with inspiring role models still underlay much of the programming. For instance, "Makin' Good in the Hood" was a mentoring program established at the turn of the twenty-first century under the leadership of Alexis Brent. Brent was a seminary student pursuing ordination in the United Methodist Church, and she was a key employee at the center for a number of years prior to her first appointment in the pastorate. Designed "to encourage and support the future leaders of New Orleans' inner-city communities," the program was intended to give one hundred youth between the ages of eleven and seventeen "special mentoring by caring adults" and to allow the youth to "participate in weekend training events, African-American history and cultural arts, community projects, and lots of celebrations." A promotional brochure promised that the youth would be "listened to; helped with problems with school, home or friends; shown how to turn their dreams into reality." Parents or guardians were required to sign a contract stating that they would attend four celebratory "rite-of-passage" award dinners during the year. A rap printed in the brightly colored document offers insight into the center's ideas about the target group:

> Sick of tryin' and cryin'
> always gettin' dissed.
> bin' told the way you're doin's
> gettin' everybody pissed?
> Rather be a Supastar,
> make money with no risk
> of bein' messed with by gangstas
> or taken in and frisked?
> If you know what I'm saying' [*sic*]
> then what you need is this—
> Makin' Good in the Hood!
>
> Ain't no gangin' or bangin'
> goin' on down here.
> We hangin' with the brothers
> and the sisters who be near,
> gettin' special 'sideration
> for the things we got planned
> from older folks who been there,
> bros who really jammed—
> Makin' Good in the Hood!

After additional verses, it concludes: "the cool soja's the one Makin' Good in the Hood!"[32] The rap might be seen as an indication that St. Mark's was still, a century after its establishment, trying to reach a population by using the language most comfortable for them.

THE POST-KATRINA ST. MARK'S

On August 29, 2005, Hurricane Katrina made landfall in Louisiana, and subsequent levee breaks devastated the city of New Orleans. Only a few small sections of town were not flooded. The French Quarter was among the areas least affected, but St. Mark's is on the very edge of the Quarter, and some water did come into one area of the first floor, underneath the sanctuary. The building also sustained significant wind damage, and broken windows in various locations allowed rain to enter unimpeded for months.

The portion of the building used by the congregation is on the second floor and sustained no significant damage. According to the Reverend Ms. Anita Dinwiddie, pastor of St. Mark's UMC since 2005, the congregation has gained members in the time since Katrina. The congregation played host the next spring to Elizabeth Stroud, a former United Methodist pastor from Pennsylvania who lost her clergy credentials in 2005 after coming out as a practicing lesbian involved in a monogamous relationship. Stroud preached at worship on May 21, 2006, and also spoke at a "Coffee and Conversation" event on May 22.[33]

The Sunday worship services are attended by a complex mix of longtime members, new residents in the city, and street people. The population of people who are homeless is thought to have tripled in New Orleans since the storm, and the congregation provides a free hot meal every Sunday immediately after worship. Unlike some churches that provide free meals, St. Mark's makes no demand that those who eat attend the religious service ahead of time; anyone who wishes to is free to eat. Still, most do join the congregation for worship each week.

At the center itself, programming halted temporarily after Katrina, not so much because of damage to the building as because the clientele was no longer present in the city. Seven months later, in March 2006, most families with children still had not returned to New Orleans, in part because only a handful of elementary schools had reopened. Board members who lived nearby kept the swimming pool maintained; this may sound frivolous until one considers that there were individuals around the city who reported that they did not drown in the flooding solely because of swimming lessons they had received at St. Mark's. As soon as children began to return to the city, some programming was offered for them.[34]

The center's administration has been reorganized under a new board of directors, and it is now called the North Rampart Community Center. In the summer of 2006, the building was leased by its owner, the Women's Division of the UMC's General Board of Global Ministries, to the Louisiana Annual Conference, and it underwent transformation into a staging area for teams who came to New Orleans to do volunteer repair work on residences. Various rooms were filled with newly constructed bunk beds, and shower facilities were installed and/or revamped.

For the first time since 1966, a deaconess has been appointed to the ministry. The space that was originally the pastor's apartment, long devoted to an office suite for the director, has been reclaimed as living space for deaconess Joanne Finley. Finley is part of a growing group of women who wish to hold professional status within the UMC but who do not believe that ordination is the right choice for them. These women are creating some resurgence within the deaconess movement. They commit to "function through diverse forms of service directed toward the world to make Jesus Christ known in the fullness of his [ministry and] mission," following a mandate that his followers should: "a) Alleviate suffering; b) Eradicate causes of injustice and all that robs life of dignity and worth; c) Facilitate the development of full human potential; and d) Share in building global community through the church universal."[35]

9

CONCLUSION

WOMEN AND THE SOCIAL GOSPEL—
WHO COUNTS?

In 2003, Wendy Deichmann Edwards and Carolyn De Swarte Gifford's anthology, *Gender and the Social Gospel,* called for more research on the women who were the movement's practitioners. The call was not precisely a new one—White and Hopkins had noted as early as 1976 that women had been "neglected" in previous studies.[1] However, Edwards and Gifford took a crucial step in moving women's work from its toehold on the margin into the center of our understanding of the Social Gospel movement. They were specific about the need for studies by scholars who would not rely solely on "theological treatises, sermons, and philosophical monologues" written by men, but who would do primary research in minutes of women's meetings; the publications produced by women's home missionary, temperance, and other organizations; women's periodicals; and various first-person accounts of women's lives.[2] As detailed in appendix A, the eleven-year journey of collecting information for this volume required persistence, creativity, and a list of sources that surpassed those suggested by Edwards and Gifford. One of the more important contributions of this study is the evidence it presents that the stories of churchwomen's endeavors can be recovered and told.

For several reasons, that matters quite a lot. One is that the recovery of women's stories is valuable in and of itself, for the historian and for the women who will read those histories and learn who women have been and what women have done in the past. In a larger sense, however, the omission of women from the category of actors has skewed the answers to important questions asked by historians of the twentieth century. A problem larger still is that it has skewed the questions themselves.

As shown in this study, the settlement house work of MECS women was undeservedly discounted both by many of their contemporaries and by historians. This occurred in part simply because it was the work of women, but scholars also constructed a barrier between religious and nonsectarian settlements that resulted in their overlooking the place of the religious settlement in southern history. Religious settlements run by MECS women were bracketed out of studies by historians Allen Davis and Judith Trolander precisely because of the religious aspects of that work. They saw religious settlements as just "modified missions" that engaged in social service primarily as a means to evangelize and convert the recipients of their aid. On the other hand, the settlements and the women who ran them were not taken seriously by the church because of the social services aspects—or as a pastor put it in 1912, "the secularizing evil"—of their work.

It is ironic that the women's settlement work has been so profoundly neglected, because a more nearly perfect demonstration of Social Gospel ministries cannot be found. Yet the individual men whose theological treatises are considered to be the Social Gospel "classics" were considered by many historians to have *been* the Social Gospel movement. Because these men taught and wrote in the North, and because Methodist women's efforts were dismissed and undocumented, researchers framed their questions and compiled their answers about the Social Gospel as though there were no manifestations of it in the South. As I began this project, much more data was needed about women's religious settlement work and about what its absence from historical considerations might mean. Examining the Social Gospel through the lens of St. Mark's provided clarity about several issues and confirmed that important assumptions needed refining.

This study has highlighted some of the gender-related issues that surrounded Methodist women's work in New Orleans. The women had to overcome significant challenges to their authority from clergymen who had power in the larger church. Jean Miller Schmidt's typology of the "True Methodist Woman" characterized the ways that women could deal with the "Cult of True Womanhood" and its insistence that women be pious, domestic, and submissive, and that they confine their activities to the proper "women's sphere." She noted that they could react: a) by accepting the sphere and staying within it; 2) by rejecting the whole notion of a proper sphere; or 3) by remaining within the sphere but working constantly to enlarge its boundaries. Analysis of the New Orleans MECS women's work showed that the local lay leaders largely remained within the proper "women's sphere" but constantly worked both overtly and subversively to expand that sphere. For instance, the woman's society members in New Orleans participated in the political battle for women's suffrage in the United States and for laity rights (voting rights) for women within the structure of the church. They worked openly, as when they endorsed resolutions to be brought before church bodies, and in more subtle ways, as when they worked behind the scenes to obtain the appointment of Mary Werlein's brother, an advocate of laity rights for women, to take the place of a pastor who would not work with deaconess Margaret Ragland and who was sabotaging the women's efforts.

The collaborative nature of the women's work contributed both to the lack of attention paid it by historians and to its success; no individual women became prominent enough to lift the work as a whole out of historical obscurity, but on the other hand, no one leader had to endure so much opposition to her stances that the whole work faltered because of her inability to stay the course. Even when head resident Margaret Ragland lost her position in New Orleans in the 1912 controversy, the church relocated her to a post in another city, and another deaconess came to New Orleans to continue the work with something approaching a fresh slate.

The "troublemaker" label that was attached to Methodist deaconesses was well deserved, and they endured significant conflict when their work pitted them over against the norms of Deep South society. This is not to say that the MECS women received no rewards for their work. Both the deaconesses and the women in lay leadership like Elvira Beach Carré, Mary Werlein, and Hattie Parker received many things: the satisfaction of doing important work that they could believe mattered, especially as they saw women gaining more power over their own lives; the admiration and gratitude they received from many individuals for what they accomplished; the close fellowship and friendship they shared with like-minded women; and other intangible benefits.

The deaconesses engaged in full-time paid work had the additional opportunity to choose a lifestyle other than marriage and motherhood that still let them enjoy respectability and even appear to most as selfless and giving women. Overall, the deaconess movement proved a major avenue for the development of women's leadership in Methodism until 1956, when ordination for women finally arrived in The Methodist Church. Despite current uncertainty regarding whether the creation of the office of deaconess proved a help or a hindrance toward ordination, in the mid-1960s, editors of a national Methodist women's publication were convinced it had been a help. They recalled that in 1902, when the office of deaconess was being created in the MECS, both its advocates and its opponents saw it as a wedge that would open further doors for women. In the "long and bitter debate" at that early conference, some expressed fear "that such an office would lead women to aspire to the ministry, and even to the Episcopacy. Others feared that it was intended to displace ministers. One delegate declared that such action could only be called heresy. But none of this dissuaded the women."[3]

Exploration of this kind of twentieth-century women's leadership has much to offer twenty-first-century women who aspire to innovative service. The congruence of the collaborative venture that was St. Mark's with the most current thinking about women's leadership styles is significant.[4] The increasing acceptance of the feminist critique of hierarchical structures is beginning to open space for women who choose to work cooperatively instead of imitating the individualism that male leaders have often brought to positions of leadership. While their public language was often about "a brotherhood of man," the leaders of St. Mark's actually created "a sisterhood of women" that allowed them to accomplish what none of them could have done alone. The recovery of the history of their innovative and creative ministries could be helpful in the same ways that feminist biblical scholars' recovery of women's stories in the New Testament has been.

NOT JUST CHURCHWOMEN—
METHODIST WOMEN

MECS women acted as they did not simply because they were churchwomen, but rather because they were Methodist women. In recent years, United Methodist scholars have discussed the "Hatch thesis," the theory that there has been relatively little historical work performed on such a large phenomenon as Methodism in the United States because Methodist history mirrors so closely the rest of the country's history. There is a case to be made for that idea.[5]

However, what defines the history of Methodist women is that so many were precisely so *counter*-cultural in thought and action. As John Patrick McDowell noted, the MECS women were influenced both by their religion and by the culture in which they lived. The Methodist women whose stories are written here had ideas about Christianity that put it in tension, not agreement, with white southern culture, and when the two were in conflict, as they were with issues of race, the women allowed their religion to trump their culture's expectations for them. Even the most socially elite of the New Orleans women, like Elvira Beach Carré, chose to operate counter to culture and the norms of the city's upper class, and their Methodist heritage was far more congruent with the work they were engaged in than were their social backgrounds. Further, Elvira Carré's strong support from the MECS women who elected her, and then reelected her as their president an amazing eighteen times, shows plainly that the majority of the MECS women who belonged to the mission societies approved of and appreciated her willingness to lead organizations that broke racial and class taboos.

The deaconess's training program steeped them not just in theological studies, but more specifically in Wesleyan holiness. The Methodist societies that John Wesley founded in England were not strongholds of the rich and powerful. His own father, an Anglican clergyman, had been put in debtor's prison, and John Wesley never forgot the financial hardships that his mother Susanna faced. All his life, his heart was with the poor; he established health clinics and a school for poor children, and he spent much of his time preaching in the open air to coal miners and laborers. He actually hoped that after reaching a higher level of spirituality, Methodist societies would be moved to hold their goods in common like the early church described in Acts 2:44 and 4:32–37.[6]

The ability to cross class and other social lines is considered to have been a major benefit for the earliest Christians and one of the factors, along with care for the poor and hungry, that accounted for the success of the Jesus movement. Some of the same claims can be made with regard to the early days of the fast-growing Methodist movement. However, during his own lifetime,

Fig. 19. Elvira Beach Carré later in her
life. Photos courtesy of Isabel Gardner
Larue and Susan Larue.

Wesley was disturbed to watch the discipline he promoted resulting in a rise
in the socioeconomic status of many of his followers. Additionally, there were
always a certain number of wealthy people who were Methodists. One of them,
Miss March, corresponded with Wesley a number of times in an effort to convince him that she could not follow his advice to spend time visiting with poor
people. She protested that she needed to be around morally uplifting people
of good character, but Wesley denied that those in need were more likely to
possess poor character or prove less uplifting than the rich. He maintained
that she could not fulfill her Christian responsibility without building actual
relationships with those who were in need.[7] The "friendly visiting" in which
the deaconesses were trained and their focus on visiting the home of everyone
who entered the center was absolutely in keeping with John Wesley's ideas of
what Christian living demanded.

Wesley is often quoted as saying, "there is no holiness but social holiness."
In fact, he probably did not mean exactly what many who quote him think
that he did, because the recognition that individuals could band together to ac-

complish structural change in society was not common in his lifetime. Though Wesley would have been in favor of Methodists working for justice, his concept of what that meant was not the same one we have come to hold in the twenty-first century. He did believe that how Christians treat other people matters, and he would have made no exception depending on the class or wealth of the one with whom the Christian was dealing. He believed that love was a way of acting toward others, and that every Methodist should strive to be more holy in heart every day.

In fact, Wesley espoused a doctrine of "Christian perfection" that was the source of much confusion during his lifetime, and that may have contributed somewhat to the later confusion of Methodist activities in the Social Gospel era with those of the Progressive movement. For Wesley, perfection was just a part of the process of sanctification that began when a person was converted. He thought that individuals could achieve momentary states where they acted from nothing except the motive of Christian love. Of crucial importance is his teaching that even if a person *were* operating only from the motive of love, she or he could still make a mistake about what the best course of action might be. Human beings could never free themselves from ignorance—from not knowing everything there was to know about a situation—and therefore, the thing one did from love could turn out to have been the wrong thing to do. Furthermore, even if a Christian were able to achieve such a state of "perfection," Wesley did not expect him or her to be able to remain in it. And, significantly, Wesley insisted that he himself had never attained it even briefly.

This concept is markedly different from the idea that humanity is improving itself and might eventually possess the ability to solve its own problems simply through the acquisition of greater knowledge. The fact that persons who are about to be ordained as United Methodist clergy are asked if they are going on to a state of perfection and whether they expect to reach it does not at all mean that it would shock Wesley to learn that the "progress" of the human race has failed to take us to a utopian state. Nevertheless, many individuals confuse his doctrine of perfection with something more nearly like the Progressive agenda, and this contributed to the common failure to distinguish between the motivations of Methodist Christians and the dreams of the Progressive movement.

Kathryn Kish Sklar has lamented the widespread failure to recognize religious motivations among the women of the settlement house movement, such as Jane Addams and Florence Kelley. She also objected to the overall paradigm of maternalism because it "permits historians to characterize many of women's reform efforts as an extension of white, Protestant, middle-class domesticity, without exploring these reformers critiques of class-based exploitation and oppression." She was concerned that historians were missing "the power of religious discourse to define political agendas, especially those associated with 'social justice' for working people."[8] Sklar was particularly interested in demonstrating the ability of the women of the *secular or nonsectarian* settlement movement to use religious language and concepts to further their work.

In contrast, I am particularly interested in pointing out the power of religious belief and experience that underlay the work of the *unabashedly religious* settlement workers and thereby emphasizing how the practitioners of the Social Gospel in the South differed from other kinds of reformers in the Progressive Era. St. Mark's joined the New Orleans Council of Social Agencies when it organized in 1921, and the women demonstrated in other ways that they saw the work at St. Mark's as compatible with that of other "social agencies." However, even when the establishment of the Community Chest occasioned the administrative separation of St. Mark's Community Center from the worshiping congregation in 1925, the center did not sever its relationship with the larger Methodist church. The decision not to abandon the matrix of the church for nonsectarian status, as many settlements (including Kingsley House) chose to do, resulted in the women's work being discounted by the world of social work and its later historians.

Understanding the particular kind of religious motivation that needs to be recognized in the MECS women is crucial. We can ascertain this only by discovering something about how they regarded the task and even the identity of the church. What did they see as the purpose for its existence? Anthropologists and social historians, among other kinds of scholars, tend to see religion as a form of "glue" that holds societies together in ordered ways. They are not wrong in that belief, and it is that which has brought so many people, both inside and outside the church, to see religious institutions as enforcers of cultural mores and upholders of a society's status quo. There is no denying that the church has often served in that role and even gloried in it. As a result, researchers like Paul Boyer worked from the viewpoint that religious reformers were primarily interested in maintaining social order and control.

However, there exists in the canon of Christian scripture a different way of viewing the followers of Jesus, as evidenced by accusations that the earliest Christians were "these [people] that have turned the world upside down."[9] In this view, Christianity is an agent for radical social change, worlds away from a repressive entity that suppresses nonconformity and enforces social order. Although John Wesley's "social holiness" might have been a less activist phrase than some have wished, he never saw Methodism as a religion that should engage in enforcing social standards or the status quo—the kind of religion that scholars who talk about the "social order" and "moral order" aspects of reformers seem to have in mind. The MECS deaconesses who followed Wesley embraced the "turn the world upside down" kind of Christianity and allowed it to drive them into settings where it is otherwise unlikely that they ever would have gone.

The mandates in the Hebrew scriptures and the New Testament to offer hospitality to the stranger were in sharp conflict with the xenophobia and racism that characterized much of the culture at large in the early decades of the twentieth century. White female reformers have been criticized for "band-aiding" symptoms rather than eradicating underlying causes of social ills, but to the exact extent that they saw the underlying problem as the existence of the immigrants and people of color in their midst, their *failure* to address the problem at the root (which would have required exterminating minority groups, as the *New Orleans States* editor once proposed, or urging that our borders be closed to all immigrants) must be viewed as a Christian, as over against a cultural, response.

The "Americanization" of immigrants can legitimately be termed a conservative practice, but along with helping immigrants adapt to the United States and become citizens, the deaconesses worked hard to adapt their congregation, the larger church, and the city to the immigrants' presence. They also celebrated—rather than attempting to eradicate—the cultures the immigrants brought with them to New Orleans. Endeavoring to meet what the immigrants whom they lived among presented as their greatest needs was not a conservative response, especially when viewed against the Ku Klux Klan and other violently anti-immigrant groups that arose or resurfaced around the turn of the twentieth century. If the women retained racist or classist views (as no doubt at least some did, at least to some extent), the fact that they devoted their lives to living with, listening to, learning from, and serving an amazingly hybrid, multiethnic, mixed-race, urban, immigrant community of people who were mostly poor is a testament to their commitment to follow Jesus, who they understood to have preached a Gospel of racial equality and justice for all.

Some historians have judged the motives of reformers by their achieved results—consider those who maintain that if the New Deal kept a full-fledged revolution from occurring, then the motives of those who fashioned it must have been to prevent radical social change. This process ignores the deep truth underlying the adage, "Politics is the art of the possible." Marsha Wedell recalled Marx's assertion that men make history not completely as they choose but rather in the context of the past as they have received it, and she applied that recognition helpfully to the work that women reformers were able to accomplish within the limited choices available to them.[10] Some historians have looked at reformers, decided what would have been in the best interest of those individuals, and concluded that that end—whether it is what they achieved or not—must have been what the reformers were seeking. They have asserted that female reformers were conservative because the livelihoods of their husbands or fathers (and therefore their own) depended on preserving the status quo. Others posit that the reformers were conservative because the real motive behind philanthropic endeavor was the preservation of the elite social class; indeed, that is probably true for some female philanthropists who worked through the kinds of organizations studied by Diana Kendall, but not for those who worked through the Methodist women's societies.[11]

There is a need for much more nuanced consideration of "conservative" and "liberal" labels, particularly when they are applied to actions motivated by religious convictions. The "conservative" label applied to Social Gospel reformers and the assertions that their agenda was preserving the capitalist status quo and moral order are belied by careful examination of the MECS deaconesses' training program and their personal theologies and ideologies. This story of the MECS women of New Orleans demonstrates that on the theoretical level, they were actively engaged in a serious questioning of class structures, and on the practical front, they were actively engaged in promoting frequent contact and cooperation between privileged women and women who were poor. The deaconesses' own "critiques of class-based exploitation and oppression" came directly from their training in Christian theology. Methodist deaconesses were, for instance, required to study Walter Rauschenbusch's call for a radical remaking of society, including common ownership of all natural resources and a dramatic redistribution of wealth by means of taxation, and his belief that the rich had to be converted so that they would share their resources with the poor. Deaconesses who studied economic theory from the viewpoint of such a theologian were most unlikely to accept uncritically the idea that workers in urban industries did not deserve to earn a living wage or that poor people suffered because that was how God intended things to be.

Despite all this concern with the impetus behind the reformers' work, few researchers have delved deeply into the area of women's religious motivation. Several errors have resulted. One is the already mentioned bracketing of Methodist settlement workers *out of* studies of reformers in the Progressive Era. Just as unhelpful has been the impulse to collapse Social Gospel workers *into* Progressivism, and it is this latter error that has been primarily responsible for placing the end of the Social Gospel movement too early, at the end of World War I.

The Progressive movement was associated in the minds of many with the idea that humankind was "making progress"—that is, getting better—and that social ills of all kinds would be solved as scientists and scholars continued to advance in knowledge about the world and about the evolution of humanity itself. The facts that scientific advances were used not to prevent war but rather toward the service of the particularly gruesome new killing and maiming techniques of World War I, that the reasons for the conflict were particularly unclear, and that the hope to avoid further conflict was dashed when the United States refused to join the League of Nations are understood to have resulted in a widespread disenchantment with the idea of "progress" and a concomitant loss of interest in the Progressive reform movement. To understand why the Social Gospel did not lose its underpinnings as a result of these phenomena (and thus end when Progressivism did), it is necessary to understand that it was never based on faith that humanity could improve itself.

The earlier date also resulted in part from an identification of the movement with several northern male theologians who happened to die—and hence stop publishing—during World War I rather than with the women who were practicing it. Like the rest of the country, New Orleans and the ministries at St. Mark's were affected by World War I, but it hardly resulted in a cessation of the Social Gospel. The Methodist women of New Orleans who were manifesting Social Gospel thought, theology, and principles were still very much on the upswing of the arc of their work in the 1920s. The structure at 1130 North Rampart Street dedicated in 1924 contained many features clearly intended for Social Gospel ministries. The height of the St. Mark's manifestation of Social Gospel activities was thus beginning at the time when the movement is thought to have expired, and it proceeded unabated throughout the 1920s and the opening years of the Great Depression. It was rather the coming of the New Deal that signaled the decline of the Social Gospel, because many deaconesses and other Methodist leaders saw government attempts to meet the needs of poor citizens as more effective than the efforts of the church.

METHODISTS IN KINGDOMTIDE

The most important theological concept required for evaluating the Social Gospel or the work of the MECS deaconesses is the doctrine of the Kingdom of God, and it is also the most essential for discovering the differences between the Social Gospel and the Progressive movement. Overall, the Kingdom is one of the most puzzling, or put another way, mystical aspects of Christian theology.[12] It is common to speak of its "already-but-not-yet" nature in order to point simultaneously to the teaching of Jesus that "the Kingdom is at hand" and to the understanding that the Kingdom is expected to become manifest only in the future. There is an oddly shared responsibility for its in-breaking; Christians understand that while the Kingdom of God is something that God alone will be able to bring about, this does not obviate the Christian's task to work toward the Kingdom as though human beings have the ability to establish it—as though "the only hands God has to work with are ours." Methodists have traditionally placed more emphasis on this doctrine than other mainline Protestant denominations. It is linked with, but by no means identical to, what theologians call eschatology (that is, the study of "last things" or what might occur at the "end of the world" or the "end of time") and soteriology (that is, the study of salvation—what "being saved" might mean, either before or after death, and whether and how one might obtain that state).

The primary alteration in widely accepted Christian theology that accompanied the Social Gospel had to do with salvation. Protestant Christianity had become closely focused on the idea of salvation of the individual or "personal salvation," with the term "salvation" usually understood to mean that one would be rewarded, rather than punished, in an afterlife. Historian Christopher Evans maintained that it is the idea of "social salvation" that has been most thoroughly integrated into American Protestantism from Social Gospel thought.[13] He lamented that many today forget that the Social Gospel propagated theologies that "challenged churches to promote an awareness of how God was present through the *zeitgeist* of modern culture, and called upon Christians to work for major institutional changes that would lead to an egalitarian, democratic society."[14] By the year 2000, Evans believed, the question of whether the church should meet human need that was otherwise unmet was no longer a topic of widespread debate. "Even as historical circumstances over the past one hundred years have changed, the social gospel's insistence that Christian faith must engage contemporary social issues in order to utilize the full force of the gospel remains a central, and taken-for-granted, principle among many denominations at the opening of the twenty-first century."[15] The moves of late twentieth- and early twenty-first-century Republican administrations toward "faith-based initiatives," which implied that responsibility for treating social ills lay primarily with church-run charities, show how thoroughly secular society has processed the concept.

The existence of corporate or structural sin has also become an accepted part of mainstream Christian theology today. It is not just personal actions that can be sinful; Christians can participate in sin as part of a society or institution that is acting in sinful ways. Failing to speak out against obvious instances of institutional racism or sexism, profiting from stock in a company that exploits its workers, or belonging to a club that refuses to admit those who practice a particular religion might present instances of participating in structural sin.[16]

Again, these ideas are linked to a greater awareness of how societies function than was common a century ago. The mandate for the original deaconesses consecrated in 1888 was to minister to the poor, visit the sick, pray with the dying, care for the orphan, seek the wandering, comfort the sorrowing, and save the sinning.[17] An assessment of deaconess work at the mid-twentieth century noted, "The first deaconesses went forth impelled by the desire to share the love of Christ with the lonely, the sick and the forgotten. In a world so different it is scarcely possible to believe that only 75 years have passed, they still go forth impelled by the same desire." By 1998, however, a recruitment brochure promised the new deaconess opportunities to:

> Share the love of God with those on the margins of society.
> Serve the needs of the whole person.
> Participate on the cutting edge of mission.
> Work to address the root causes of poverty.
> Belong to a supportive community of women.[18]

Note that deaconesses were no longer expected just to "minister to the poor" but rather to attack the "root causes of poverty." The change in terminology regarding the deaconess's tasks reflects more recent understandings of what mission in urban areas should consist of and how it should be conducted, but it also reflects the assimilation of social salvation into the portfolio of the church.

It is fitting that Belle Bennett, the president of the MECS women's organization when St. Mark's was founded, dealt with the issue in the guise in which it was then presented to the women (posing evangelism for the salvation of souls over against social services for the material body and world) by dismissing it as the false choice it was. What the women wanted, she explained, was "Eternal life for the individual, the kingdom of God for humanity."[19]

Social salvation—the in-breaking of the Kingdom—was an important goal, but so was meeting the needs of the particular people they served. Counting their successes on the individual or family-unit basis, Methodist deaconesses were able to assess the work at St. Mark's positively. Annie Rogers, who came to New Orleans in 1923, said the "visionary" women who established and funded the new center on North Rampart Street "were women with brilliant minds and a deep commitment to Jesus Christ, and they knew what was going on in the world." Further, their national leaders were aware of the needs of mountain people and black residents of southern cities, and of various kinds of urban problems that many individuals had not even recognized in the 1920s. Rogers emphasized the women's desire to bring "life more abundant" to the people they served every day, and in the deaconesses' view, life abundant did not consist just in knowing Christ, but also in "having what you need, an opportunity to have your children get education, for you to grow physically and spiritually the most you can."[20]

The same kinds of activities that St. Mark's was engaged in during the 1920s are often held up as cutting-edge urban ministry today. It is not as surprising as it should be that the organized church's twenty-first-century methodologies for achieving social salvation are, at least in the United States, primarily still those used by the early deaconesses—a subtle subversion of the social order and an attempt to influence individuals and to lift them from poverty in units no larger than a family. The programming St. Mark's provided when it was first established as a religious settlement house was in some ways not dissimilar to that which the community center offered when Katrina made landfall. The clientele itself was different; in 2005, that clientele was almost entirely black, while the early twentieth-century work was conducted primarily with white immigrants. Basic instruction in standard English was an important facet of the services that helped immigrant families become self-sufficient and survive in the urban environment. Computer literacy and basic educational competencies that would help young people succeed in the mainstream educational system and basic job skills that would help them succeed in the workplace were important parts of the work in 2005. As the deaconesses knew, the success of any individual who has been served by St. Mark's is still a cause for celebration, and no doubt will ever be.

SOCIAL GOSPEL AND CIVIL RIGHTS

Another avenue of historical inquiry considered in *St. Mark's and the Social Gospel* is whether white Social Gospel practitioners were racists. What the story reveals about race relations is an important contribution to the history of the Social Gospel movement, because the evidence from New Orleans Methodism shows a strong, positive connection between active adherents of the Social Gospel and the later civil rights movement.

The Social Gospel practice of the Methodist deaconesses was a direct outgrowth of and inextricable from their understanding of the Christian gospel as presented in the New Testament. That understanding was shaped by their educations at deaconess training schools. The majority studied at Scarritt College under professors like New Testament scholar Albert Barnett, a social activist, a strong supporter of labor unions, and a white member of a national committee of the NAACP. As a result of their theological training, which included interchange with historically black Fisk University, the white deaconesses who came to work at St. Mark's were actively engaged in subversion of racial taboos. In the 1930s, head resident Nettie Stroup widely publicized the fact that "Negroes" had open, first-come-first-served access to medical and dental care in the health clinic. Mixed meetings of all sorts of civic and religious groups from around the city were held at St. Mark's, because it was one of the few organizations (many individuals maintain it was the only one) that would allow integrated groups to meet in its facilities.

Deaconesses were among the key lay leaders in the St. Mark's congregation, and many of the members had joined and remained affiliated with St. Mark's because of their relationships with these spiritual mothers. The deaconesses shaped a worshipping congregation that offered its public support when the white pastor, Andy Foreman, defied those who implemented a white boycott of William Frantz Elementary because a black girl began attending there in November 1960. It was the women who had made space for Foreman to take his stand, and women who led the congregation to support him.

Foreman's motivation lay in part in his upbringing, but it was even more deeply rooted in his own theological education. He was pursuing a doctorate at Methodist-affiliated Boston University and was profoundly influenced by his advisor, Allan Knight Chalmers, who like Albert Barnett was a prominent white member of the NAACP. The first time I interviewed Foreman for this project, I began with a completely open-ended question on the order of "Tell me about what happened," and the first sentence Foreman spoke included Chalmers's name.[21]

Ron White asserted almost twenty years ago that the relationship between the Social Gospel and racial reform is "more multifaceted than previously suggested," and subsequent research has proved his point.[22] Though it might once have been a novel idea, it is surely evident today that various groups of people practiced the Social Gospel in different ways. Considering that practice varied based on the gender, race, social class, and motives of the practitioners, a given group's inclusion or exclusion from an assessment of the Social Gospel will automatically shift how the entire movement's relationship to issues of race is perceived.

In the early 1990s, White and Ralph Luker explored the intersection of the Social Gospel and race relations. Luker hoped to demonstrate that Social Gospelers were not as racially prejudiced as some suggested, but his study, *The Social Gospel in Black and White,* had mixed success in achieving this goal; he had to admit that prominent writers like Josiah Strong did have racist views, and it was not until the end of his book, when he turned to Walter Rauschenbusch, that Luker made a particularly convincing case for truly progressive racial views among well-known Social Gospel thinkers. He makes only a passing reference to the settlement work of Methodist women, which is a major reason he was not more successful at defending his thesis.[23]

In his *Liberty and Justice for All: Racial Reform and the Social Gospel,* Ronald White made a stronger case for the racial openness of Social Gospel workers. However, because the period he wrote about ended in 1925, observing direct links to the later civil rights movement was not a part of his project.[24]

Other historians linked the two movements without seeing a need to explain or prove the connection. Taylor Branch linked the theological education of Martin Luther King Jr., which was grounded in Social Gospel thought, to King's later work. Black liberation theologian James Cone saw all King's work as stemming from his religious convictions and education. Kim Lacy Rogers reported several persons connected to the civil rights movement in New Orleans who credited their Social Gospel backgrounds for their involvement.[25] Yet, other scholars continued to debate the question of how Social Gospelers leaned on racial matters. Darryl M. Trimiew argued against historian Susan Hill Lindley's contention that the Social Gospel's definition should be broadened to include the work of women, blacks, and others excluded in previous assessments.[26] Lindley called that process "Deciding Who Counts," and both she and Trimiew recognized that the method chosen for "counting"—in other words, the inclusion or exclusion of various practitioners of the Social Gospel—would inevitably affect the movement's definition. While Lindley lifted up previously overlooked groups to broaden understanding of the Social Gospel, Trimiew narrowed it, arguing that anyone who was not a racist white male did not and indeed could not "count." Because nonracist praxis could not be included in the Social Gospel without altering Trimiew's definition of it as a thoroughly racist doctrine linked inherently to white supremacy, he disputed Dr. Martin Luther King Jr.'s contention that he (King) was an adherent of the Social Gospel. Because King was not a racist, Trimiew maintained, it could not have been the Social Gospel that King was carrying forward, despite King's own belief that it was.[27]

Trimiew's insistence that nonracists could not have sprung from the Social Gospel is not supported by the evidence. True, a limited perception of whose experiences represented the Social Gospel movement did lead its early historians to confine their research mainly to persons who actually were *not* linked to progress in racial issues. Through working around what was then a blind spot, like Luker, or through working in a deliberately exclusionary way, like Trimiew, scholars have used constricted pictures of the Social Gospel that omitted the practitioners who were most demonstrably committed to it, Methodist deaconesses who lived and worked in urban settlement houses such as St. Mark's. Admittedly, these women were operating from understandings that would not bear close scrutiny using twenty-first-century standards for enlightened racial attitudes. Maternalism can definitely be found within their words and actions. Yet these white southern women who lived in the early twentieth century took what then amounted to radical actions, such as joining the NAACP, volunteering to work in centers serving a black clientele, and publicizing the fact that St. Mark's provided something so intimate as medical and dental care to both blacks and whites in a setting where no separate rooms, equipment, or instruments were maintained. The local white laywomen's societies called for improved race relations as early as 1917 (and for voting rights for blacks as early as 1946). Further, there is no question that all these women perceived themselves as operating from a Social Gospel mindset, and that they actually were.

Enrique Dussel, a historian of the liberation theology movement, has maintained that Christianity exists *only* as it is actually enacted in human history.[28] I would maintain that this principle applies to the Social Gospel and civil rights movements, as well. The embodiment of these sweeping and profoundly important movements—indeed, sea changes—in the United States existed in the lives, thoughts, and actions of real people. The best and most effective way to examine the connections between the Social Gospel and civil rights movements is to examine the people who literally were those connections—precisely the people whom previous studies have not included. The women of St. Mark's physically bridged the Social Gospel and civil rights movements through their lived embodiment of both movements and through the enactment of their understandings of the Gospel.

"By Both Word and Deed"

Attributing the decisions of the heroines of St. Mark's to their belief that their actions answered a call of God on their lives may seem suspect to some, but other, equally sufficient answers for their behavior are lacking. The religious forces and the cultural forces that acted on the women of St. Mark's were sometimes congruent but often at odds. When the influences pulled in different directions, MECS deaconesses and the early WP&HMS leaders in New Orleans made choices that reflected not their cultural backgrounds, but rather their willingness to answer what they saw as a divine call to pursue justice. The extensive focus in this study on the theological educations of the women who served at St. Mark's, their reactions to that education, and how they adapted what they learned into their real-life experiences on North Rampart Street allows me to speak with some degree of surety about what they thought they were doing and why they thought they were doing it. They were prompted precisely by their understandings of Christianity to desire profound alterations in the class-ridden and racially biased social structure around them.

St. Mark's required a commitment of enormous proportions from the women who established and ran it, and its history calls into question the assumption that all women of similar social status shared the same motivations. It is crucial that sufficient weight be given to the ways that religious beliefs and motivations can alter behavior. These vibrant Methodist women were taught, and they willingly absorbed, ideas that were radical in the 1920s and 1930s (and some that would still be deemed radical today) about economic theory and race relations. They moved not only themselves but also Methodism and as much of society as they could tow along with them toward their vision of the Kingdom, a vision that would require a dramatic restructuring of society.

In one sense, both church and secular history would profit from a blurring of the arbitrary sacred/secular discriminations that kept religious settlements from achieving full acceptance in either church or secular society in the early twentieth century and in later historical treatments. Yet it is also the case that more careful distinctions need to be drawn between the two areas; this study stands as a corrective to subsuming the Social Gospel uncritically into a Progressive agenda that was bound inextricably with the idea that humanity as a whole is improving. The Methodist women who believed they were engaged in facilitating the in-breaking of the Kingdom of God were not discouraged by the evidence World War I presented that humanity was apparently not capable of digging itself out of its own morass, after all. The Christian might be saddened but was not surprised by the outcome of the conflict.

To deem any human undertaking a failure because it did not bring about the Kingdom of God is simply foolish. It is equally unwise to try to assess the success or failure of the Social Gospel movement without paying sufficient attention to the participants' spiritual lives, motivations, and religious training and to their belief that it was the Kingdom of God toward which they were ultimately working. The people of St. Mark's were undoubtedly afflicted by lack of information and lack of enlightenment, by lack of ability to discriminate between Christian teaching and southern culture, by a desire to be accepted by their communities, by failures of nerve, and by a host of other human frailties that hindered their work. However, their failure to bring about a complete transformation of society was not from a lack of desire.

Like the women who founded St. Mark's and like the women who for a century have mellowed its stair railings with their hands, Christians today are still called to make earth more like what the dream of what heaven would be. The conviction that it is indeed society that needs to change, or in different language, society that needs to obtain salvation, is as present today as it was a century ago. The first superintendent of St. Mark's Hall, Nicolas Joyner, wrote in 1909, "We are trying to preach the gospel by both word and deed, believing that the latter is as effective as the former."[29] One hundred years later, the proclamation of a saving Gospel and the attempt to meet the whole spectrum of human needs remained the methods of choice for action in the congregation and at the community center. On North Rampart Street, the Kingdom of God is as close to hand as it has ever been, and just as far away.

APPENDIX A

SOURCES FOR RESEARCH ON MECS WOMEN'S WORK

This is the first study of its kind of which I am aware. I hope it has revealed how much can be learned about the larger work of Methodism's white southern women with regard to the Social Gospel and to race relations through a very long-range, in-depth study of their work at one facility.

A truly comprehensive study from a scholarly viewpoint has not been written for other missions run by women of the Methodist Episcopal Church, South, but this is not surprising, given the daunting nature of the task. While researching St. Mark's, I discovered that most seemingly obvious methods for obtaining documentation were not productive. Furthermore, I strongly suspect that this would be the case at all, or nearly all, of the women's missions. I hope this summary of the methods through which I accumulated enough data to tell the St. Mark's story may benefit other researchers who choose the important undertaking of constructing narratives about churchwomen's work.

The footnotes throughout this volume point to many helpful secondary sources. A good literature review relevant to almost any study of Methodist women's institutions exists in *Gender and the Social Gospel,* edited by Wendy J. Deichmann Edwards and Carolyn De Swarte Gifford.[1] Research specifically on the work of Methodist deaconesses is scant. In the second half of the twentieth century, Elizabeth Meredith Lee and Barbara Campbell published brief works.[2] Another major contribution was Mary Agnes Dougherty's expansion of her doctoral dissertation into *My Calling to Fulfill: Deaconesses in the United Methodist Tradition;* it is, as its title suggests, an overview that does not follow the specific work of women in any particular location. Scholars Carolyn De Swarte Gifford, Susan Hill Lindley, Rosemary Skinner Keller, Barbara Campbell, Laceye Warner, and more recently Alice Knotts have published some results of their research, but all have focused mainly on women in the MEC and the northern training schools.[3]

Although the quality of local recordkeeping no doubt varies, most religious settlement houses are likely to present similar problems for researchers, because even when deaconesses fully appreciated the need to preserve records for historians, they lacked sufficient personnel for the task. They almost invariably chose to devote limited resources to immediate assistance for their neighbors rather than to documentation of their own efforts for posterity. Records at the national level also proved largely nonexistent. Although this may be due in part to understaffing, it also reflects the lack of importance the church at large has attached to "women's work." In secular society, the practice of writing women out of history has been so well documented that it need not be revisited here. Because of their prolonged resistance to the ordination of females, churches have been even more prone than the rest of society to ignore the contributions of women.

For at least thirty years, since the United Methodist Church created GCAH—the General Commission on Archives and History—personnel in other church agencies have been able to believe that if they packed up material and sent it to GCAH, they had dealt with the issue of historic preservation. As any historian knows, creating an archive is not a miracle cure that automatically makes documentation usable and available; however, it is understandable that other agencies would want to avoid duplicating work that GCAH "should" be doing. GCAH is located on the campus of Drew University in New Jersey and has archival space there. Thus, "we sent it to Drew" is often Methodist-speak for, "I think maybe someone sometime put some stuff in a box and sent it—or at least meant to send it—somewhere else."

My own quest to recover the stories of the women of Methodism's Social Gospel movement in New Orleans began as a research paper for a New South history class taught by Clarence Mohr, then of the Tulane faculty. Sarah Kreutziger, a member of the School of Social Work's faculty who wrote her dissertation about how Methodist deaconesses contributed to the professionalization of the field of social work, suggested the settlement house named St. Mark's as a topic. The paper grew over the years into a doctoral dissertation at Tulane and still later into this book. The first step toward the construction of that first paper was to ascertain what material was available at St. Mark's itself. Various types of records were stored in the offices of the St. Mark's congregation, but they were mainly related to its own history (as over against that of the community center).[4] These included some early membership directories, some pastors' reports, and minutes from a few Quarterly Conferences and annual Charge Conferences. The majority of years of the century-long history were not represented by any documents at all.

Housed in the office were materials compiled in 1978-79 when a member of the congregation, Margery Freeman, received a grant from GCAH for an oral history project on St. Mark's. The publication that resulted from her project was a narrative that appeared in installments with the Sunday worship bulletin over the course of several weeks, and a copy of this narrative was there. Transcripts of twenty-two interviews she conducted were present; these valuable resources are discussed below. Some materials that members or former members had donated for her project were present, including copies of various programs, brochures, letters, bulletins, and newspaper and magazine articles. In addition, there were copies of the most comprehensive history of St. Mark's ever compiled outside Freeman's work—a six-page typed manuscript produced in 1971 by Mary Morrison, a prominent member of the congregation. The materials in the church office also included the script of a historical play entitled *Opening Doors* written by a former deaconess, Lillian Day, and performed in 1949.[5] Among the most valuable resources were the original architect's drawings for the facility at 1130 North Rampart Street. These indicated the intended use of every room on all three floors and supplied important evidence about the extension of the women's Social Gospel agenda into the 1920s.

The most obvious location to check for any existing records from the community center (as over against those of the congregation) was the center itself. However, the director stated that no such records existed when he came to St. Mark's in 1995. After repeated inquiries among current and former St. Mark's personnel and a personal (and fruitless) inspection of the attic and an elevator shaft where records might have been stored, I learned that a previous director moved all the records to her home during her tenure in the 1970s, after the last deaconess appointed there in the twentieth century had left.[6] This director later moved out of state and has since died. Inquiries with her family and acquaintances and with personnel at a camp in Mississippi where some of her papers were reposited yielded no records from St. Mark's.

Several other sources that seemed likely to produce written records also led to dead ends. For instance, the center had been supported by United Way and its predecessors, the United Fund and the Community Chest, since 1925, and I expected that the United Way would retain reports on funded agencies. However, an employee told me that the records had been discarded.[7]

When the insufficiency of records in New Orleans became evident, I was not too discouraged because I expected that the denomination-wide women's organizations and mission boards would require annual reports, which should still reside in their archives. My most devastating discovery was that the reports the St. Mark's deaconesses filed annually with their arm of the Board of Home Missions (now the Women's Division of the General Board of Global Ministries), which still owns the Community Center, were no longer extant. An archivist at GCAH stated that many of the records housed at the national office of the Board of Home Missions in Philadelphia were destroyed in a fire, and that many of those records that remained were discarded when the agency moved to New York City in 1972.[8]

Inquiries with the national deaconess office at the GBGM in New York City confirmed this and revealed that all paper records that had survived the fire and the move had been sent to GCAH at Drew University. Deaconess Betty Purkey, who then headed the deaconess program, provided what assistance she could, but she had little data. She said that deaconess records are only very slowly being computerized. Data about deaconesses had never been organized in such a way that they could be sorted by facilities at which the women served, and no institutional mechanism was in place to determine which deaconesses might have been working at St. Mark's in any given year.[9] Despite the extensive research undertaken for this project, it is possible that women who served there have still escaped my notice.

Because of the lack of local records and the destruction of written reports filed with the national mission board, records at other archives were crucial. One such source was the Scarritt archives. Many of the deaconesses who served at St. Mark's received their training at Scarritt College for Christian Workers, which moved from Kansas City to Nashville in 1924. No longer a degree-granting institution, Scarritt is operated as a continuing education/retreat center known as the Scarritt-Bennett Center, but it continues to house what has recently evolved into the Virginia Davis Laskey Research Library. Scarritt had sent many documents, including records for students and faculty, to GCAH, but GCAH could not locate them at the time of my visit there.[10]

Materials that remain in the Scarritt archives include long runs of most of the magazines for Methodist women. They hold bound copies of minutes from many (but not all) of the national meetings of the Women's Division's predecessors; a short report on St. Mark's was included almost every year. This would be an important source for historical data on any operation run by Methodist women.

Research at the General Commission on Archives and History (GCAH) at Drew University revealed additional bound copies of minutes not present in the Scarritt collection. There were other relevant resources, such as copies of the daily newsletter issued during national conferences of the women's groups and runs of Methodist periodical literature not held by Scarritt's library.[11]

In Louisiana, the conference-level organization of the United Methodist Women (UMW) houses the records of their predecessor societies at the Wesley Conference Center at Woodworth. When I used them, they were located in an area without climate control, in a storage room sectioned off with chicken wire. Fortunately, the bound minutes of state meetings, arguably the most important type of resource housed there, have been placed in archival-quality boxes. Minutes from 1940 onward are located there.

The archives of the Louisiana Annual Conference housed at Centenary College in Shreveport, which might have been presumed to be a major source of material, were disappointing. Because St. Mark's is not an agency of the Louisiana Conference, the annual conference journals did not usually contain a report on St. Mark's. The archives did hold bound minutes of conference-level meetings of women's organizations from 1911 through 1939, which was the period not included among the minutes at Woodworth, and they included a few paragraphs about St. Mark's almost every year. Archivists did not know of any other helpful documents among the large amount of uncatalogued material they held. If the records benefit from better organization as time and resources permit, it is quite possible that documents about other women-sponsored missions might turn up. Unfortunately, one could also argue the opposite side, that records are *less* likely to surface as time goes on; I urge any researcher who wants to document any nineteenth- or twentieth-century institution run by churchwomen to begin their work as soon as possible.

Some archives of the Louisiana Annual Conference are housed at the Dillard University library. These are primarily, but not exclusively, records from MEC churches before 1939 and records from the black-membership conference affiliated with the race-based Central Jurisdiction, which existed between 1939 and 1972. One online finding aid listed some MECS material that would have been relevant, but the archivist could not locate it, and he said that finding aid was no longer in use, even though it was still accessible on the Web. However, it is possible that some material about various women-sponsored ministries could exist at Dillard; this would seem likelier for missions of the MEC rather than the MECS.

Purely by happenstance, in the course of a trip made to conduct interviews with women who had served at St. Mark's, I discovered that the Brooks-Howell Home for retired deaconesses in Asheville, North Carolina, has a library. Though it is small, it consists primarily of materials that were still in the personal collections of deaconesses and missionaries when they moved to the home; it is therefore skewed toward church history in general, and church women's history in particular. It also includes scores of brochures and pamphlets and other publications issued by the General Board of Global Ministries and its predecessor agencies throughout the twentieth century. I would not be surprised to learn that GBGM itself is unaware that some of these documents exist.

Further, the home maintains scrapbooks, which include a one-page "Life Story" for each person who has lived in any of the Methodist-run homes for retired deaconesses, even those residences that are no longer in operation. These self-prepared summaries of the deaconesses' work promise a fertile field for study and might furnish a great deal of data for other types of studies about female church professionals.

At one time, the Louisiana Annual Conference and the two Annual Conferences in Mississippi sponsored a weekly newspaper, the *New Orleans Christian Advocate.* This publication began in broadsheet format and later changed to a tabloid. It contained news from around the three conferences and included regular reports of the activities of the Women's Parsonage and Home Mission Societies (WP&HMS). Unfortunately, a complete collection of these newspapers does not seem to exist in Louisiana. Microfilm of a partial set, ending in

1900, is owned by the Louisiana Annual Conference archives, and microfilm copies of some of the marriage notices and obituaries were in the Louisiana collection at the public library in New Orleans. However, the Methodist archives at Millsaps College in Jackson, Mississippi, contain a complete run, both in hard copy and on microfilm, from the antebellum era through 1947, when it ceased publication. This periodical proved one of the most significant sources of data about women's work at St. Mark's. It had a regular Louisiana WP&HMS column, which appeared approximately every other issue (with Mississippi news occupying the space in alternate weeks). No doubt because of its proximity to the editor, the society in the New Orleans District received the lion's share of the coverage on Louisiana women.

Oral history played a very important role in this study, in an unexpectedly layered way. Most of the twenty-two interviews recorded by Margery Freeman in the course of her 1978-79 study focused on questions about the pastors of the St. Mark's congregation. However, her work was nevertheless absolutely crucial to the success of this project, because a number of the people she interviewed died before my study began. These included Fae Daves, the last deaconess to serve at St. Mark's, and Mary Morrison, who was one of the most active laypeople in the congregation and who also served on the board of directors for the center for many years. I would not have had the rich information on their long involvements with St. Mark's if Freeman's interviews had not been recorded over two decades previously. I urge laywomen reading this to capture the stories of their older colleagues and to have those recordings transcribed, considering that some recording media have limited life spans. All recordings need particular kinds of care if they are to remain useful in the future. The Oral History Association can provide guidelines that will help nonhistorians make the interviews more useful for researchers, but even if the conversations are not conducted in accordance with historians' standards, some oral record is far better than no record at all. A number of the still-surviving individuals that Freeman interviewed, including Laura Smith, Warren Calvin, and David Billings, consented to being reinterviewed, and having had access to their earlier remembrances enriched my own work with them.

More than a dozen persons who had not originally been interviewed by Freeman also agreed to discuss their experiences at St. Mark's with me. Three of the most important were deaconess Mary Lou Barnwell, who was head resident at St. Mark's in the late 1930s and who later became executive secretary of the Commission on Deaconess Work for the general church; Deaconess Helen Mandlebaum, a native of New Orleans who grew up in the St. Mark's congregation and who later served in the New York office of the deaconess program; and the Reverend Mr. Lloyd Anderson Foreman, who was pastor at St. Mark's during the school desegregation crisis in 1960.[12]

When I was already years into my research, I learned that the Women's Division of GBGM possessed a number of oral histories that historian Hilah Thomas recorded with deaconesses. A list of the women interviewed is not in the possession of the Women's Division, and it is necessary to send them the name(s) of a subject(s) to find out whether a tape might be available. The tapes have not been transcribed, and they are available for listening only in the New York offices.[13]

With regard to the history of St. Mark's during the civil rights era, the S.O.S. Collection on file at Tulane University's Amistad Center is the largest single repository of information about the controversial role St. Mark's played in the New Orleans school desegregation crisis. It contains the papers of the Save Our Schools, Inc., organization, which tried to avert the closing of public schools in New Orleans. Along with various internal S.O.S. documents and several of the organization's publications, there is an extensive group of newspaper clippings that deal with school desegregation. Many of these discuss the experiences of Lloyd Anderson "Andy" Foreman, the pastor at St. Mark's who broke the white boycott of William Frantz Elementary by keeping his daughter in school with Ruby Bridges.[14] Foreman also had an extensive private collection of materials from that era. It contained newspaper clippings from many states and even some foreign countries, along with letters and other kinds of documents. He was gracious enough to allow me access to these for my research.

Supplemented with the published work cited elsewhere, these sources yielded significant data on St. Mark's. Despite the lack of records at the facility itself, a fairly comprehensive picture of its history and its place in the Social Gospel movement of the South and in the school desegregation crisis in New Orleans emerged.

It is my hope that historians with interest in other women-run facilities will find this study encouraging. Though there is usually an eagerness on the part of individual informants to help with the writing of women's history, many of them have very little confidence that data about their own lives and work is worth recording. Encouraging them about the importance of their histories, and being willing to persevere in tracking down small leads they offer toward other sources, can result in a wealth of previously unrecovered data. Even some women who have lost cognitive function can contribute to the study. I contacted descendants of some of the women who worked at St. Mark's, and had joint interviews with mothers and daughters in two instances. One mother had saved a shoebox of memorabilia on a shelf in a closet, and when her daughter brought it out, it stirred enough memory for her to help interpret it. They kindly let me make copies of their material, which included clippings about other deaconesses from out-of-state newspapers (usually in the deaconesses' home towns), which I would never have otherwise encountered, and brochures that I did not discover anywhere else. Another woman had advanced Alzheimer's when I visited with her and her daughter, and though she had no short-term memory at all, she was able to admonish my husband that whenever he took a photograph, he should write the name of the people in it on the back. She spoke from a position of authority, too, because she had kept detailed scrapbooks throughout her adult life; thus, even though she married a pastor and left St. Mark's after a fairly brief tenure there, she possessed correspondence and other material that proved of assistance to me, and her care in preserving materials in chronological order let her daughter and me discover it. Indeed, the researcher who is willing to seek small amounts of information from many sources and weave them with care into a coherent story may reap the same reward as the women through the centuries who have quilted, piecing small bits of fabric into what finally becomes a beautiful and useful product.

APPENDIX B

A CHARTER OF RACIAL POLICIES

A·CHARTER·OF·RACIAL·POLICIES

WOMAN'S DIVISION OF CHRISTIAN SERVICE
BOARD OF MISSIONS OF THE METHODIST CHURCH

·WE BELIEVE·

1. We Believe that God is the Father of all people and all are His children in one family.

2. We Believe that the personality of every human being is sacred.

3. We Believe that opportunities for fellowship and service, for personal growth, and for freedom in every aspect of life are inherent rights of every individual.

4. We Believe that the visible church of Jesus Christ must demonstrate these principles within its own organization and program.

5. We Believe that the Woman's Division as an agency of The Methodist Church must build a fellowship and social order without racial barriers in every area it may touch.

·WE WILL·

1. Commit ourselves as individuals called by Jesus Christ to witness by word and deed to the basic rights of every person regardless of cost.

2. Unite our efforts with all groups in the church toward eliminating in The Methodist Church all forms of segregation based on race whether in basic structure or institutional life.

3. Create in local churches opportunities for inclusive fellowship and membership without restriction based on race.

4. Act with other groups and agencies to involve families in new experiences with other races and cultures.

5. Share in creative plans that challenge youth, students and young adults of all races to new understanding of the Church's mission and ministries.

6. Interpret and strengthen recruitment and employment practices of the Woman's Division consistent with our belief in the oneness of God's family.

7. Open the facilities and services of all Woman's Division institutions without restriction based on race and make such policies clearly known.

8. Establish all Schools of Missions and Christian Service and all leadership development and enrichment programs on a regional basis without restriction based on race.

9. Seek to change community patterns of racial segregation in all relationships including education, housing, voting, employment and public facilities.

10. Work for national policies that safeguard the rights of all the nation's people.

11. Support world-wide movements for basic human rights and fundamental freedoms for peoples everywhere.

12. Join with others who seek in church and community justice and freedom for all members of the family of God.

As we begin this New Decade, the Woman's Division of Christian Service calls with new urgency on the Woman's Society of Christian Service and Wesleyan Service Guild to study the principles and goals stated in this Charter, looking toward early ratification. Such ratification will constitute a commitment to work for the speedy implementation of those principles and goals within jurisdiction, conference, district and local Woman's Society or Guild.

Pamphlet published by Women's Division of Christian Service of the Methodist Church, 1962, 9, in Records of the Women's Division of the General Board of Global Ministries, United Methodist Church Archives—General Commission on Archives and History, Madison, New Jersey.

NOTES

INTRODUCTION

1. Valerie Saiving Goldstein, "The Human Situation: A Feminine View," *Journal of Religion* 40, no. 2 (April 1960): 100–112.

2. See Christopher H. Evans, "From Militant Methodism to Secular Christianity: The Social Gospel in American Methodist Historical Narratives," *Methodist History* 38 no. 3 (April 2000): 147–59; Susan Hill Lindley, "Deciding Who Counts: Toward a Revised Definition of the Social Gospel," in *The Social Gospel Today*, ed. Christopher H. Evans (Louisville, Ky.: Westminster John Knox, 2001), 17–26; Wendy J. Deichmann Edwards and Carolyn De Swarte Gifford, *Gender and the Social Gospel* (Urbana: University of Illinois Press, 2003).

3. Jean Miller Schmidt, *Grace Sufficient: A History of Women in American Methodism, 1760–1939* (Nashville, Tenn.: Abingdon Press, 1999), 79–98. Schmidt, following Barbara Welter's classic definition of the "True Woman," refines it specifically for the women of Methodism, thus creating the apt description, "True Methodist Women."

4. John Patrick McDowell, *The Social Gospel in the South: The Woman's Home Mission Movement in the Methodist Episcopal Church, South, 1886–1939* (Baton Rouge: Louisiana State University Press, 1981), 100; Susan Hill Lindley, *You Have Stept Out of Your Place: A History of Women and Religion in America* (Louisville, Ky.: Westminster John Knox Press, 1996).

5. Because the restructuring of the organization is so recent, the designation "North Rampart Community Center" is not used at any point in this history. After Hurricane Katrina, much of the building was temporarily leased to the Louisiana Annual Conference to serve as a dormitory and staging area for volunteer work teams helping the city recover from the 2005 storm and subsequent levee breaks.

6. See the clarifications about the use of the term "women's society," both with regard to official nomenclature and with regard to race later in this introduction.

7. Katrina brought another generation of deaconesses to St. Mark's; at the time of this writing, Deaconess Joanne Finley administers the community center and lives on the third floor of the building.

8. Elizabeth Meredith Lee, *As Among the Methodists: Deaconesses Yesterday, Today and Tomorrow* (New York: Woman's Division of Christian Service, Board of Missions of the Methodist Church, 1973), 37; *Journal of the General Conference, Methodist Episcopal Church, 1888*, 435, cited in Schmidt, *Grace Sufficient*, 201.

9. Alice Cobb, *"Yes, Lord, I'll Do It": Scarritt's Century of Service* (Nashville, Tenn.: Scarritt College, 1987), 40–41; Lee, *As Among the Methodists*, 50–52.

10. Alice Knotts, *Lifting Up Hope, Living Out Justice: Methodist Women and the Social Gospel* (San Diego: Frontrowliving Press, 2007), 8; Elke Adams, Offices of Deaconess, Home Missioner and Home Missionary, e-mail to the author, July 7, 2010.

11. Sarah Sloan Kreutziger, "Going on to Perfection: The Contributions of the Wesleyan Theological Doctrine of Entire Sanctification to the Value Base of American Professional Social Work through the Lives and Activities of Nineteenth Century Evangelical Women Reformers," D.S.W. diss., Tulane University, 1991.

12. Schmidt, *Grace Sufficient*, 192, 216–19.

13. Mary Agnes Dougherty, *My Calling to Fulfill: Deaconesses in the United Methodist Tradition* (New York: Women's Division, General Board of Global Ministries, United Methodist Church, 1997), 20–21.

14. Lucy Rider Meyer quoted in Eleanor P. Clarkson, "Deaconesses Then," *World Outlook* 53, no. 1 (January 1963): 39; Dougherty, *My Calling to Fulfill*, 24–28.

15. Catherine Wessinger, ed., *Religious Institutions and Women's Leadership: New Roles Inside the Mainstream* (Columbia: University of South Carolina Press, 1996), 5.

16. Barbara Welter, "The Cult of True Womanhood: 1820–1860," *American Quarterly* 18 (1966): 151–74; Barbara J. MacHaffie, *Her Story: Women in Christian Tradition* (Philadelphia: Fortress Press, 1986); Schmidt, *Grace Sufficient*, 212.

17. Edwards and Gifford, *Gender and the Social Gospel*, 6–9.

18. Lindley, "Deciding Who Counts," 18–22.

19. Edwards and Gifford, *Gender and the Social Gospel*, 9, 12, 14.

CHAPTER 1

1. *New Orleans States*, May 4, 1940, 4.

2. Fae L. Daves, "'Opening Doors' at St. Mark's Community Center," *The Methodist Woman*, January 1950, 8–9; Mary Morrison, "Looking Back at St. Mark's," 1971, manuscript on file at St. Mark's United Methodist Church; Margery Freeman, "The St. Mark's Family: A Story of Change," 1979, manuscript on file at St. Mark's United Methodist Church.

3. *Journal of the Louisiana Annual Conference*, 1894, 32–33. Journals of the proceedings of the annual conference were given slightly different titles at various times in the nineteenth and twentieth centuries. To prevent confusion, slight title variations are ignored in this study, and all references to these documents use the nomenclature *Journal of the Louisiana Annual Conference*.

4. Mrs. H. A. Kennedy, "P. and H. M. Work in the Louisiana Conference," *New Orleans Christian Advocate*, October 3, 1895, 4. Her article contains a typographical error; the society was actually established in 1891.

5. Ibid.

6. Although no documentation on the industrial school at the Tchoupitoulas Mission is available, an industrial school operated at Kingsley House, a nonsectarian settlement house located nearby. At the Kingsley House school, girls took sewing, English, physical culture, and singing classes, while boys enrolled in manual training, clay modeling, and mechanical drawing. The mechanical drawing instructor said, "In working drawings I wish the boys to learn . . . to measure accurately. In geometrical drawing the problems are the best kind of mental gymnastics." The manual training instructor's goal was "to teach the boys to lay out work systematically and handle tools properly; these are the essentials to practical work on leaving the school." From Katharine Hardesty, "Eleanor McMain, Trail-Blazer of Southern Social Work," M.S.W. thesis, Tulane University, 1936, 57.

7. Program of the Second Annual Meeting of the Woman's Board of Home Missions, Methodist Episcopal Church, South, April 11–18, 1900. In the personal collection of Beach Carré.

8. Ibid.; "Louisiana Conference P. and H. M. S.," *New Orleans Christian Advocate*, February 7, 1895, 7.

9. Despite the fact that this kind of acronym is not usually applied to newspapers, the *New Orleans Christian Advocate* is hereafter referred to within the text as *NOCA*. The name "Christian Advocate" has traditionally been used for Methodist publications at many levels, including publications at General Conference. Further, a *Southwestern Christian Advocate* was also published in New Orleans for MEC readers, many of whom were African Americans. Shortening the *New Orleans Christian Advocate's* name to *Christian Advocate* or *Advocate* would not only invite confusion on the part of many readers, but also assign "normative" status to the white-readership version. I have judged it better to use an unusual abbreviation than to risk implying that the *New Orleans Christian Advocate* was the only *Christian Advocate* published in Louisiana. This source is further discussed in Appendix A.

10. *New Orleans Christian Advocate*, February 28, 1895, 2.

11. Ibid.

12. *New Orleans Christian Advocate*, April 25, 1895, 4.

13. *New Orleans Christian Advocate*, October 3, 1895. Advertisers included the WCTU Restaurant, located on Gravier Street between St. Charles Avenue and Camp Street. Run by the Woman's Christian Temperance Union, it sold lunches for fifteen cents, apparently as a fund-raiser for the organization.

14. Kennedy, "P. and H. M. Work," 4.

15. Ibid.

16. Florence Russ, "P. and H.M.S. Report," *New Orleans Christian Advocate*, April 8, 1897, 2. Werlein's father, Philip, was an immigrant from Germany who became one of the country's first publishers of sheet music. Werlein Music was a prominent New Orleans business in the late nineteenth and throughout the twentieth centuries.

17. Parham Werlein, telephone interview by the author, September 3, 2001; Betty Werlein Carter and Lorraine Moore, telephone interview by the author, April 24, 1998. Betty Werlein Carter, who was married to publisher Hodding Carter, was a noted author and activist who advocated racial justice in the South. Her mother, Elizebeth Werlein, was a noted preservationist of the Vieux Carré (the French Quarter), a volunteer at Kingsley House, and an activist for numerous causes.

18. Leila Werlein Stone, telephone interview by the author, October 12, 2001.

19. Ibid.

20. Mary Werlein, "Be Prompt," *New Orleans Christian Advocate*, May 2, 1895, 2.

21. Ibid.

22. Mary Werlein, letter to Lucinda B. Helm, June 26, 1895, *New Orleans Christian Advocate*, July 11, 1895, 2.

23. Ibid.

24. Ibid.

25. Ibid.

26. Ibid.

27. *New Orleans Christian Advocate*, February 6, 1896, 4.

28. Ibid., 5.

29. Ibid.

30. Russ, "P. and H.M.S. Report," 2.

31. Mary Noreen Dunn, *Women and Home Missions* (Nashville, Tenn.: Cokesbury Press, 1936), 26–27.

32. Russ, "P. and H.M.S. Report," 2.

33. Sara Joyce Myers, "Southern Methodist Women Leaders and Church Missions, 1878–1910," Ph.D. diss., Emory University, 1990; Ben Logan, *A Lost History*, produced by Patricia Mauger, NBC News, in association with the World Council of Churches, 1984, videocassette; Rosemary Skinner Keller, "Conversions and Their Consequences: Women's Ministry and Leadership in the United Methodist Tradition," in Catherine Wessinger, ed., *Religious Institutions and Women's Leadership*, 115; Annette K. Baxter, "Preface," in Karen J. Blair, *The Clubwoman as Feminist: True Womanhood Redefined, 1868–1914* (New York: Holmes & Meier, 1980), xii.

34. Mrs. E. R. Kennedy, "Report of the Louisiana Conference Woman's Home Mission Society, *Journal of the Louisiana Annual Conference*, 1901, 66; *Journal of the Louisiana Annual Conference*, 1903; Mrs. J. Benton Hobb, "Woman's Home Mission Society," *Journal of the Louisiana Annual Conference*, 1906, 46.

35. Kreutziger, "Going on to Perfection."

36. *Journal of the Louisiana Annual Conference*, 1907, 36. In the 1926 *Journal of the Louisiana Annual Conference* and thereafter, there is no mention of the Mary Werlein Mission, and presumably it ceased to exist as a separate entity at that time. Margery Wright, Methodist Archives, Centenary College, Shreveport, e-mail to the author, September 30, 2002.

37. *Twenty-First Annual Report of the Woman's Home Mission Society, MECS*, 1907, 108.

38. *New Orleans Christian Advocate*, May 9, 1940, 7.

39. "Devout Church Worker Expires," *New Orleans States*, May 4, 1940, 3; "Mary Werlein," *New Orleans States*, May 4, 1940, 4.

40. Eric F. Goldman, "Books That Changed America," *Saturday Review*, July 4, 1953, 9, cited in Ronald C. White Jr., *Liberty and Justice for All: Racial Reform and the Social Gospel (1877–1925)* (San Francisco: Harper & Row, 1990), 31.

41. McDowell, *The Social Gospel in the South*, 26; see also Dana L. Robert, "Bennett, Belle Harris," *Biographical Dictionary of Christian Missions*, ed. Gerald H. Anderson (New York: Simon & Schuster, Macmillan, 1998; Grand Rapids, Mich.: Wm. B. Eerdmans, 1999), 55.

42. Belle H. Bennett, "The Woman's Home Mission Society," address delivered at the General Missionary Conference at New Orleans, April 27, 1901, pamphlet in the records

of the Women's Division of the General Board of Global Ministries, United Methodist Church Archives—General Commission on Archives and History, Madison, New Jersey, 8.

43. Ibid.; The officers of the New Orleans City Mission Board as listed in the *Journal of the Louisiana Annual Conference*, 1903, 12, were Mrs. W. W. Carré, president; Mrs. F. A. Lyons; first vice president; Mrs. S. A. Montgomery, second vice president; Mrs. L. P. Jackson, third vice president; Miss Margaret Beasley, corresponding secretary; Mrs. A. Bartels, recording secretary; and Mrs. J. G. Rowland, treasurer. The *Journal of the Louisiana Annual Conference*, 1901 reported that eight congregations' societies were represented on the board.

44. See, for instance, Jean Miller Schmidt's *Grace Sufficient*, 228–29, and Robert W. Sledge, *"Five Dollars and Myself": The History of Mission of the Methodist Episcopal Church, South, 1845–1939* (New York: General Board of Global Ministries, 2005), 300–302.

45. Bennett, "Woman's Home Mission Society" address, 1901, 8, GCAH.

46. Harry W. Rickey, secretary, board of missions, *Journal of the Louisiana Conference*, 1903, 65.

47. Ibid.

48. "Episcopal Address," *Journal of the General Conference of 1906*, 24, cited in John Olen Fish, "Southern Methodism in the Progressive Era," Ph.D. diss., University of Georgia, 1969, 71.

49. William Ivy Hair, *Carnival of Fury: Robert Charles and the New Orleans Race Riot of 1900* (Baton Rouge: Louisiana State University Press, 1976).

50. Ibid.

51. Arnold R. Hirsch and Joseph Logsdon, eds., *Creole New Orleans: Race and Americanization* (Baton Rouge: Louisiana State University Press, 1992); Louise Reynes Edwards-Simpson, "Sicilian Immigration to New Orleans, 1870–1910: Ethnicity, Race and Social Position in the New South," Ph.D. diss., University of Minnesota, 1996.

52. Edwards-Simpson, "Sicilian Immigration to New Orleans," 113.

53. "In 1930, for example, Atlanta had only 509 out of a total population of 270,366; Dallas had 1913 out of a total population of 260,475; Houston had 4931 out of a total population of 292,352; Cincinnati, a city outside the south about the same size as New Orleans, had 7432 out of a population of 451,160; New Orleans stood far ahead of these cities with 24,011 out of a total population of 458,762." George M. Reynolds, *Machine Politics in New Orleans, 1897–1926*, Studies in History, Economics and Public Law, no. 421 (New York: Columbia University Press, 1936), 13, quoting Twelfth Census 1900, "Population," vol. 1, 800; Fourteenth Census 1920, "Population," vol. 3, 928.

54. Edwards-Simpson, "Sicilian Immigration to New Orleans," 13.

55. Ibid., 38; Rowland Berthoff, "Southern Attitudes Toward Immigration, 1865–1914," *Journal Of Southern History* 17, no. 3 (1951): 328–60.

56. John Olen Fish, "Southern Methodism and the Accommodation of the Negro," *Journal of Negro History* 55, no. 3 (July 1970): 202–3.

57. Edwards-Simpson, "Sicilian Immigration to New Orleans," 11–12.

58. Ibid., 43.

59. "Louisiana Conference," *New Orleans Christian Advocate*, December 17, 1908, 4.

60. Lillian Day, *Opening Doors: A Pageant*, play performed at St. Mark's Community Center on September 29, 1949, script on file at St. Mark's United Methodist Church. Day was a deaconess at St. Mark's.

61. New Orleans residents will know that during the four years the settlement spent at 619–21 Esplanade, it was technically in the Faubourg Marigny; its next location, 908 Esplanade, which it occupied for ten years, was on the opposite side of the street and thus technically in the French Quarter.

62. Virginia A. Shadron, "Out of Our Homes: The Woman's Rights Movement in the Methodist Episcopal Church, South, 1890–1918," M.A. thesis, Emory University, 1976, 3; Walter N. Vernon, *Becoming One People: A History of Louisiana Methodism* (Bossier City: Commission on Archives and History, Louisiana Annual Conference of the United Methodist Church, 1987), 108.

63. *Sixteenth Annual Report of the General Board of Managers of the Woman's Home Missionary Society, MEC,* 1896–97, 97; "Italian Kindergarten," *Woman's Home Missions*, April 1936, 11.

64. Paul Boyer, *Urban Masses and Moral Order in America, 1820–1920* (Cambridge, Mass.: Harvard University Press, 1978).

65. N. E. Joyner, "Italians in New Orleans and Vicinity," *The Missionary Voice*, April 1911, 46–47; "A Help to Italian Immigrants," *The Missionary Voice*, April 1911, 63.

66. *The Council Daily* 7, no. 4 (April 18, 1917), records of the Women's Division of the General Board of Global Ministries, United Methodist Church Archives—General Commission on Archives and History, Madison, New Jersey, 3–4.

67. "Mrs. W. W. Carré Dies at Home of her Nephew: Family Present as Faithful Church Worker Passes," *New Orleans Times-Picayune*, May 29, 1924, 6; "What Women Are Doing: Gifted Louisiana Women," *New Orleans Louisiana Review*, April 29, 1891, 6; "Dr. E. D. Beach Dies Aged Eighty-Seven," *New Orleans Daily Picayune*, August 6, 1902, 4.

68. E. P. Moskie, "In Memoriam—Erasmus Darwin Beach," resolution adopted by the Official Board of Carondelet Methodist Episcopal Church, South, August 23, 1902. In the personal collection of Beach Carré.

69. "What Women Are Doing," *New Orleans Louisiana Review*, April 29, 1891, 6.

70. Welter, "Cult of True Womanhood," 151–74; Schmidt, *Grace Sufficient*, 79–98; Ellen Blue, "True Methodist Women: Reflections on the Community at St. Mark's, 1895–1939," in *Louisiana Women: Their Lives and Times*, ed. Janet Allured and Judith F. Gentry (Athens: University of Georgia Press, 2009), 215–36.

71. Carré was president of the Christian Woman's Exchange for five years, providing "effective leadership" before resigning in 1915 because of ill health and "frequent long absences from the city." Charles L. "Pie" Dufour, *Women Who Cared: The 100 Years of the Christian Woman's Exchange* (New Orleans: Christian Woman's Exchange, 1980), 23–24.

72. One of her sons, Henry Beach Carré, went on to become ordained, serve as president of Centenary College, and hold the Chair of Biblical Theology and English Exegesis at Vanderbilt's School of Religion.

73. "What Women Are Doing," *New Orleans Louisiana Review*, April 29, 1891, 6.

74. Isabel Gardner Larue, telephone interview by the author, May 30, 2006; Alcée Fortier, ed., *Louisiana: Comprising Sketches of Parishes, Towns, Events, Institutions, and Persons, Arranged in Cyclopedic Form* (Madison, Wis.: Century Historical Association, 1914), 3:502–3; *Council Daily* 7, no. 4 (April 18, 1917), 3–4; "Mrs. W. W. Carré Dies at Home of her Nephew: Family Present as Faithful Church Worker Passes," *New Orleans Times-Picayune*, May 29, 1924, 6.

75. Sylvia Robbins, "A History of the New Orleans Council of Social Agencies, 1921–1941," M.S.W. thesis, Tulane University, 1941, 16, 26. One official representative was Mrs. J. G. Snelling of the Methodist Home for Women, a facility established to care for unwed mothers, when Storyville, the section of New Orleans where prostitution was licensed and legal, was closed down. Snelling's grandson, the Reverend Mr. Clarence H. Snelling Jr., whose mother was a deaconess, played a prominent role in the history of Methodist race relations in the city during the time period covered in chapter 5.

76. Sonora Towles Marsh, "A History of the New Orleans Community Chest, 1924–1940," M.S.W. thesis, Tulane University, 1940, 139.

77. Elizabeth Hayes Turner, *Women, Culture, and Community: Religion and Reform in Galveston, 1880–1920* (New York: Oxford University Press, 1997); see also Marsha Wedell, *Elite Women and the Reform Impulse in Memphis, 1875–1915* (Knoxville: University of Tennessee Press, 1991).

78. Diana Kendall, *The Power of Good Deeds: Privileged Women and the Social Reproduction of the Upper Class* (Lanham, Md.: Rowman and Littlefield, 2002).

79. Rayne Memorial Year Book, 1908, issued by the Woman's Home Mission Society, cited in Fannie Rayne Russ and Georgie Russ Ross, *One Hundred Years of Rayne Memorial* (New Orleans: privately published, 1975), 93-94.

80. Ibid., 94.

81. Acts 2:44; Randy Maddox, "'Visit the Poor': John Wesley, the Poor, and the Sanctification of Believers," in *The Poor and the People Called Methodists*, ed. Richard P. Heitzenrater (Nashville, Tenn.: Kingswood, 2002), 66-67.

82. Maddox, "Visit the Poor," 77-79. Emphasis in the original.

CHAPTER 2

1. *New Orleans Christian Advocate*, January 24, 1907, 5.

2. R. E. Smith, "Nicolas E. Joyner: February 15, 1871-January 25, 1959," *Journal of the Louisiana Annual Conference*, 1959, 210-13, available at <www.iscuo.org/memoirs/m59njoyner.htm>, accessed October 24, 2008.

3. *New Orleans Christian Advocate*, January 24, 1907, 5.

4. *New Orleans Christian Advocate*, February 4, 1909, cover. Institutional churches were those that had broadened their focus to include the meeting of human needs and instituted a wide range of charitable and social works as part of their programming.

5. Reverend N. E. Joyner, "St. Mark's Hall, Institutional Plant, in New Orleans," *Go Forward* 9, no. 5 (November 1909): 3-4, records of the Women's Division of the General Board of Global Ministries, United Methodist Church Archives—General Commission on Archives and History, Madison, New Jersey.

6. Ibid.

7. Ibid. Emphasis added.

8. Margery Freeman, "The St. Mark's Family: A Story of Change," 1979, manuscript on file at St. Mark's United Methodist Church; church membership rolls on file at St. Mark's United Methodist Church.

9. *New Orleans Christian Advocate*, March 4, 1909, 5.

10. "Woman's City Mission Board," *New Orleans Christian Advocate*, March 3, 1910, 5.

11. Ibid.

12. Ibid.

13. Robert A. Woods and Albert J. Kennedy, eds., *Handbook of Settlements* (New York: Charities Publication Committee, 1911), 92.

14. *Minutes of the Second Annual Meeting*, Louisiana Conference Woman's Missionary Society, 1912, 32, on file at Magale Library, Centenary College.

15. *Minutes of the Third Annual Meeting*, Louisiana Conference Woman's Missionary Society, 1913, 68, on file at Magale Library, Centenary College.

16. *Minutes of the Second Annual Meeting*, Louisiana Conference Woman's Missionary Society, 1912, 4, 8, on file at Magale Library, Centenary College.

17. J. W. Moore, letter to Bishop Warren Candler, July 9, 1912, box 19, folder 6, Warren A. Candler Papers, Special Collections, Robert W. Woodruff Library, Emory University, Atlanta. As noted elsewhere, Meekins was a widow and not a deaconess, but rather a city missionary, an important distinction that the designer of the letterhead apparently had not grasped.

18. Mabel Katherine Howell, *Women and the Kingdom: Fifty Years of Kingdom Building by the Women of the Methodist Episcopal Church, South, 1878–1928* (Nashville, Tenn.: Cokesbury Press, 1928), 191.

19. J. W. Moore, letter to Bishop Warren Candler, July 9, 1912, Emory.

20. Fish, "Southern Methodism in the Progressive Era," 43–44.

21. *Twenty-Fourth Annual Report of the Woman's Home Mission Society, MECS*, 1910, 165; *Second Annual Report of the Woman's Missionary Council, MECS*, 1911–12, 358; *Third Annual Report of the Woman's Missionary Council, MECS*, 1911–12.

22. Gail Bederman, "'The Women Have Had Charge of the Church Work Long Enough': The Men and Religion Forward Movement of 1911–1912 and the Masculinization of Middle-Class Protestantism," *American Quarterly* 41, no. 3 (September 1989): 432–65.

23. Robert Watson Sledge, *Hands on the Ark: The Struggle for Change in the Methodist Episcopal Church, South, 1914–1939* (Lake Junaluska, N.C.: Commission on Archives and History, United Methodist Church, 1975), 44.

24. Isabelle Dubroca, *Good Neighbor Eleanor McMain of Kingsley House* (New Orleans: Pelican Publishing, 1955), 41. The move toward diversity did not extend to gender; the members of the Kingsley House board of directors in 1916 were all men.

25. Allen F. Davis, *Spearheads for Reform: The Social Settlements and the Progressive Movement, 1890–1914* (New York: Oxford University Press, 1967), 15, 23.

26. Helen Dore Boylston, *Sue Barton, Visiting Nurse* (Boston: Little Brown and Company, 1938), 115–19.

27. Maureen Fastenau, "Maternal Government: The Social Settlement Houses and the Politicization of Women's Sphere, 1889–1920," Ph.D. diss., Duke University, 1982, 254.

28. *Minutes of the Third Annual Meeting*, Louisiana Conference Woman's Missionary Society, 1913, 68, on file at Magale Library, Centenary College.

29. *Third Annual Report, Woman's Missionary Council, MECS*, 1912–13, 161; *Fourth Annual Report, Woman's Missionary Council, MECS*, 1913–14, 446; *Fifth Annual Report, Woman's Missionary Council, MECS*, 1914–15, 362.

30. *Fourth Annual Report of the Woman's Missionary Council, MECS*, 1913–14, 153; *Journal of the Louisiana Annual Conference*, 1913; Robert Henry Harper, *Louisiana Methodism* (Washington, D.C.: Kaufmann Press, 1949), 109.

31. *Fifth Annual Report of the Woman's Missionary Council, MECS*, 1914–15, 285; "Memorial to the Woman's Missionary Council," *Fourth Annual Meeting, Woman's Missionary Society of the Louisiana Conference*, 1914, 60. One signer was Mrs. J. G. Snelling, who with her husband, a Methodist clergyman, ran the Methodist home for unwed mothers in the city. She was the grandmother of the Reverend Dr. Clarence H. Snelling Jr., who would play a role in the portion of the civil rights movement detailed in chapter 5; his mother was a deaconess assigned to the Methodist Home.

32. *Sixth Annual Report of the Woman's Missionary Council, MECS*, 1915–16, 94.

33. "Mrs. Lily [*sic*] Meekins, Charity Worker, Dragged by Car: 'The Angel of Tchoupitoulas' Is Victim of Peculiar Accident," *New Orleans Times-Picayune*, January 3, 1916, 10.

34. Ibid.

35. "Mrs. Lily [*sic*] Meekins, Charity Worker, Dies of Her Hurts," *New Orleans Times-Picayune*, January 10, 1916, 1.

36. Ibid.

37. "Mrs. Lily [*sic*] Meekins, Charity Worker, Dragged by Car," *New Orleans Times-Picayune*, January 3, 1916, 10.

38. *The Council Daily* 7, no. 4 (April 18, 1917), 3–4.

39. Undated clipping from a New Orleans newspaper, in the collection of Parker Schneidau. The groom's brother, Franklin Nutting Parker, later dean of Candler School of Theology at Emory University, officiated, and a prayer of blessing was offered by another brother, Fitzgerald S. Parker, who later worked with the MECS Publishing House.

40. John William Leonard, ed., *Woman's Who's Who of America: A Biographical Dictionary of Contemporary Women of the United States and Canada, 1914–1915* (New York: American Commonwealth, 1914), 621.

41. *The Picayune's Guide to New Orleans*, 5th ed., revised and enlarged (New Orleans: Daily Picayune, 1903), 165, accessed September 20, 2008 at <http://books. google.com/books?id=jU8UAAAAYAAJ&pg=PA193&lpg=PA193&dq=picayune's+guide +to+new+orleans+1903&source=web&ots=ZTSXQmHkVz&sig=FUktaUE1agH61MxL njjCwKh5uyk&hl=en&sa=X&oi=book_result&resnum=2&ct=result#PPA164,M1>.

42. Elna C. Green, *Southern Strategies: Southern Women and the Woman Suffrage Question* (Chapel Hill: University of North Carolina Press, 1997), 132, 238.

43. Parker Schneidau, interviews by the author, April 2, 2007, and September 25, 2008, Metairie, Louisiana. Schneidau said Hattie Parker frequently wrote things that appeared in the *Times-Picayune*. After she was quite old, she was stopped one day while driving for going through a stop sign. She told the officer that she had slowed into second gear and that no other cars were coming, so she was not going to accept a ticket. He told her that if she did not, he would take her to jail. She responded, "Oh, good, I've never been there, and I've always wanted to go!" When they arrived, she saw cockroaches and a rat and found the odor horrible, and kept commenting on what a wonderful story it was going to make for the newspaper. "It wasn't long," Schneidau said, "before they called my uncle and said, 'Can you please come and get your mother?'"

44. *The Council Daily* 7, no. 4 (April 18, 1917), 3–4.

45. Louise Marie Lester, "A History of Travelers Aid Society in New Orleans," M.S.W. thesis, Tulane University, 1940, 1.

46. Green, *Southern Strategies;* Pamela Tyler, *Silk Stockings & Ballot Boxes: Women & Politics in New Orleans, 1920–1963* (Athens: University of Georgia Press, 1996).

47. "The New Orleans Reforms Movement," *New Orleans Christian Advocate*, February 1, 1917, 8.

48. Fortier, ed., *Louisiana*, 460–61; Alecia P. Long, *The Great Southern Babylon: Sex, Race, and Respectability in New Orleans, 1865–1920* (Baton Rouge: Louisiana State University Press, 2004), 211–14.

49. Lester, "History of Travelers Aid Society," 1.

50. Nicholas Kristof, "A Heroine from the Brothels," *New York Times*, September 25, 2008.

51. Long, *Great Southern Babylon*, 225–28.

52. *New Orleans Christian Advocate*, March 29, 1917, 14.

53. Helen Gibson, "St. Mark's Hall," *Seventh Annual Report, Woman's Missionary Council, MECS*, 1917, 297.

54. Joyner, "St. Mark's Hall," 3–4, GCAH.

55. Reverend W. E. Thomas, "New Orleans and Some of Its Missionary Needs," *New Orleans Christian Advocate*, April 12, 1917, 4.

56. "Notes from St. Mark's Hall, New Orleans La.," *New Orleans Christian Advocate*, September 6, 1917, 14; "Woman's Home Missionary Society," *New Orleans Christian Advocate*, October 11, 1917, 14.

57. "Woman's Home Missionary Society," *New Orleans Christian Advocate*, November 15, 1917, 14.

58. "Deaconesses Volunteer, Report No. 6," *The Council Daily* 7, no. 6 (April 20, 1917).

59. Jane Addams, *The Second Twenty Years at Hull-House* (New York: MacMillan, 1930), 12.

60. Kathryn Kish Sklar, "Beyond Maternalism: Protestant Women & Social Justice Activism, 1890–1920," *Women and Twentieth-Century Protestantism* 3 (Winter 1999): 2–7; Eleanor J. Stebner, *The Women of Hull House: A Study in Spirituality, Vocation, and Friendship* (Albany: State University of New York Press, 1997).

61. Nathan O. Hatch, "The Puzzle of American Methodism," in *Methodism and the Shaping of American Culture*, ed. Nathan O. Hatch and John H. Wigger (Nashville, Tenn.: Kingswood Books, 2001), 23–40.

CHAPTER 3

1. Schmidt, *Grace Sufficient*, 227–31.

2. Jerald C. Brauer, ed., *The Westminster Dictionary of Church History* (Philadelphia: Westminster Press, 1971), 360, 692, 777, 791.

3. Helen Mandlebaum, interview by the author, Asheville, North Carolina, August 25, 2000.

4. Lucy Rider Meyer quoted in Clarkson, "Deaconesses Then," 39.

5. Dorothy Lorena Lundy Smira, interview by the author, Metairie, Louisiana, March 8, 2001.

6. Luke 4:18–19, King James Version (hereafter KJV); Isaiah 61:1, KJV.

7. Program for Consecration Service of Missionary and Deaconess Candidates, Wesley Memorial Methodist Episcopal Church, South, Atlanta, Georgia, March 14, 1932; Program for Consecration Service of Missionary and Deaconess Candidates, First Methodist Episcopal Church, South, Dallas, Texas, March 22, 1936, in records of the Women's Division of the General Board of Global Ministries, United Methodist Church Archives, General Commission on Archives and History, Madison, New Jersey.

8. Judith Ann Trolander, *Settlement Houses and the Great Depression* (Detroit: Wayne State University, 1975), 27, 145. Emphasis added.

9. Helen Mandlebaum, a deaconess who grew up as part of the St. Mark's congregation, worked with the National Federation of Settlements in New York as part of her deaconess career. Mandlebaum, interview by the author, August 25, 2000.

10. Robbins, "History of the New Orleans Council," 16, 26. One official representative was Mrs. J. G. Snelling of the Methodist Home for Women. Snelling's grandson, the Reverend Mr. Clarence H. Snelling Jr., whose mother was a deaconess, played a prominent role in the history of Methodist race relations in the city during the time period covered in chapter 5.

11. Rev. Marion Browning, Pastor's Report to Quarterly Conference, March 23, 1921, on file at St. Mark's United Methodist Church; Rev. and Mrs. Marion Browning, "Mary Werlein Mission," *Minutes: Eleventh Annual Session of the Woman's Missionary Society of the Louisiana Conference*, February 1921, 71.

12. Berta Ellison, "Annual Report for St. Mark's Hall," *Minutes, Eleventh Annual Session of the Woman's Missionary Society of the Louisiana Conference*, February 1921, 90.

13. Ibid., 64–65.

14. Ruth Byerly, "Annual Report for St. Mark's Hall," *Minutes, Twelfth Annual Session of the Woman's Missionary Society of the Louisiana Conference*, February 1922, 72.

15. Elmer T. Clark, "Centenary Fund, The Missionary," in *The Encyclopedia of World Methodism*, ed. Nolan B. Harmon (Nashville, Tenn.: United Methodist Publishing House, 1974), 1:432–33.

16. Winans Drake, P. E., "News from the Districts," *New Orleans Christian Advocate*, January 25, 1923, 4.

17. "Woman's Missionary Society," *New Orleans Christian Advocate*, April 5, 1923, 14.

18. Berta Ellison, "A Dream Come True," *New Orleans Christian Advocate*, May 24, 1923, 14. Regarding the individuals involved in the establishment of St. Mark's Community Center, Ellison wrote: "Just who dreamed first and when, I do not know. In the beginning and for many years, Miss Bennett and Mrs. MacDonell, Miss Mary Helm and some consecrated local women, among whom was Mrs. W. W. Carré, were interested in St Mark's. They worked for it, they prayed for it, they loved it. There were others, of course, and when history is written their names should appear; but this short sketch is not meant to be historical primarily."

19. Ibid.

20. "St. Mark's Hall," *New Orleans Christian Advocate*, May 31, 1923, 8.

21. Sherry Gordon Smyth, interview by the author, Harahan, Louisiana, March 22, 2001.

22. Annie Rogers, presentation at the Brooks-Howell Home in Asheville, North Carolina, March 1976, tape recording in possession of deaconess Helen Mandlebaum.

23. Ibid. The other side of the cassette tape on which Rogers's presentation was recorded contained a talk by deaconess Lola Timms at a Brooks-Howell Home vespers service in the fall of 1975. She recounted that the Methodist church closed the northern center where she served because they had not been successful at converting the Polish Catholics who made up most of their clientele. "We hadn't tried," she said, noting that the women of the center did not see converting practicing Catholics as part of their mission to the people.

24. "Mr. Roosevelt and the Pope," *New Orleans Christian Advocate*, April 14, 1910, 8.

25. *New Orleans Christian Advocate*, March 4, 1909, 5.

26. Leila Werlein Stone, telephone interview by the author, October 12, 2001.

27. Annie Rogers, tape recording.

28. The convent, completed in 1752, is the oldest surviving building in the Mississippi River valley.

29. David Cuthbert, "Unlocking a Landmark," *New Orleans Times-Picayune*, August 1, 1995, D-1; "Archbishop Antoine Blanc Memorial Including Old Ursuline Convent, Oldest Building in the Mississippi Valley, and St. Mary's Church, Ancient Chapel of the Archbishops," brochure distributed at the Old Ursuline Convent, 1100 Chartres Street, New Orleans.

30. "I am come that they might have life, and that they might have it more abundantly," (John 10:10b, KJV).

31. Annie Rogers, tape recording.

32. Ibid.; Boyer, *Urban Masses and Moral Order;* Trolander, *Settlement Houses*.

33. Berta Eliison [*sic*], *New Orleans Christian Advocate*, December 21, 1923, 13.

34. Delores Prickett, transcript of interview conducted in 1979 by Margery Freeman, on file at St. Mark's United Methodist Church.

35. Minutes of Quarterly Conference, January 12, 1927, on file at St. Mark's United Methodist Church. The same minutes indicated that the church began the year with 189 members on the roll, but that 107 were removed by conference action; this action is taken only with totally inactive members. Twenty-five persons had joined the church by profession of faith, and eleven others had transferred their membership to St. Mark's. The pastor reported that fifteen adults and five infants had been baptized. The Woman's Missionary Society had fifteen members. Other progress during the

year included the organization of a men's Bible class and the commitment of "several" persons to lives of Christian service, a term that implied acknowledging a full-time, vocational-level calling rather than just a commitment to live a Christian life as a layperson. The pastor reported holding frequent "cottage" prayer services in homes, sometimes praying in French, and giving some participants the opportunity "to sing Christian hymns for the first time in their lives."

36. Margery Wright, Methodist Archives, Centenary College, Shreveport, e-mail to the author, September 30, 2002.

CHAPTER 4

1. Roma C. Cupp, "Deaconesses . . . 'Loving Trouble-Makers.'" *Methodist Woman* 25, no. 11 (July–August 1965): 22–24.

2. Mary Lou Barnwell, interview by the author, Asheville, North Carolina, August 25, 2000; "Mary Lou Barnwell," personal entry for "Life Stories Book" at Brooks-Howell Home, Asheville. After the 1939 denominational merger, she was elected executive secretary of urban work in the Woman's Division of Christian Service of the Board of Missions and Church Extension. She served in that capacity until 1948, when she was named executive secretary of the Commission on Deaconess Work. In 1964, when that commission merged into other portions of the denomination-wide mission agency, she became the assistant general secretary of the National Division and served there until she retired in 1968.

3. *They Went Out Not Knowing . . . : An Encyclopedia of 100 Women in Mission* (New York: Women's Division of the General Board of Global Ministries, The United Methodist Church, 1986), 35.

4. Mary Lou Barnwell, interview by the author, August 25, 2000.

5. Ibid.

6. Virginia Lieson Brereton, "Preparing Women for the Lord's Work: the Story of Three Methodist Training Schools, 1880–1940," in *Women in New Worlds: Historical Perspectives on the Wesleyan Tradition*, ed. Hilah F. Thomas and Rosemary Skinner Keller (Nashville, Tenn.: Abingdon Press, 1981), 188–89.

7. Clinton Howell, ed., *Prominent Personalities in American Methodism* (Birmingham: Lowry Press, 1945), vol. 1:18.

8. Cobb, *"Yes, Lord, I'll Do It,"* 49.

9. Helen Mandlebaum, e-mail to the author, February 8, 2001.

10. Boone M. Bowen, *The Candler School of Theology: Sixty Years of Service* (Atlanta: Candler School of Theology, Emory University, 1974), 178–79.

11. *Journal of the Alabama–West Florida Annual Conference*, 1962, 232, cited in Bowen, *Candler School of Theology*, 178–79.

12. Albert E. Barnett, *Andrew Sledd: His Life and Work*, monograph originally presented as a paper to the Andrew Sledd Study Club of the Alabama–West Florida Conference of The Methodist Church, Spring 1956, copy on file at the Perkins Library, University of Florida, Gainesville (privately printed, n.d.), 3.

13. Ibid., 16. Emphasis in the original. Sledd went on to say that while SMU would do well to get Barnett, he thought it would not necessarily be good for Barnett to expose himself to the process of "being digested" by SMU. Again, it is important not to confuse Bishop John M. Moore with the Rev. John W. Moore who clashed with head resident Margaret Ragland in 1912.

14. Julia Southard Campbell, letters to the author, n.d. (received February 5, 2001); n.d. (received February 16, 2001); March 22, 2001.

15. Albert E. Barnett, "The Kingdom of God and the Church's Task," *Social Action* 22 (September 1955): 21–25 (originally published in *Christian Advocate*, July 7, 1955).

16. Julia Southard Campbell, letter to the author, March 22, 2001. Vida Scudder, the lone woman whose name occasionally appears on lists of prominent Social Gospel writers, was a self-proclaimed socialist, and her 1917 volume, *The Church and the Hour: Papers by a Socialist Churchwoman* (New York: E. P Dutton, 1917), should alone be enough to refute any contention that all religious reformers/activists were motivated by the aim of social control or maintenance of the status quo. Scudder, an active Episcopalian laywoman, was convinced that Christianity required the adoption of socialism, and at the very least, a benign approval of class struggles by the proletariat, which could lead to revolution.

17. Kenneth Edwin Barnhart, "The Evolution of the Social Consciousness in Methodism," Ph.D. diss., University of Chicago, 1924, 5–6, 139.

18. Wallace MacMullen, L. F. W. Lesemann, and Miss A. M. King, *Directions and Helps: Course of Study for Deaconesses* (New York: The Methodist Book Concern, 1922), 168–70.

19. Walter Rauschenbusch, *Christianizing the Social Order* (New York: Macmillan, 1921), 394, 398, 405.

20. Ibid., 405, 412, 429–31, 464–65.

21. MacMullen, Lesemann, and King, *Directions and Helps*, 168–70.

22. Pastor's Report to Quarterly Conference, October 1928, on file at St. Mark's United Methodist Church.

23. Doris Alford Branton, interview by the author, Shreveport, Louisiana, June 2001.

24. Ibid.

25. Daisy Weinberg, "Her Work Touches Lives of 6000," photocopy of undated clipping from unknown Texas newspaper, in possession of the author, original in collection of Dorothy Lundy Smira. Smira gave up her work as deaconess when she married a New Orleans resident, Eddie Smira, in 1935. Inspired by her aunt, also a deaconess, to study at Scarritt, Smira had been in charge of work with boys and the athletics program. She coached the basketball and baseball teams, working with youngsters up to about age ten.

26. Nettie Stroup, "Glimpsing Our Work at St. Mark's Community Center, New Orleans," *World Outlook* 25, no. 8 (August 1935): 19.

27. Weinberg, "Her Work Touches Lives."

28. Stroup, "Glimpsing Our Work," 18.

29. Ibid.

30. Ibid.

31. Ibid., 18–19.

32. Doris Alford Branton, interview by the author, June 7, 2001.

33. Julia Southard Campbell, telephone interview by the author, February 13, 2001; letter to the author, n.d. (received February 5, 2001).

34. Ibid.

35. Stroup, "Glimpsing Our Work," 22.

36. Ibid.; Doris Alford Branton, interview by the author, June 7, 2001.

37. "Estimates—1937: Education and Promotion/Home Field/Foreign Fields," pamphlet for use at meeting of the Women's Missionary Council, MECS, at First Methodist Episcopal Church, South, Dallas, Texas, March 1936, in records of the Women's Division of the General Board of Global Ministries, United Methodist Church Archives, General Commission on Archives and History, Madison, New Jersey. The pastor of the congregation would have been paid from the congregation's funds; these monies would not have been mingled with the community center's, nor raised by the women's societies.

38. Helen Mandlebaum, interview by the author, August 25, 2000.

39. In another example, Methodist Protestants had ordained women but agreed that the unified body would not do so.

40. James S. Thomas, *Methodism's Racial Dilemma: The Story of the Central Jurisdiction* (Nashville, Tenn.: Abingdon, 1992); Peter C. Murray, *Methodists and the Crucible of Race, 1930–1975* (Columbia: University of Missouri Press, 2004); Morris L. Davis, *The Methodist Unification: Christianity and the Politics of Race in the Jim Crow Era* (New York: New York University Press, 2008).

41. James B. Bennett, *Religion and the Rise of Jim Crow in New Orleans* (Princeton, N.J.: Princeton University Press, 2005), 234.

42. Sledge, *Hands on the Ark*.

43. Sara Estelle Haskin, "Women of the Left Wing," *World Outlook* 23, no. 1 (February 1933): 30. Settlements that served whites were usually called "Wesley Houses." St. Mark's was unusual in having a different name.

44. Mrs. Luke Johnson's report on attending the biennial session of the National Colored Woman's Federation in 1921, cited in Haskin, "Women of the Left Wing," 30.

45. Alice G. Knotts, *Fellowship of Love: Methodist Women Changing American Racial Attitudes, 1920–1968* (Nashville, Tenn.: Kingswood Books, 1996); Alice G. Knotts, "Thelma Stevens, Crusader for Racial Justice," in *Spirituality & Social Responsibility: Vocational Vision of Women in The United Methodist Tradition*, ed. Rosemary Skinner Keller (Nashville, Tenn.: Abingdon Press, 1993), 231–47.

46. Haskin, "Women of the Left Wing," 30.

47. Robert R. Moton, "When Women Will," *World Outlook* 23 no. 1 (February 1933): 31; Ellison, "A Dream Come True," 14.

48. Mary Morrison, interview by Margery Freeman, July 24, 1979, transcript on file at St. Mark's United Methodist Church, 23–24. Hale Boggs was the United States representative from the New Orleans area and served as the majority leader of the House of Representatives at the time his airplane disappeared in Alaska in 1972.

49. Ibid., 24–25.

50. Tooke was one of the women who left because she had to relinquish her status as a deaconess when she married. She spent much of her adult life as a pastor's spouse.

51. Mary Frances Fairchild Tooke and Mary Tooke Kitchens, interview by the author, Crystal Springs, Mississippi, February 1, 2001.

52. Julia Southard Campbell, telephone interview by the author, February 13, 2001.

53. *New Orleans Christian Advocate*, January 22, 1942.

54. Laura Smith, interview by the author, Adamsville, Alabama, May 16, 2000; Brochure, "St. Mark's Community Center, 1948," in possession of Dorothy Lundy Smira.

55. Maureen Honey, *Creating Rosie the Riveter: Class, Gender, and Propaganda during World War II* (Amherst: University of Massachusetts Press, 1984).

56. Brochure, "St. Mark's Community Center, 1948," in possession of Dorothy Lundy Smira.

57. Ibid.

58. Helen Mandlebaum, interview by the author, August 25, 2000; Fae Daves, interview by Margery Freeman, November 21, 1978, transcript on file at St. Mark's United Methodist Church; Laura Smith, interview by the author, May 16, 2000.

59. Mrs. John B. Pollard, "Louisiana Conference," *New Orleans Christian Advocate*, July 25, 1946, 10.

60. Laura Smith, interview by Margery Freeman, July 27, 1979.

61. Laura Smith, interview by the author, May 16, 2000.

62. Kreutziger, "Going on to Perfection."

63. Catherine Wessinger, "Key Events for Women's Religious Leadership in the United States—Nineteenth and Twentieth Centuries," in Catherine Wessinger, ed., *Religious Institutions and Women's Leadership*, 367.

64. *Journals of the Louisiana Annual Conference*, 1956–72. Carole Cotton later married John Winn, who is discussed later in chapter 5; her name is now Carole Cotton-Winn. The Reverend Miss Lea Joyner was a clergy member of the Louisiana Annual Conference during the 1940s and 1950s, but she was ordained by the Methodist Protestant denomination immediately before the 1939 merger and thus "grandmothered" in as clergy. Until the mid-1990s, United Methodist clergy were first ordained as deacons, and after a probationary period, ordained again as elders. Now, deacons and elders are on separate permanent clergy tracks, and both are commissioned as probationary members before a permanent ordination as either deacon or elder.

65. Dougherty, *My Calling to Fulfill*, 230

66. Helen Mandlebaum, interview by the author, August 25, 2000.

67. "Born of a Restlessness," *World Outlook*, September 1941, cited in "'Salty Methodist Characters' at the United Nations," *World Outlook* 53, no. 10 (October 1963): 34.

CHAPTER 5

1. McDowell, *Social Gospel in the South*, 100.

2. Fae Daves, interview by Margery Freeman, November 21, 1978.

3. Elisabeth Lasch-Quinn, *Black Neighbors: Race and the Limits of Reform in the American Settlement House Movement, 1890–1945* (Chapel Hill: University of North Carolina Press, 1993), 23.

4. C. Vann Woodward, *The Strange Career of Jim Crow* (New York: Oxford University Press, 1955), 8–9.

5. Samuel Hill, "The Southern Church as Conservator," in *Major Problems in the History of the American South*, vol. 2, *The New South*, ed. Paul D. Escott and David R. Goldfield (Lexington, Mass. and Toronto: D. C. Heath, 1990), 302.

6. Lasch-Quinn, *Black Neighbors*, 33.

7. Ibid., 111, 126.

8. An adjunct organization, the Wesleyan Service Guild, was created to serve women who were employed outside the home and therefore needed a night meeting.

9. "The Charter for Racial Justice: A History," film (now transferred to videotape), 14 minutes, 55 seconds, with "A Study/Action Guide for the Filmstrip: Pre- and Post-Viewing Discussion and Activities," developed by the Council on Interracial Books for Children for the Women's Division of the General Board of Global Ministries, New York, n.d., 6.

10. Alice G. Knotts, "Thelma Stevens, Crusader for Racial Justice," in Keller, ed., *Spirituality & Social Responsibility*, 237. Pauli Murray would later become the first African American woman to be ordained an Episcopal priest.

11. "The Charter for Racial Justice," with "A Study/Action Guide," 9.

12. Mrs. E. R. Kennedy, "Woman's Missionary Council," *New Orleans Christian Advocate*, April 5, 1917, 14.

13. Lily H. Hammond, *In Black and White: An Interpretation of Southern Life* (New York: Fleming H. Revell, 1914), 203–4, cited in McDowell, *Social Gospel in the South*, 102.

14. Executive Committee of the Louisiana Conference of the WSCS, "WSCS Louisiana Conference," *New Orleans Christian Advocate*, July 25, 1946, 10.

15. Ibid.

16. "Segregation Void in Public Schools" and "Kennon Is Calm on School Edict," *New Orleans Times-Picayune*, May 18, 1954, 1. The article also notes that Hebert lamented, "Why can't people be sensible and realistic even if you are a member of the supreme court."

17. Ibid.

18. "Catholic Board Favors Ruling: Backs High Court Stand Against Segregation," *New Orleans Times-Picayune*, May 28, 1954, 1.

19. Liva Baker, *The Second Battle of New Orleans: The Hundred-Year Struggle to Integrate the Schools* (New York: HarperCollins, 1996), 472.

20. "Segregation Void in Public Schools" and "Kennon Is Calm on School Edict," *New Orleans Times-Picayune*, May 18, 1954, 3.

21. "Catholic Board Favors Ruling: Backs High Court Stand Against Segregation," *New Orleans Times-Picayune*, May 28, 1954, 1.

22. "Churches Back Schools Ruling," *New Orleans Times-Picayune*, June 22, 1954, 1.

23. Those sources include Baker, *Second Battle of New Orleans;* Adam Fairclough, *Race and Democracy: The Civil Rights Struggle in Louisiana, 1915–1972* (Athens: University of Georgia Press, 1995); Morton Inger, *Politics and Reality in an American City: The New Orleans School Crisis of 1960* (New York: Center for Urban Education, 1968); Joseph B. Parker, *The Morrison Era: Reform Politics in New Orleans* (Gretna, La.: Pelican Publishing, 1998); Edward F. Haas, *DeLesseps S. Morrison and the Image of Reform: New Orleans Politics, 1946–1961* (Baton Rouge: Louisiana State University Press, 1974); Glen Jeansonne, *Leander Perez: Boss of the Delta*, 2d ed. (Lafayette: Center for Louisiana Studies at University of Southwestern Louisiana, 1995).

24. "Segregation?" advertisement, *New Orleans Times-Picayune*, November 2, 1954, 5.

25. Tyler, *Silk Stockings & Ballot Boxes;* Lindy Boggs with Katherine Hatch, *Washington Through a Purple Veil: Memories of a Southern Woman* (New York: Harcourt Brace & Company, 1994); Haas, *DeLesseps S. Morrison;* Parker, *The Morrison Era*.

26. "Rainach Strikes Back at IWO," *New Orleans Times-Picayune*, October 27, 1954, 3.

27. "Women Deplore Rainach Attack: IWO Demands Withdrawal of His Remarks," *New Orleans Times-Picayune*, October 29, 1954, 43.

28. Pamela Tyler, telephone interview with the author, June 1, 2001; Tyler, *Silk Stockings & Ballot Boxes*, 1, 5. Admittedly, in later years, there were those who considered Mary Morrison as much of a hindrance as a help in moving the community center toward integration (Warren Calvin, interview by the author, New Orleans, August 1, 2000).

29. John M. Glen, *Highlander: No Ordinary School*, 2nd ed. (Knoxville: University of Tennessee Press, 1996); Numan V. Bartley, "The Southern Conference and the Shaping of Post–World War II Southern Politics," in *Developing Dixie: Modernization in a Traditional Society*, ed. Winfred B. Moore Jr., Joseph F. Tripp, and Lyon G. Tyler

Jr., Contributions in American History Series, ed. Jon L. Wakelyn, no. 127 (New York: Greenwood Press, 1988), 179-97; Anthony P. Dunbar, *Against the Grain: Southern Radicals and Prophets, 1929-1959* (Charlottesville: University Press of Virginia, 1981); Linda Reed, *Simple Decency and Common Sense: The Southern Conference Movement, 1938-1963*, Blacks in the Diaspora Series, ed. Darlene Clark Hine, John McCluskey Jr., and David Barry Gaspar (Bloomington: Indiana University Press, 1991); Morton Sosna, *In Search of the Silent South: Southern Liberals and the Race Issue*, Contemporary American History Series, ed. William E. Leuchtenburg (New York: Columbia University Press, 1977); Kim Lacy Rogers, *Righteous Lives: Narratives of the New Orleans Civil Rights Movement* (New York: New York University Press, 1993).

30. Howell, ed., *Prominent Personalities*, 18; Frank T. Adams, *James A. Dombrowski: An American Heretic, 1897-1983* (Knoxville: University of Tennessee Press, 1992), 24.

31. Dunbar, *Against the Grain*, 6-10.

32. Dunbar, *Against the Grain*, 39-41; Adams, *James A. Dombrowski*, 79; James Dombrowski, *The Early Days of Christian Socialism in America* (New York: Columbia University Press, 1936), vii. See also David Nelson Duke, *In the Trenches with Jesus and Marx: Harry F. Ward and the Struggle for Social Justice* (Tuscaloosa: University of Alabama Press, 2003).

33. Adams, *James A. Dombrowski*, 45-49.

34. Charles W. Eagles, "The Closing of Mississippi Society: Will Campbell, *The $64,000 Question*, and Religious Emphasis Week at the University of Mississippi," *Journal of Southern History* 67, no. 2 (May 2001): 331-72.

35. *Southern Patriot* 12, no. 3 (March 1954): 3. An account of this hearing from the viewpoint of a participant can be found in Virginia Durr's autobiography, Hollinger F. Barnard, ed., *Beyond the Magic Circle: The Autobiography of Virginia Durr* (University: University of Alabama Press, 1985).

36. Frank Adams and Myles Horton, *Unearthing Seeds of Fire: The Idea of Highlander* (Winston-Salem, N.C.: John F. Blair, 1975), 194, cited in Reed, *Simple Decency and Common Sense*, 159.

37. I remember a billboard in my small central Louisiana hometown that showed Martin Luther King Jr. sitting at a desk in a classroom. The caption claimed he was at a Communist training session. As a child, I thought it proved that Dr. King was a Communist and that integration was "a Communist plot." A child's limited reasoning capabilities and a strongly racist environment contributed to my willingness to accept this linkage. Taylor Branch later wrote about the billboards labeled "King at Communist Training School" and the photo, which actually showed MLK at a training session

at Highlander Folk School. King had been there to deliver a speech, but he did not want to disclaim having been "trained" there because it would denigrate the school. "The state of Tennessee had destroyed Highlander because it 'brought Negroes and whites together in a way they would have never been brought together ... they live together,' King said, adding that from fearful hysteria about integration, Highlander 'suffered what many white liberals suffer in the South, the Communist tag.... SCEF has suffered the same thing.'" Taylor Branch, *Pillar of Fire: America in the King Years, 1963–65* (New York, Simon & Schuster, 1998), 189.

38. Alfred H. Kelly, Winfred A. Harbison, and Herman Belz, *The American Constitution: Its Origins and Development*, 6th ed. (New York: W. W. Norton, 1983), 597; Adams, *James A. Dombrowski*, 273–76; Fairclough, *Race and Democracy*, 323–25.

39. Julian Feibelman, *The Making of a Rabbi* (New York: Vantage Press, 1980), 448–49.

40. "Uphold Integration!" advertisement, *New Orleans Times-Picayune*, July 6, 1954, 58.

41. John Murray Winn, interview by the author, New Orleans, December 19, 2000.

42. Ibid.

43. Ibid.

44. Baker, *Second Battle of New Orleans*, 345.

45. John Murray Winn, interview by the author, December 19, 2000.

46. Clarence H. Snelling Jr., interview by the author, New Orleans, January 19, 2001.

47. Ibid.

48. "School Board Hears Desegregation Plea," *New Orleans Times-Picayune*, September 13, 1955, 1; "N.O. Integration Petition Proves Decency's Strength," *Southern Patriot* 13, no. 8 (October 1955): 1; Feibelman, *Making of a Rabbi*, 448ff.; Rosa Freeman Keller, interview by Kim Lacy Rogers, November 9, 1978, quoted in Rogers, *Righteous Lives*, 44.

49. John Murray Winn, interview by the author, December 19, 2000.

50. Ibid.

51. Ibid.

52. "St. Louis Pastor Forum Speaker," *New Orleans Times-Picayune*, December 16, 1955, 30.

53. John Murray Winn, interview by the author, December 19, 2000.

54. Clarence H. Snelling Jr., interview by the author, January 19, 2001.

55. Ibid.

56. Ibid. For more on Storyville, see Long, *Great Southern Babylon*.

57. Clarence H. Snelling Jr., interview by the author, January 19, 2001.

58. Ibid.

59. Clarence H. Snelling Jr., e-mail to the author, October 16, 2001.

60. Clarence H. Snelling Jr., interview by the author, January 19, 2001.

61. "NAACP Condemns All Segregation," *New Orleans Times-Picayune*, October 31, 1954, 6.

62. Adams, *James A. Dombrowski*, 238.

63. Clarence H. Snelling Jr., interview by the author, January 19, 2001. Snelling enjoys telling the story of Dombrowski's visit to the hospital when Snelling's son, David, was born. Dombrowski brought a toy he had bought as a baby gift. Having forgotten that he had placed it on the top of his car while he was stowing some other items, he drove all the way across the city with a stuffed dachshund on his roof.

64. Ibid.

65. Ibid.

66. Ibid.

67. Ibid.

68. Ibid.

69. "Rabbis Approve School Decision," *New Orleans Times-Picayune*, June 26, 1954, 9; "Council Works on Segregation: Leaders Refer to Issue as 'Great Scandal,'" *New Orleans Times-Picayune*, August 22, 1954, 22; "Synod Raps Forced Racial Segregation," *New Orleans Times-Picayune*, September 3, 1954, 14; "Church Magazine Hits Segregation," *New Orleans Times-Picayune*, September 29, 1954, 6; "'Nonsegregated Church' Is Urged," *New Orleans Times-Picayune*, November 1, 1954, 7.

70. McDowell, *Social Gospel in the South*, 100.

71. Edward L. Pinney and Robert S. Friedman, *Political Leadership and the School Desegregation Crisis in Louisiana*, Eagleton Institute Cases in Practical Politics, Case 31, ed. Paul Tillett (New York: McGraw Hill, 1963).

72. Hill, "Southern Church as Conservator," 302.

73. Bea Fucich, Minutes, Board of Christian Education, St. Mark's Methodist Church, June 13, 1958, from the personal collection of Laura Smith, in possession of the author.

74. Darryl M. Trimiew, "The Social Gospel Movement and the Question of Race," in Evans, ed., *Social Gospel Today*, 27–37.

75. John Murray Winn, interview by the author, December 19, 2000.

76. Tyler, *Silk Stockings & Ballot Boxes*, 1–5.

77. Gerald N. Grob and George Athan Billias, eds., "The Progressive Movement: Liberal or Conservative?" in *Interpretations of American History: Patterns and Perspectives, Since 1977*, 6th ed. (New York: The Free Press, 1992), vol. 2: 216–34.

CHAPTER 6

1. The politics involved in those decisions and various other aspects of the events surrounding them have been explored in sources such as Baker, *Second Battle of New Orleans;* Fairclough, *Race and Democracy;* Morton Inger, *Politics and Reality;* and Pinney and Friedman, *Political Leadership*.

2. Laura Smith, interview by the author, May 16, 2000; Morrison, "Looking Back at St. Mark's," 2.

3. Lloyd Anderson "Andy" Foreman, interview by the author, Harahan, Louisiana, July 31, 1998. Redeemer was one of the churches that the MEC planted in New Orleans after the Civil War, and it was just a few doors down from the original St. Mark's location.

4. The story of Ruby Bridges Hall has been told by Robert Coles, by Hall herself, and in a made-for-television movie. Robert Coles, *Children of Crisis: A Study of Courage and Fear* (Boston: Little, Brown, 1967); Robert Coles, *The Story of Ruby Bridges* (New York: Scholastic, 1995); Ruby Bridges Hall, "The Education of Ruby Nell," *Guideposts*, March 2000, 3–7; Ruby Bridges, *Through My Eyes*, ed. and comp. Margo Lundell (New York: Scholastic Press, 1999); Toni Ann Johnson, *Ruby Bridges*, a Marian Rees Associates Production for Walt Disney Television, released by Walt Disney Home Video, Marian Rees, executive producer, Anne Hopkins, producer, 89 min., 1997. She has also appeared on television shows such as the *Today* show, where she saw for the first time in person the Norman Rockwell painting of her walking to William Frantz Elementary, and Oprah Winfrey's talk show, Harpo Productions, "35 Years Later: Black & White Student Reunions," transcript of *The Oprah Winfrey Show*, June 3, 1996 (originally aired January 15, 1996), prepared and distributed by Burrelle's Information Services, Livingston, New Jersey.

5. Lloyd Anderson "Andy" Foreman, interview by the author, July 31, 1998.

6. Ibid.

7. Ibid.; "A Look at the World's Week," *Life* 29, no. 4 (December 12, 1960): 25.

8. Lloyd Anderson "Andy" Foreman, interview by the author, July 31, 1998.

9. "Father Drolet to Get Award: Louisiana Priest's Aid to Cane Workers Cited," *New Orleans Times-Picayune*, August 12, 1954, 2; "Father Drolet Receives Honor: Priest's Aid to Southern Workers Cited," *New Orleans Times-Picayune*, October 10, 1954, 16.

10. John Steinbeck, *Travels with Charley: In Search of America* (New York: Viking Press, 1962), 227–28.

11. Ibid.

12. Conner, a Roman Catholic, sought the advice of her parish priest and found him unwilling to make a commitment to support her. She said, "He did not make any commitment. He did not help me at all. He was like, 'Please, you are tainted, don't come here. I hope no one sees you going out.'" Roman Catholic children were to be brought from school to catechism class in procession, and when Mrs. Conner's three children were the only Catholic children, they were taken by themselves. The Conners once received a threat that the children would be killed as they went to catechism class at church. The FBI brought the children to their home but said they could not escort them to the church. As Conner was taking the children to the class, they were met by a priest. She said, "He was the only one in the church who had come to see me. He did it on his own. Here he comes with his robes flowing and two altar boys at his sides. He was coming to meet us and get the kids to catechism." This priest is referred to in Wieder's article as Father Smith, which Wieder calls "a fictitious name used for this article." There is no hint as to why he does not use the priest's real name. Alan Wieder, "One Who Stayed: Margaret Conner and the New Orleans School Crisis," *Louisiana History* 26, no. 2 (Spring 1985): 196–97.

13. Although this video shows news footage of Foreman and his daughter walking into William Frantz Elementary, their names are not mentioned. *A House Divided*, video produced by Drexel Center at Xavier University, Burwell Ware, author, director, and producer; Sybil A. Morial, executive producer, 1987, on file at the Xavier University Library, New Orleans.

14. Laura Smith, interview by the author, May 16, 2000.

15. Gene M. Faurie, interview by the author, Harahan, Louisiana, September 13, 2001.

16. Ibid. Faurie now sees his disregard for the people of St. Mark's as dehumanization and said, "to go along with everyone else, we begin to dehumanize the object of

our hate, to be able to excuse our behavior." Overall, he admits, "It's a part of my life I'm not proud of. I really regret [being] so tied up in racism." Faurie, who entered the Methodist ministry in 1988, dates his conversion to Christianity to 1982, and says that his attitude toward people of color changed on the same day: "The day God saved me, it was a miraculous healing. . . . I was convicted that day of my racism and knew that that was not of God. . . . It wasn't just about racism; it was treating people, period, equally and in the love of God. And from that time on, it was nothing but repentance and asking forgiveness from my black brothers and sisters, whom I love. I think it's a great testimony God's given me to talk to others who are still caught in that bondage of racism, to say, 'If God can heal me, He can heal you, but you've got to be willing.'"

17. Ed Barksdale, interview by the author, Covington, Louisiana, February 1, 2001.

18. Ibid.

19. Donice W. and Julie Alverson, interview by the author, New Orleans, January 29, 2001.

20. The missing signature was not because of the minister's unavailability, but his refusal to sign.

21. Donice W. and Julie Alverson interview.

22. Ibid.

23. Robert N. Kelso, "Orleans Weathers Its Second Week of Integration," undated, unidentified newspaper clipping, box 5, folder 17, S.O.S. Collection, Amistad Research Center, Tulane University.

24. Unidentified clipping, box 4, folder 2, S.O.S. Collection, Amistad Research Center, Tulane University.

25. Edward F. Haas, "The Expedient of Race: Victor H. Schiro, Scott Wilson, and the New Orleans Mayoralty Campaign in 1962," *Louisiana History* 42, no. 1 (Winter 2001): 5–29.

26. Pinney and Friedman, *Political Leadership*, 1–2.

27. Leander Perez was reinstated, apparently secretly, into the Roman Catholic communion at some point before his death, and his funeral was held at Holy Name of Jesus Church on St. Charles Avenue, adjacent to the campus of Loyola University. Glen Jeansonne, *Leander Perez: Boss of the Delta*, 2d ed. (Lafayette: Center for Louisiana Studies at University of Southwestern Louisiana, 1995); James Conaway, *Judge: The Life and Times of Leander Perez* (New York: Alfred A. Knopf, 1973).

28. Lloyd Anderson "Andy" Foreman, interview by the author, July 31, 1998.

29. Letterhead for Save Our Schools, Inc., 1520 Jefferson Avenue, New Orleans 15,

La., box 1, folder 1, S.O.S. Collection, Amistad Research Center, Tulane University; Rogers, *Righteous Lives*, 60–61.

30. "Women's Unit Attacks Davis on Tax Plans," unidentified clipping, hand-dated December 16, 1960, S.O.S. Collection, box 1, Dec. 14–19 folder, Amistad Research Center, Tulane University.

31. "School Board Given Support: Independent Women's Organization Acts," unidentified clipping, hand-dated December 8, 1960, S.O.S. Collection, box 1, Dec. 14–19 folder, Amistad Research Center, Tulane University.

32. Claude Sitton, "New Orleans Tension: Violence in Wake of First School Integration Stirs Fears of Prolonged Racial Unrest," *New York Times*, November 19, 1960.

33. "A Concurrent Resolution," undated clipping from the *New Orleans States-Item*, box 2, folder 1, S.O.S. Collection, Amistad Research Center, Tulane University.

34. *A House Divided*, Xavier University.

35. Mrs. E. Weiss, letter to the *New Orleans States-Item* editor, December 20, 1960, box 4, folder 4, S.O.S. Collection, Amistad Research Center, Tulane University.

36. "Church Against Mixed Schools," unidentified clipping, hand-dated December 1, 1960, box 4, folder 4, S.O.S. Collection, Amistad Research Center, Tulane University.

37. *A House Divided*, Xavier University.

38. "Catholic Group Is Challenged," unidentified clipping, box 4, folder 4, S.O.S. Collection, Amistad Research Center, Tulane University.

39. Lloyd Anderson "Andy" Foreman, interview by the author, July 31, 1998.

40. Ibid.

41. Ibid.

42. Allan Knight Chalmers, *They Shall Be Free* (Garden City, N.Y.: Doubleday, 1951); Minnie Finch, *The NAACP: Its Fight for Justice* (Metuchen, N.J.: Scarecrow Press, 1981); Charles Flint Kellogg, *NAACP: A History of the National Association for the Advancement of Colored People*, vol. 1, *1909–1920* (Baltimore: Johns Hopkins Press, 1967). The Scottsboro Boys were a group of young black transients arrested and imprisoned for life for the rape of a white woman, an act that supposedly occurred on a freight train during the Depression era.

43. Lloyd Anderson "Andy" Foreman, interview by the author, July 31, 1998.

44. Charles Marsh, *God's Long Summer: Stories of Faith and Civil Rights* (Princeton, N.J.: Princeton University Press, 1997), 121–22.

45. Lloyd Anderson "Andy" Foreman, interviews by author, Harahan, Louisiana, July 31, 1998, and Lockport, Louisiana, March 6, 2001.

46. Ibid.

47. Ibid.

48. Lloyd Anderson "Andy" Foreman, interview by the author, July 31, 1998.

49. Ibid.

50. Coles, *Children of Crisis*, 335.

51. Lloyd Anderson "Andy" Foreman, interview by the author, July 31, 1998; Robert Coles, letter to the author, April 2, 2001.

52. Lydia and Odette Mickal, interview by Margery Freeman, July 18, 1979, transcript on file at St. Mark's United Methodist Church, 1.

53. Ibid., 2.

54. Ibid., 4. Their departure was linked to feelings that kept them from using the center once blacks began attending it; Odette Mickal told the interviewer in 1979, "I wouldn't go swimming in a pool with a negro."

55. Eva Perez, interview by the author, Arabi, Louisiana, August 12, 1999.

56. In an ironic twist on the common southern claim that "outside agitators" were responsible for stirring up a desire for integration, Foreman told the reporter that he blamed "outside agitators" for the protests against integration. He insisted that hate "isn't natural" in New Orleans, which had always been a cosmopolitan city: "I feel that if people had been left alone, they would have quietly taken their children to school. I have no evidence to prove it, but I am certain there are agitators here—people who are egging others on. . . . I question if many of [the ringleaders] have any direct involvement with the schools as parents." Cited in "Pastor Sees Slow Death of the School Boycott He Defied," *Chicago Sun-Times*, December 8, 1960, 22; photocopy; original in personal collection of Lloyd Anderson "Andy" Foreman.

57. John Murray Winn, interview by the author, December 19, 2000; Clarence H. Snelling Jr. interview by the author, January 19, 2001.

58. Samuel Butler, personal communication to the author; Lloyd Anderson "Andy" Foreman, interview by the author, July 31, 1998.

59. Harpo Productions, "35 Years Later: Black & White Student Reunions."

60. Ibid.

61. Lloyd Anderson "Andy" Foreman, interview by the author, July 31, 1998.

Chapter 7

1. Mary Morrison, "Looking Back on St. Mark's," addendum stapled to page 1.

2. Sherry Gordon Smyth, interview by the author, March 22, 2001.

3. Eva Perez, interview by the author, August 12, 1999.

4. Morrison, "Looking Back on St. Mark's," 3.

5. Ibid.

6. Ibid.

7. Sherry Gordon Smyth, interview by the author, March 22, 2001.

8. Biographical information sheet on Fae L. Daves, one typed page, on file at St. Mark's United Methodist Church.

9. Lloyd Anderson "Andy" Foreman, interview by the author, July 31, 1998.

10. Coles, *Children of Crisis;* Lloyd Anderson "Andy" Foreman, interview by the author, July 31, 1998.

11. Lloyd Anderson "Andy" Foreman, interview by the author, July 31, 1998; Laura Smith, interview by the author, May 16, 2000.

12. John Murray Winn, interview by the author, December 19, 2000.

13. Wieder, "One Who Stayed," 199.

14. Lloyd Anderson "Andy" Foreman, interview by the author, July 31, 1998.

15. Clarence H. Snelling Jr. interview by the author, January 19, 2001. After an initial telephone conversation, Spencer Wren did not follow through on repeated requests that he grant an interview, in person or by telephone, or to send his written remembrances of the events of the era. However, there is little reason to doubt that Snelling's recollections are accurate, especially in the essential facts of the threat from a north Louisiana layperson and the lack of support from the church hierarchy. Wren is now deceased.

16. Jewel Brown, "Opportunities of a Lifetime," *Methodist Woman* 23, no. 1 (September 1962), 5.

17. Mary Lou Barnwell, "Deaconesses Are Needed, Too: Seventy-five New Deaconesses by 1963!" *Methodist Woman* 21, no. 10 (June 1961): 14.

18. Ibid.

19. Ibid.

20. Daves, "Opening Doors," 8–9.

21. "'Deaconess Work Better Known in 1963': Barnwell," *Christian Advocate* 7, no. 25 (December 5, 1963): 23.

22. Ibid.

23. In Romans 16:1, Paul speaks of Phoebe, whom he refers to as a deacon (diakonos) in the congregation at Cenchreae. In this verse, where it refers to a woman, the term is usually translated into English as "deaconess," although the noun carries the male gender in the Greek. It is exactly the same word that is used elsewhere in Pauline and pseudo-Pauline letters to describe males, and even to describe Paul himself (see Colossians 1:23, Ephesians 3:7). The standard Greek-English lexicon in use in seminaries notes that when the word 'diakonos' is used in a masculine sense (in other words, when it refers to males, because there is otherwise no distinction in the word itself), it can refer to servants, or helpers, or apostles and other prominent Christians, or an official of the church. In its feminine form (in other words, when it is used for Phoebe, because again, there is no distinction in the Greek word used), the definitions are limited to "deaconess," "helper," and "agent." William F. Arndt and F. Wilbur Gingrich, *A Greek-English Lexicon of the New Testament and Other Early Christian Literature*, 2d edition (Chicago: University of Chicago Press, 1979), 184–85.

24. Mary Lou Barnwell, "75 in '63: Women of Great Ideas," *Methodist Woman* 23, no. 6 (March 1963): 5–6.

25. Lindley, *"You Have Stept,"* 88; Schmidt, *Grace Sufficient*, 178.

26. "Deaconess Work Better Known in 1963," *Christian Advocate* 7, no. 25 (December 5, 1963): 23.

27. Mary Lou Barnwell, "Two Wonderful Years," *Methodist Woman* 24, no. 2 (October 1963): 7–8.

28. Mary Lou Barnwell, "Deaconesses Explore International Affairs," *Methodist Woman* 23, no. 1 (September 1962): 15.

29. "Study Book Projects—1961–1962: Churches for New Times," *Methodist Woman* 21, no. 10 (June 1961): 18.

30. Fae L. Daves, Report to the Annual Meeting of the Louisiana Annual Conference of the Woman's Society of Christian Service, March 10-12, 1965, on file at St. Mark's United Methodist Church.

31. Fae Daves, interview by Margery Freeman, November 21, 1978.

32. Ibid., 9.

33. Dorothy Schneider and Carl J. Schneider, *American Women in the Progressive Era, 1900–1920* (New York: Facts on File, 1993), 110.

34. Sherry Gordon Smyth, interview by the author, March 22, 2001.

35. Laura Smith, interview by the author, May 16, 2000.

36. It is ironic that it was pressure from United Way that finally moved the center's board, considering that Judith Trolander's research on Depression-era settlements, primarily in the Northeast and in Chicago, led her to conclude that funding from a community chest (a United Way predecessor organization) drove workers at non-sectarian settlements in the 1930s to be more conservative, not less so. She saw the professionalization of social work as another reason for conservative trends. Trolander, *Settlement Houses*, 27.

37. Laura Smith, interview by the author, May 16, 2000.

38. "St. Mark's Community Center Points Way to Fuller Life," *Together News Edition, Louisiana Area* 9, no. 2 (February 1965): A2–A3, in records of the Women's Division of the General Board of Global Ministries, United Methodist Church Archives, General Commission on Archives and History (GCAH), Madison, New Jersey.

39. Ibid.

40. Fae L. Daves, Report to the Annual Meeting of the Louisiana Annual Conference of the Woman's Society of Christian Service, March 10-12, 1965.

41. "St. Mark's Community Center Points Way to Fuller Life," *Together News Edition*, A2–A3, GCAH.

42. Fae Daves, interview by Margery Freeman, November 21, 1978.

43. Ibid., 5.

44. Ibid., 16.

45. Daves, "Opening Doors."

46. Laura Smith, interview by Margery Freeman, July 27, 1979.

47. Ibid.

48. Warren Calvin, interview by the author, August 1, 2000.

49. Fae Daves, interview by Margery Freeman, November 21, 1978.

50. Donald E. Devore and Joseph Logsdon, *Crescent City Schools: Public Education in New Orleans, 1841–1991* (Lafayette: Center for Louisiana Studies, University of Southwestern Louisiana, 1991), 239–40.

51. Ibid.

52. Ibid., 243.

53. Pinney and Friedman, *Political Leadership*, 32. Their study links the religious affiliation of state legislators to their voting records, and they conclude that being Roman Catholic had the greatest effect on legislators' likeliness to vote against extreme measures for maintaining segregation.

54. "Segregation Void in Public Schools" and "Kennon Is Calm on School Edict," *New Orleans Times-Picayune*, May 18, 1954, 1. Hebert was comparing the *Brown* decision to the cases of *Cherokee Nation v. Georgia* (1831) and *Worcester v. Georgia* (1832).

55. John Murray Winn, interview by the author, December 19, 2000; Lloyd Anderson "Andy" Foreman, interview by the author, July 31, 1998.

56. Trimiew, "Social Gospel Movement," 27–37; Ralph Luker, *The Social Gospel in Black and White: American Racial Reform, 1885–1912* (Chapel Hill: University of North Carolina Press, 1991); White, *Liberty and Justice for All*.

57. Lloyd Anderson "Andy" Foreman, interview by the author, March 6, 2001.

58. Bobbie Malone, *Rabbi Max Heller: Reformer, Zionist, Southerner, 1860–1929*, Judaic Studies Series, Leon J. Weinberger, ed. (Tuscaloosa: University of Alabama Press, 1997); Mark K. Bauman and Berkley Kalin, *The Quiet Voices: Southern Rabbis and Black Civil Rights, 1880s to 1990s*, Judaic Studies Series, Leon J. Weinberger, ed. (Tuscaloosa: University of Alabama Press, 1997); Feibelman, *Making of a Rabbi*, 445–47, 502.

59. Clarkson, "Deaconesses Then," 39.

60. Ibid.

61. Lloyd Anderson "Andy" Foreman, interview by the author, July 31, 1998.

62. Ibid.

63. Cupp, "Deaconesses " 24.

CHAPTER 8

1. "St. Mark's Gangplank," Fall 1967, on file at St. Mark's United Methodist Church; Wilma Snare Reinhardt, interview by the author, Nashville, Tenn., September 22, 2000.

2. Bella Jarrett, "Community Centers Are No Longer Child's Play," *Response*, April 1972, 6.

3. Warren Calvin, interview by the author, August 1, 2000; David Billings, interview by the author, New Orleans, August 4, 2000.

4. Fae Daves, interview by Margery Freeman, November 21, 1978.

5. Warren Calvin, interview by the author, August 1, 2000; Laura Smith, interview by the author, May 16, 2000. Both attributed the removal of the records to "paranoia" on Sharp's part about leaving them in the building with the black clientele.

6. "The Second Annual Operation Understanding: Dedicated to the sacred memory of His Excellency Archbishop Joseph Francis Rummel 1876–1964," program for event held January 31, 1965, on file at St. Mark's United Methodist Church.

7. "Resolution of St. Mark's United Methodist Church," presented to the Administrative Board but not adopted, May 21, 1972, on file at St. Mark's United Methodist Church.

8. Mary Morrison, unpublished press release, June 1972, on file at St. Mark's United Methodist Church.

9. David Billings, interview by the author, August 4, 2000; David Billings, telephone interview by the author, November 1, 2001.

10. Ibid.

11. Ibid.

12. Scholar Janet Allured is currently completing a book on second-wave feminism in Louisiana that will include information from her interviews with Freeman and Watts.

13. Susie C. Stanley, "The Promise Fulfilled: Women's Ministries in the Wesleyan/Holiness Movement," in Wessinger, ed., *Religious Institutions and Women's Leadership*, 150.

14. Susan Laurie, outreach coordinator, Reconciling Ministries Network, telephone interview, July 28, 2005.

15. Margery Freeman to Greater New Orleans Federation of Churches, n.d., letter on file at St. Mark's United Methodist Church.

16. Bruce Nolan, "Service Remembers Upstairs Fire Victims," *New Orleans Times-Picayune*, June 25, 1998, B1; David Cuthbert, "Where There Was Smoke: Sifting Through the 'Grief, Shock and Ashes' of the Upstairs Lounge Fire, *New Orleans Times-Picayune*, June 20, 1998, E1; Susan Finch, "Fire of '73: Tragedy United Gays," *New Orleans Times-Picayune*, June 24, 1993, A1.

17. In September 2008, the National Gay and Lesbian Task Force meeting in New Orleans honored St. Mark's. The NGLTF's faith work director, Rev. Rebecca Voelkel, said that "[a]midst the deafening silence of so many religious leaders and the vocal

hatred of others" the people of St. Mark's opened their doors for the memorial service. She noted that "Their witness bore life in the moment, but it also planted seeds that have, 35 years later, come to life as the Welcoming Church Movement. Now there are some 3,100 congregations across the U.S. that are publicly welcoming and affirming of LGBT people." <http://www.thetaskforce.org/press/releases/pr_070108 and http://gaycitynews.com/site/index.cfm?newsid=19829165&BRD=2729&PAG=461&dept_id=568864&rfi=8>.

18. Rev. Jerry M. James, "On Homosexuality and Christianity," *New Orleans Times-Picayune*, June 26, 1977, clipping on file at St. Mark's United Methodist Church; Mrs. Jacob H. Morrison to the Editor, *New Orleans Times-Picayune*, June 28, 1977, copy on file at St. Mark's United Methodist Church.

19. The Reverend Mr. Robert Carter, personal communication to the author; Pamela Tyler, telephone interview by the author, June 1, 2001.

20. Undated letter from the United Klans of the Crescent City Chapter 30. Photocopy in possession of the author.

21. Ibid.

22. Gene M. Faurie, interview by the author, September 13, 2001.

23. Joan Treadway, "Anti-racism group receives death threats," *New Orleans Times-Picayune*, July 30, 1999, B-1. The director of the Southern Poverty Law Center's investigative unit also told a reporter in November 2008 that the organization did not know of "the Sons of Dixie or any other Klan branches in Washington Parish before now," although the occasion of the reporter's inquiry was the alleged murder by the Sons of Dixie of an initiate who belatedly changed her mind. Jeff Adelson, "Klan initiation turns deadly, sheriff says," *New Orleans Times-Picayune*, November 12, 2008, A-1, A-6.

24. Alexis Brent, personal communication to the author.

25. In the fall of 2001, when an organization that publicly advocated a nonviolent response to the World Trade Center bombings of September 11 was asked to stop meeting at another local (non-Methodist) congregation, they were welcomed to meet at St. Mark's. Few, if any, problems arose as a result of this decision.

26. St. Mark's Community Center, Year 2000 Annual Report, copy in possession of the author.

27. Elizabeth Donze, "Little Victories in the Big Easy: New Orleans Center Works Miracles Among People Living on the Margins," *Interpreter* 43, no. 5 (July–August 1999): 14–17.

28. Ibid; St. Mark's Community Center, Year 2000 Annual Report.

29. St. Mark's Community Center, Year 2000 Annual Report.

30. Barri Bronston, "Big Gig," *New Orleans Times-Picayune*, April 20, 1998, C-1.

31. Donze, "Little Victories," 15.

32. The Reverend Mr. Gregor Dike, personal communication to the author; list in possession of the Reverend Ms. Alexis Brent at the time of her death, now in possession of the author; "Makin' Good in the Hood," brochure, n.d., in possession of the author. In 1999–2000, St. Mark's received over $131,000 in grants for the "Makin' Good" program, and sources included the Institute of Mental Hygiene and the Louisiana State Department of Social Services.

33. Anita Dinwiddie, personal communication, March 14, 2006; personal communication, May 20, 2006; e-mail to the author, August 3, 2006; <www.frenchquarterumc.org>, accessed August 3, 2006.

34. Peg Culligan, personal communication, March 14, 2006; personal communication, May 18, 2006.

35. Paragraph 1313, *The Book of Discipline of the United Methodist Church, 2004* (Nashville, Tenn.: United Methodist Publishing House, 2004), 563, cited in "Deaconess: Is this a calling for you?" undated brochure from the General Board of Global Ministries, stock number 5294. Information about the current program can be obtained from the Deaconess Program Office at the General Board of Global Ministries, 475 Riverside Drive, #320, New York, NY 10115, 212-870-3850, deaconess@gbgm-umc.org or at the GBGM Web site, <http://gbgm-umc.org/about/us/mp/deaconesshomemissioner/calling>.

Chapter 9

1. Edwards and Gifford, *Gender and the Social Gospel*, 1–17; Ronald C. White and C. Howard Hopkins, *The Social Gospel: Religion and Reform in Changing America* (Philadelphia: Temple University Press, 1976), 119–26, cited in Susan Hill Lindley, "Gender and the Social Gospel Novel," in Edwards and Gifford, eds., *Gender and the Social Gospel*, 187.

2. Edwards and Gifford, *Gender and the Social Gospel*, 9, 12, 14.

3. "Salute to the Deaconess Movement," *Methodist Woman* 23, no. 5 (January 1963): 15–16.

4. See, for instance, Katharine Rhodes Henderson, *God's Troublemakers: How Women of Faith Are Changing the World* (New York: Continuum, 2006).

5. Hatch, "Puzzle of American Methodism," 36.

6. Maddox, "Visit the Poor," 66–67.

7. Maddox, "Visit the Poor," 77–79.

8. Sklar, "Beyond Maternalism," 2–7.

9. Acts 17:6, KJV.

10. Wedell, *Elite Women*, 6, 8.

11. Kendall, *Power of Good Deeds*.

12. It is becoming customary to speak of the "Reign of God" or the "Kin-dom of God" as the need for inclusive language is more widely accepted. However, because this is a historical treatment, I have continued with the "Kingdom" language that the early deaconesses would have used.

13. Christopher Evans, "Historical Integrity and Theological Recovery: A Reintroduction to the Social Gospel," in Evans, ed., *Social Gospel Today*, 5.

14. Ibid., 5.

15. Christopher Evans, "Toward a New Social Gospel?" in Evans, ed., *Social Gospel Today*, 172.

16. Today, the rituals of the United Methodist Church acknowledge the reality of corporate sin; in baptism, the candidate is asked, "Do you accept the freedom and power God gives you to resist evil, injustice, and oppression in whatever forms they present themselves?" *The United Methodist Hymnal* (Nashville, Tenn.: United Methodist Publishing House, 1989), 34.

17. Lee, *As Among the Methodists*, 37.

18. "Deaconesses: Pioneers Yesterday and Today," brochure issued by the General Board of Global Ministries, Cincinnati, Ohio, stock #5294, February 1998.

19. Laceye Warner, "Redemption and Race: The Evangelistic Ministry of Three Women in Southern Methodism," *Wesleyan Theological Journal* (Fall 2005): 21.

20. Annie Rogers, tape recording.

21. Lloyd Anderson "Andy" Foreman, interview by the author, July 31, 1998.

22. White, *Liberty and Justice for All*, xiii.

23. Luker, *Social Gospel;* White, *Liberty and Justice for All*. The southern reformers whom Luker described as being relatively open on racial matters included Edgar Gardner Murphy, an Episcopalian clergyman who became director of the Southern Education Fund. However, Murphy's Southern Education Fund must not be confused with the Southern Conference Educational Fund (SCEF), the offshoot of the Southern

Conference on Human Welfare (SCHW) headed by James Dombrowski, which was both grounded in the Social Gospel and deeply committed to racial justice during the civil rights movement, and which is discussed at length in chapter 5. No mention is made in Luker's book of either Dombrowski or the SCEF.

24. White, *Liberty and Justice for All*. Of the eighty-two "Social Gospel" leaders White considers, only ten are women, and several of these had no formal religious affiliation.

25. Taylor Branch, *Parting the Waters: America in the King Years, 1954–63* (New York: Touchstone, 1988); James H. Cone, *Martin & Malcolm & America: A Dream or a Nightmare* (Maryknoll, N.Y.: Orbis, 1992); Rogers, *Righteous Lives*.

26. Trimiew, "Social Gospel Movement"; Lindley, "Deciding Who Counts."

27. Trimiew, "Social Gospel Movement," 28.

28. Enrique Dussel, *A History of the Church in Latin America: Colonialism to Liberation (1492–1979)*, trans. and rev. Alan Neely (Grand Rapids, Mich.: William B. Eerdmans, 1981), 17.

29. Joyner, "St. Mark's Hall," 3, GCAH.

Appendix A

1. Edwards and Gifford, eds., *Gender and the Social Gospel*, 1–9.

2. Lee, *As Among the Methodists;* Barbara E. Campbell, *United Methodist Women In the Middle of Tomorrow*, 2d ed. (New York: Women's Division, General Board of Global Ministries, United Methodist Church, 1983).

3. Mary Agnes Dougherty, *My Calling to Fulfill;* Mary Agnes Dougherty, "The Social Gospel According to Phoebe: Methodist Deaconesses in the Metropolis, 1885–1918," in Thomas and Keller, eds., *Women in New Worlds*, 1:200–216; Carolyn De Swarte Gifford, ed., *The American Deaconess Movement in the Early Twentieth Century* (New York: Garland Publishing, 1987); Knotts, *Lifting Up Hope*. Keller, Lindley, and Campbell's research focusing specifically on deaconesses has not yet been published in separate form, and neither has Warner's dissertation, which was completed in England.

4. The community center and the congregation housed in its building were separated administratively in 1925 when the center began receiving funds from the agency known today as the United Way. When the terms "center" or "community center" or "settlement house" are used with regard to St. Mark's, they refer to St. Mark's Community Center,

while references to the St. Mark's "church" or "congregation" refer to the worshipping congregation known today as St. Mark's United Methodist Church.

5. Margery Freeman, "The St. Mark's Family: A Story of Change," manuscript on file at St. Mark's United Methodist Church; Mary Morrison, "Looking Back at St. Mark's," 1971, manuscript on file at St. Mark's United Methodist Church; Lillian Day, *Opening Doors: A Pageant*, play performed at St. Mark's on September 29, 1949, on file at St. Mark's United Methodist Church.

6. Warren Calvin, interview by the author, August 1, 2000.

7. United Way employee Mary Ambrose, personal communication, March 26, 2001.

8. Mark Shenise, associate archivist, General Commission on Archives and History (GCAH), e-mail to the author, June 18, 1999.

9. Betty Purkey, e-mail to the author, October 12, 2001.

10. Mark Shenise, e-mail to the author, June 18, 1999.

11. GCAH has prepared and posted generalized finding aids at <http://www.gcah.org>.

12. Ruby Bridges Hall, the first black child to enter William Frantz Elementary, where the daughter of the pastor at St. Mark's Methodist Church attended school during the school desegregation crisis, was kept isolated from the white students and did not meet the Foremans until the mid-1990s.

13. In 2005, I went to New York City and listened to Thomas's 1982 and 1988 interviews with Mary Lou Barnwell; however, the Women's Division was not able to locate the release forms and grant me permission to use the small additional amount of material on Barnwell that I obtained there soon enough for it to be included in this book.

14. The Amistad Research Center contains a collection of materials called the St. Mark's Project. In the late 1970s under the auspices of St. Mark's, Tom Dent recorded oral histories and compiled other types of information on the culture of the Tremé neighborhood. Persons to be interviewed were chosen because of a connection to Tremé, not because of a connection to St. Mark's; thus, the contents were actually not profitable for this study.

Index

Southern Conference on Human Welfare
(SCHW), 143–45, 276n29
Southern Methodist University, 112, 147
Southern States Women Suffrage Conference
(SSWSC), 74–75
Southwestern Christian Advocate, 151, 257n9
Spearheads for Reform, 67, 264n25
St. Anna's Asylum, 30, 38
St. Luke's Methodist Church, 178
St. Paul's Methodist Church, Harahan, 166–67
Stafford, Mrs., 36
Stanley, Susie, 214, 289n13
Starr, Ellen Gates, 67
"States' Laws on Race and Color," 138
Stebner, Eleanor, 80, 267n60
Steinbeck, John, 163–65, 281n10–11
Stevens, Thelma, 138, 273n45, 275n10
Stone, Leila Werlein, 30, 32, 98, 258n18, 269n26
Storyville , 76–78, 150, 262n75, 279n56
Strong, Josiah, 29, 83, 239
Stroup, Nettie, 3, **4**, **117,** 117–19, 121–22, 185, 201,
238, 272n26
Sue Barton, Visiting Nurse, 68, 264n26
Sunday school, 28, 34, 40, 46, 79, 90–91, 117, 167,
184; and Allan Knight Chalmers, 176; and
J. W. Moore, 63–64; refusal to let White
Citizens Council member teach, 154; using
Center's rooms, 95

Tackaberry, Carmel, 197
Taylor, Prince, 151
Temple Sinai, 146, 202
They Shall Be Free, 175, 283n42
Thomas, Hilah 252, 270n6, 293n3, 294n13
Thomas, James S., 125, 273n40
Thomas, Norman, 114
Thomas, W. E. 61, 64, 79, 267n55
Tippy, Worth, 88
Tooke, Mary Frances Fairchild, 130, 273n50–51
Touro Synagogue, 170
Toynbee Hall, 58, 144
Travelers' Aid Society, 38, 77, 266n45, 266n45
Travels with Charley, 163–64, 281n10

Tremé, 136, 161, 210, 294n14; and Corner Café,
218
Trimiew, Darryl, 239–41, 280n74, 288n56,
293n26–27
Trinity Episcopal Church, 66
Trolander, Judith, 86, 224, 268n8, 269n32, 287n36
"True Methodist Women," 5, 10, 21, 48–49, 224,
255n3, 262n70
Tulane University, 246; Amistad Research Center,
173, 252; and CFI, 147–49, 151–52, 246;
and Era Club, 74, 76; and Laura Smith, 132,
194, 198; medical students, 96; Newcomb
College, 98; theses and dissertations, 76,
256n11, 262n75–76, 266n45
Turner, Elizabeth Hayes, 262n77
Tuskegee Institute, 127
Tyler, Pam, 76, 215, 266n46, 276n25, 276n28,
280n76, 290n19

Union Theological Seminary, 144
UNICEF, 192
United Way, 196, 210–11, 293n4, 294n7; as
Community Chest, 16, 50, 102, 230, 248,
262n76, 287n36
Upstairs Bar fire, 215, 289n16–17
*Urban Masses and Moral Order in America,
1820–1920,* 261n64, 269n32

vandalism: of Alversons' home, 168; of Foremans'
parsonage, 166, 212; of St. Mark's, 159, 216,
165–66, 188, 212
Vatican, 97, 169
Vernon, Walter N., 261n62
Vieux Carré Courier, 212

Wald, Lillian, 1, 68
Walton, Aubrey, 177, 179, 185, 205
Ward, Harry, 83–84, 144–45, 277n32
Warner, Beverley, 66
Warner, Laceye, 245, 292n19, 293n3
Watson, Lizzie, 28
Wedell, Marsha, 232, 262n77, 292n10
Welter, Barbara, 10, 255n3, 256n16, 262n70

ST. MARK'S AND THE SOCIAL GOSPEL was designed and typeset on a Macintosh computer system using InDesign software. The body text is set in 10.5/15 Kepler Light and display type is set in Kepler. This book was designed and typeset by Chad Pelton.